REVIVE US
AGAIN

A Devotional Study of
Ezra, Nehemiah and Esther

WARREN HENDERSON

Revive Us Again – A Devotional Study of Ezra, Nehemiah and Esther
By Warren Henderson
Copyright © 2016

Cover Design by Benjamin Bredeweg

Editing/Proofreading: Randy Amos, David Dunlap, Kathleen Henderson, Laura Dunlap, Daniel Macy, and David Lindstrom

Published by Warren A. Henderson
3769 Indiana Road
Pomona, KS 66076

Perfect Bound ISBN 978-1-939770-38-7
eBook ISBN 978-1-939770-39-4

Editing/Proofreading: Mike Attwood, Kathleen Henderson, Daniel Macy, and David Lindstrom

ORDERING INFORMATION:
Gospel Folio Press
Phone 1-905-835-9166
E-mail: order@gospelfolio.com

Also available through many on-line retailers.

Other Books by the Author

Afterlife – What Will It Be Like?
Answer the Call – Finding Life's Purpose
Be Holy and Come Near– A Devotional Study of Leviticus
Behold the Saviour
Be Angry and Sin Not
Conquest and the Life of Rest – A Devotional Study of Joshua
Exploring the Pauline Epistles
Forsaken, Forgotten, and Forgiven – A Devotional Study of Jeremiah and Lamentations
Glories Seen & Unseen
Hallowed Be Thy Name – Revering Christ in a Casual World
Hiding God – The Ambition of World Religion
In Search of God – A Quest for Truth
Knowing the All-Knowing
Lessons For Life
Managing Anger God's Way
Mind Frames – Where Life's Battle Is Won or Lost
Out of Egypt – A Devotional Study of Exodus
Overcoming Your Bully
Passing the Torch – Mentoring the Next Generation
Relativity and Redemption –A Devotional Study of Judges and Ruth
Seeds of Destiny – A Devotional Study of Genesis
The Bible: Myth or Divine Truth?
The Beginning of Wisdom – A Devotional Study of Job, Psalms, Proverbs, Ecclesiastes, and Song of Solomon
The Evil Nexus – Are You Aiding the Enemy?
The Fruitful Bough – Affirming Biblical Manhood
The Fruitful Vine – Celebrating Biblical Womanhood
The Hope of Glory – A Preview of Things to Come
The Olive Plants – Raising Spiritual Children
Your Home the Birthing Place of Heaven

Endorsement

I have had the privilege of reading many of brother Warren Henderson's books and have found them to be always profitable. However, this one is without doubt my favorite for several reasons. First, I really appreciate the books of Ezra and Nehemiah. Second, I also, like brother Warren share a deep longing for revival among the people of God. Lastly, because the book is filled with outstanding quotations from those who have experienced or written on the subject of revival. I hope many take the time to read this book and that the longing for revival might grow and turn into serious prayer that the Lord might *Revive Us Again* in our lifetime.

— Mike Attwood

Table of Contents

Preface

Many believers today are wondering if the Church's present lethargic state is the final curtain call for the Church Age. While it is certainly true that apostasy will mark the "professing" Church in the latter days (2 Thess. 2:3), can we assume that the wide-open doors of the Philadelphian era have been closed? Certainly not – the Lord commissioned His disciples to continue proclaiming the gospel message until He returned for His Church (Matt. 28:18-20). Christians should therefore decline to settle into the lukewarm, uncaring, materialistic, spiritually smug Laodicean Church. No true lover of Christ can be satisfied with comfort and complacency when there are millions of hell-bound sinners in the world. Christ suffered and died for these people and the Church has been entrusted with the message (the key) to free them from the bondage of sin and eternal death!

Many of the great revivals of the last three centuries began when a few consecrated Christians, disgusted by the spiritual darkness of their time, pleaded with the Lord to do the spectacular. In response to those prayers, a great work of grace invigorated the Church, and many believers were emboldened to hazard their lives to proclaim the gospel message in mission fields worldwide. Besides the Church's zeal to fulfill the Great Commission, the Spirit of God has moved at discreet times to affect wide-sweeping revival among Christians and then to add millions to the body of Christ: The Six Mile Water Awakening in Northern Ireland (1625-1627), the First Great Awakening in England and America under the preaching of Edwards, Wesley, Whitefield, Zinzendorf, and the Moravians (1727-1750); the Second Great Awakening at Cane Ridge (1780-1810); the General Awakening in Hawaii and Jamaica under Finney (1830-1840); both the American Revival (northern states), spurred on by Finney and D. L. Moody, and the Layman's Prayer Revival in 1857-1861 (it is estimated that 500,000 souls were converted at this time); the Ulster Revival (1859), the Welsh

Revival of 1904-1905 in which 100,000 people turned from sin and confessed Christ as Savior; the revival in Korea/Manchuria in 1907; the 1950 revival in the Hebrides under Duncan Campbell's preaching; and the 1959 Ahoghill Revival in Northern Ireland under J. H. Moore. Some of these revivals were forged in the fires of adversity, but all occurred when God's people became utterly disgusted with the spiritual conditions of the day and united in one voice to petition God for a miracle.

Is it possible for the Church in the 21st century to be enflamed with that same evangelical fervor that ushered millions into the Church during the three previous centuries? This author thinks it is, but not without an awakening within the Church first. Older brethren rarely spoke about the matter of revival because they did not see the Church in Acts praying for it. However, this was no doubt due to the fact that the early Church was already in a state of revival. They expected the supernatural; the Church today generally does not expect God to do great things. Pentecost will not be repeated, but we have the same God, same Lord, same Holy Spirit, same dispensation, same gospel as those first Christians – the problem is with us; our expectations of God are too low. We should not be afraid of legitimate workings of the Holy Spirit in our time, but rather we should yearn for them!

Before the First Great Awakening in America, Christianity had sadly declined and Unitarianism had gained a social foothold. Pagan philosophy and skepticism were poisoning the minds of millions of people, and there was much indifference towards God and His Word. In fact, it may be noted that each of the above revivals occurred when those who professed to be God's people were in a spiritually pathetic condition. This same characterization would be true of both Jewish revivals during the days of Ezra and Nehemiah (Ezra 9-10; Neh. 8-9). If spiritual decline is a prerequisite for revival, the modern Church is ripe for an awakening.

Consequently, believers will benefit from an understanding of the precious truths contained in Ezra and Nehemiah concerning the authentic nature of revival, what necessitates it, and what it produces. May the study of these books encourage Christians to hold tightly to divine truth while they wait patiently for the Lord's return. May we press forward in expectation of the great things God can still do, rather than permitting a defeated foe to wrangle as many into hell as he can.

2

On this point H. A. Ironside provides the following exhortation to the Church:

> That the book of Ezra contains much-needed truth for the present time is my firm belief. A re-affirmation of early principles is necessary on account of the attempt on the part of many to set aside "that which is written" as to the gathering and fellowship of children of God in separation from evil; and this, because of break-downs on the part of some who sought, through grace, to take a scriptural position years ago. Corporate failure has been supposed (in some way incomprehensible to one who would be guided alone by the word of God) to sanction individual turning from the path of the truth. ... No amount of failure alters divine truth. We to-day are as responsible as our fathers were to go back to "that which is written" and act in faith upon it.
>
> It is true, difficulties and perplexities abound as might be expected, because of the near close of the dispensation. But "God and the word of His grace" are still all-sufficient for every peril or disaster. A careful study of the books of Ezra and Nehemiah would, I feel certain, preserve from a gloomy pessimism as to the carrying out of the truth of gathering to the Name of the Lord and furnish many needed warnings against the abounding snares of the last times.[1]

Revive Us Again is a "commentary style" devotional which upholds the glories of Christ while exploring the books of Ezra, Esther, and Nehemiah within the context of the whole of Scripture. As in *Seeds of Destiny* (Genesis), *Out of Egypt* (Exodus), and *Forsaken, Forgotten, and Forgiven* (Jeremiah), I have endeavored to include in this book some of the principal gleanings from other writers. *Revive Us Again* contains dozens of brief devotions. This format allows the reader to use the book either as a daily devotional or as a reference source for deeper study.

Historical Setting

Seven closely-linked Old Testament books describe the post-exilic circumstances of God's covenant people. Three historical books (Ezra, Nehemiah, and Esther) and four prophetic books (Daniel, Haggai, Zechariah, and Malachi) combine to provide a composite picture of the deplorable spiritual and social conditions of the Jewish nation at that time. Yet, despite these impediments, God was able to revive His people through a handful of faithful Jews who had not lost hope in Him.

The prophet Jeremiah was one of those who explicitly trusted the Lord and declared His Word through this difficult time. He warned the inhabitants of Judah for forty years that their deep-seated idolatry and general waywardness would have devastating consequences. Jehovah had punished His people with droughts, military invasions, plagues, and even smote their children, but was unable to gain their reverence and awe. Unfortunately, Jeremiah's call to repentance and Jehovah's chastening hand were ignored. For decades, God had been long-suffering with His people, but there came a time when His divine justice could no longer be tempered with His mercy, and His wrath was poured out on the Jewish nation. Yet, Jeremiah also affirmed God's love for His people and that He would cleanse the Jews of their idolatry and restore them to Himself in a future day.

So, though Jeremiah foretold that the Babylonians would invade and decimate Jerusalem and many Jews would be slaughtered and others would be hauled to Babylon, this captivity would not be the end of the nation. God promised that the Jews would be permitted to return to their homeland after seventy years (Jer. 25:11).

About a century prior to Jeremiah's declaration, Isaiah prophesied that God would raise up a Gentile king named Cyrus to end the Babylonian captivity and to rebuild His temple in Jerusalem (Isa.

44:28-45:1). Daniel confirmed the meaning of Jeremiah's seventy-year prophecy and lived throughout this period to provide an eye-witness account of its fulfillment (Dan. 9:2). Malachi brought the Old Testament narrative to a close by proclaiming God's rebuke for His rebellious people and also His future plan for them. Malachi and Nehemiah were likely contemporaries. God's next message and final Messenger to them would arrive four hundred years later in a stable located in Bethlehem; the incarnate Word, the Son of God came to call the lost sheep of Israel.

Just as there were three major deportations of Jews during the onset of the Babylonian captivity, there were also three major Jewish groups that returned to Jerusalem. Zerubbabel, under King Cyrus' authority, led approximately 50,000 Jews back to Jerusalem in 537-536 BC to rebuild the temple (Ezra 2:64-70). After the temple's foundation was laid in 535 BC, opponents were able to delay this work for fifteen years. In 520 BC, God used the prophets Haggai and Zechariah to mobilize and energize the Jews to complete the work; this was the *First Jewish Awakening*. The temple was finished in 515 BC, seventy-one years after Solomon's temple had been destroyed (Ezra 6:14).

The second group of Jews was led from Babylon to Jerusalem by the scribe Ezra in 458 BC. This was a smaller contingency, numbering 1,772 men and their families: perhaps 5,000 to 10,000 people in total. While Zerubbabel had been charged with rebuilding the temple, Ezra's duty was to rebuild the people. The Jews had lost their way and Ezra would reacquaint them with Jehovah and His Law; this was the *Second Jewish Awakening*. A fifty-seven-year gap exists between Ezra chapters six and seven. It is during this interim that the events recorded in the book of Esther occurred. King Xerxes, Esther's husband, reigned from 486-465 BC. The book of Esther highlights the "dark ages" of the Jewish nation after a hundred years of being in exile. The book does not mention God, His temple, His priests, His sacrifices, nor any aspect of His Law. There is no mention of prayer, but rather the book emphasizes the brave exploits of Mordecai and Esther in preserving their people from extermination.

Thirteen years after Ezra departed for Jerusalem, a third group of approximately 2000 Jewish captives were led home by Nehemiah in 444-445 BC. Nehemiah, the cupbearer for King Artaxerxes, had informed the king of the plight of the Jews, Nehemiah's countrymen, in

Jerusalem; they were being consistently raided by marauders. The King granted Nehemiah a twelve-year leave from his palace duties and resources to assist in the rebuilding of the wall around Jerusalem. The wall was miraculously built in fifty-two days; this was the *Third Jewish Awakening*. Nehemiah remained as governor of the region until the time appointed for him to return to Shushan (Neh. 6:15, 13:6).

Ezra

Overview of Ezra

The Author

Hebrew tradition ascribes Ezra as the author of the book entitled *Ezra* in our Bibles. Besides Jewish convention, there is also internal evidence which would indicate that Ezra is the author. First, in chapters 7 through 9, the author references Ezra in the first person. Second, as an official in the Persian court, Ezra would have had access to historical documents covering the first six chapters (538-515 BC). Third, as a scribe he would have the Jewish genealogical information contained within the book. Fourth, the writing style is similar to 1 and 2 Chronicles, which Hebrew tradition also accredits Ezra as writing; it is noted that the first two and a half verses of Ezra are quoted from the last chapter of 2 Chronicles.

Ezra was a Jewish priest-scribe. Scribes preserved the Old Testament writings and replaced deteriorated scrolls with accurate copies as needed. Their time spent reading and copying Scripture well-equipped them to teach God's Word. This passion would characterize Ezra's ministry: *"For Ezra had prepared his heart to seek the Law of the Lord, and to do it, and to teach statutes and ordinances in Israel"* (Ezra 7:10). Ezra was a godly man whom God both burdened and divinely equipped to call His people to repentance and bring revival to Israel!

The Date

The book of Ezra spans two distinct time periods. The first period, recorded in chapters 1-6, begins with the edict by King Cyrus allowing the Jews to return to Jerusalem for the rebuilding of the temple and concludes with its completion (538-515 BC). Ezra was not an eyewitness observer of these events. The second period relates to Ezra's return from Babylon and his efforts to reform the Jewish nation; these events are contained in chapters 7-10. There are, however, two exceptions to this simple outline and chronology: Ezra 4:6 is a parenthetic note which refers to a specific event which occurred during the reign of King Xerxes (Ahasuerus) who reigned from 486-465 BC, and Ezra 4:7-23 is also a parenthetic statement which supplies two letters, one to and one from King Artaxerxes (464-424 BC), whom Nehemiah served as cupbearer. King Artaxerxes gave Ezra permission to return to Jerusalem in 458 BC. The book was then likely written between 456 BC (marking the end of Ezra's ministry) and the events relating to Nehemiah's arrival from Babylon in 444 BC.

Outline
Chapters 1-6: The Rebuilding of the Temple
Chapters 7-10: The Reviving of the People

The Setting
Although Ezekiel, Daniel, and Jeremiah vividly describe the destruction of Jerusalem and the taking of Jewish captives, little is known of their actual captivity in Babylon. Other than the brief view of Jewish life in Babylon afforded by the books of Esther and Daniel, the biblical narrative is mainly silent until the Jews return home in their various groups.

Jeremiah informs us that the situation in Judah during the captivity was bleak. After the assassination of godly Gedaliah, whom Nebuchadnezzar had appointed governor of Judah, the province was dissolved and was incorporated into Samaria to the north. Few Jews dwelled in the towns and cities of Judah as these were in ruins and provided no protection against their enemies. To escape being plundered and abused, many Jews dwelt in various safe havens within the rugged foothills of Judea. The Jews were literally a dispersed people within their own homeland.

The Vision
During this time period, the Jews were a discouraged people who had lost their way; they no longer knew Jehovah in a personal way. The Law of God had been lost, their place of worship destroyed, and there were no teachers or prophets in the region to guide them back to the truth. Thus, Ezra's arrival from Babylon was paramount. The social and spiritual condition of the people was so pitiful that Ezra was moved to

pull out the hair of his head and beard, to tear his clothes, and to weep before the Lord in shame (Ezra 9:1-5). The revival of Ezra's day occurred when a few godly saints were moved to weep for a ruined people and to pray for their pathetic spiritual condition. One unmistakable fact has marked every great revival throughout the Church Age; the fervent, effectual prayers of the righteous have stoked the fires of revival.

May it be so today! May God's people be awakened from their lethargic and deplorable spiritual condition, be broken before Him, and petition Him fervently for revival within the Church. We do not want an emotional experience that merely imitates revival; we want a deep and ongoing experience with Almighty God that would embolden every soldier of the cross to storm the ramparts of hell on earth with the gospel of Jesus Christ.

Revival Meditation

A necessary precursor of any great spiritual awakening is a spirit of deep humiliation growing out of a consciousness of sin, and fresh revelation of the holiness and power and glory of God.

— John Mott

Ezra Devotions

The Decree of Cyrus
Ezra 1

The phrase *"Now the first year of Cyrus, King of Persia"* in verse 1 does not refer to the year that Cyrus became the ruler of the Medo-Persian empire (about 550 BC), but rather it relates to the year following his overthrow of Babylon (in October of 539 BC). At this point Cyrus was the uncontested king of the entire Babylonian empire. In 538 BC Cyrus would fulfill the prophecies of both Jeremiah and Isaiah. Nearly two centuries prior to this, Isaiah had foretold that a king named Cyrus would be a great conqueror and would be used of God to rebuild His temple:

> *Who says of Cyrus, "He is My shepherd, and he shall perform all My pleasure, saying to Jerusalem, 'You shall be built,' and to the temple, 'Your foundation shall be laid.'" Thus says the Lord to His anointed, to Cyrus, whose right hand I have held – to subdue nations before him and loose the armor of kings, to open before him the double doors, so that the gates will not be shut* (Isa. 44:28-45:1).

This is an incredible prophesy in that it names both this individual and his future feats at a time when Solomon's Temple still stood and when Israel was still an autonomous Jewish state. Later, but just prior to the time of the exile, Jeremiah prophesied that the Jewish captivity in Babylon would last only seventy years (Jer. 25:11-12, 29:10); with the overthrow of the Babylonian empire the Jews would be liberated and be permitted to return to their homeland. The prophet Daniel, as an elderly man who had lived through the seventy-year exile, understood that Jeremiah's prophecy was fulfilled by the Persian victory (Dan. 9:2). God had severely chastened the Jews for their idolatry, but He had also

15

kept His promise to "not make an end of them" (Jer. 30:11) and He would bring them home again.

What facilitated the fulfillment of this prophecy? First, God moved in the spirit of Cyrus not only to release the Jews, but also to rebuild God's temple in Jerusalem. Second, the Jewish historian Josephus wrote that Cyrus was shown the prophecy of Isaiah and wanted to fulfill it (*The Antiquities of the Jews* 11.1.1). Both the Word of God and the Spirit of God had an effect on Cyrus to accomplish the will of God. These two mysterious, divine Agents continue to work in the hearts of men today: *"So then faith comes by hearing, and hearing by the word of God"* (Rom. 10:17); *"'Eye has not seen, nor ear heard, nor have entered into the heart of man the things which God has prepared for those who love Him.' But God has revealed them to us through His Spirit. For the Spirit searches all things, yes, the deep things of God"* (1 Cor. 2:9-11). May the Holy Spirit continue to illuminate the minds of men to discover the vast riches of truth contained within God's Word!

Cyrus declares it was *"the Lord God of heaven"* who had given him the victory over nations and who had charged him to build His house in Jerusalem (v. 2). As Harry Ironside notes, the title which Cyrus bestows, through divine inspiration, to the God of the Jews is significant:

> In the beginning of this proclamation we see how evidently Cyrus was inspired of the Lord in the very title given to Jehovah. He is the *"God of heaven."* This is the name by which He is largely known in [Ezra, Nehemiah, and Daniel]. It was a title He took when His throne was removed from the earth, and He gave His people into the hands of the Gentiles. He went and *"returned to His place,"* as Hosea puts it. He forsook the temple at Jerusalem, dissolved the theocracy and became *"the God of heaven."* Such He is still to His ancient people, and so He will remain till He returns to Jerusalem to establish His throne again as *"the Lord of the whole earth."*[1]

Does this mean Cyrus believed that Jehovah, the God of heaven, was the one true God? Not likely. The Cyrus Cylinder (538 BC), which was discovered in 1879 AD, records Persian King Cyrus' conquest of Babylon and his subsequent release of Jewish captives. The Cylinder

16

includes this statement: "May all the gods whom I have resettled in their sacred cities daily ask Bel and Nebo for a long life for me." Cyrus worshiped Bel and Nebo, the gods of Persia. By releasing those who had been in Babylonian captivity and honoring their gods, Cyrus hoped to establish loyal buffer nations on the perimeter of his empire and ingratiate himself with the gods of these nations, including Jehovah of the Jews. Cyrus thought that by being in good standing with all proclaimed deities of the surrounding nations, it would certainly be well with him. Yet, Jehovah is no man's debtor; in fact, He was acting on the behalf of His covenant people to orchestrate the entire matter.

Though he did not realize it, Cyrus was a mere tool in Jehovah's hand, being used to fulfill God's promises to the Jews. The biblical narrative is full of examples of God using pharaohs and kings of various nations to work His will. In every case the end result is the same: God exalts His great name and blesses His people in the process. Cyrus, as a moral and a conscious being, freely chose to worship Bel and Nebo, but he had no option in how he would be used within God's unfolding design to bless the Jews. Whether or not we yield to God's call to salvation, God will be glorified through our choices; He will use us either as vessels of mercy prepared for glory, or as vessels of wrath which fit themselves for destruction (Rom. 9:14-23). God prepares yielded vessels for glory and rebellious vessels to receive His wrath.

Exodus records a good example of this truth. God did not force Pharaoh to worship Egyptian gods, but on certain occasions He did intervene to harden Pharaoh's heart to accomplish the release of His people from Egypt. The fact that Pharaoh hardened his own heart afterwards demonstrates that he still had a free choice in the matter. God would have been perfectly just to destroy a pagan like Pharaoh, but instead He designed ten specific plagues to prove to Pharaoh that He was superior to a number of specific Egyptian gods. Pharaoh rejected this revelation and hardened his own heart against the Lord – he prepared himself to be a vessel of wrath fit for destruction. Yet, in honoring Pharaoh's decision, God brought glory to His name, which was the predetermined outcome of Pharaoh's decision. This example shows how human responsibility and sovereign design ensure that God receives all the glory in every situation. It is also noted that Cyrus did not command the Jews to leave Babylon; they were permitted to leave – God does not force people against their will to worship Him. Just as

Revive Us Again

the Israelites chose to depart from Egypt long ago, many of the Jews willingly chose to leave Babylon in order to be one again with Jehovah in their homeland. Sadly, many remained in the heartland of paganism.

Besides liberating the Jews, the main focus of Cyrus' decree was the building of the temple in Jerusalem. Without a temple, the Levitical system of sacrifices and feasts could not be reinstituted, and if worship according to the Mosaic Law was not established, the vitality of the Jewish people would wane. They were a chosen nation to worship Jehovah; a temple had to be erected in Jerusalem. The Spirit of God would direct the heads of the tribes of Judah and Benjamin, the priests, and the Levites to organize the effort to rebuild the temple (v. 5).

Besides a proclamation of liberation and a command to rebuild the temple, Cyrus' edict also requested that the general population donate to them silver, gold, goods, and livestock to cover the costs of rebuilding the temple and as gifts to the Jews themselves (vv. 4-6). As in the exodus from Egypt a millennium earlier, God was delivering His people from bondage and blessing them with material wealth at the same time. King Cyrus also financially contributed to the rebuilding effort by returning all the gold and silver articles which had previously belonged to the temple, but were taken by Nebuchadnezzar during the second deportation of Jews to Babylon in 597 BC (v. 7). As Edward Dennett notes, the entire situation was being carefully orchestrated by God:

We have thus, in this chapter, all the signs of a genuine work of God. Concurrence of heart and object is produced in all concerned, whether in Cyrus, without whose permission the captives could not have returned; in the chief of the fathers of Judah and Benjamin, who were needed for the actual work of building; or in those who remained, who, in having fellowship with their brethren by their freewill offerings, contributed towards the necessary expenses. There were no preliminary meetings to arrange and to come to an agreement, but the union of heart and purpose was produced alone by the action of the Lord on the hearts of all alike. This distinguishes a divine from a human work, and is the sure proof of a real action of the Spirit of God. Every needed instrument therefore comes forward at the right moment, for the work is of God, and it must be accomplished.[2]

A Persian man called Mithredath was to oversee the transfer of all temple articles from the treasury to Sheshbazzar, who would deliver them to Jerusalem (v. 8). In all, some 5,400 original items from the temple were given to Sheshbazzar, including 2,499 more significant articles of gold and silver (vv. 9-11).

Who Sheshbazzar actually was is somewhat of a mystery. He is called the prince of Judah (v. 8), but the question arises that, if he were a Jew, why did he have a Persian name honoring a pagan deity? Many believe that Sheshbazzar is the Persian name of Zerubbabel, the grandson of King Jehoiachin, and thus a prince of Judah. Zerubbabel had apparently been assigned by Cyrus to govern the returning Jews and oversee the building of the temple in Jerusalem. Ezra mentions both names, Sheshbazzar and Zerubbabel, in association with laying the foundation of the temple (3:8-10, 5:16). This would seem to indicate that either both names refer to the same man, or that there was a Persian diplomat, Sheshbazzar, who was overseeing the temple construction effort led by Zerubbabel. The fact that the Jews solicited the testimony of Sheshbazzar to substantiate their claim of legitimacy when their rebuilding program was opposed (5:14), gives this view some credence.

As Sheshbazzar is not mentioned in later history by Ezra, it is possible that he either died or returned to Babylon shortly after the Jewish contingency arrived in Jerusalem and began building the temple. Although we may not know who Sheshbazzar was, it is evident that God used him, Cyrus, and other Persian officials to bring His covenant people back to Jerusalem at the appointed time, with great wealth, for a special purpose – to rebuild His temple. Their time of chastening was over, they were going home, and from Jerusalem revival would sweep through the Jewish nation.

A Revival Meditation

Gypsy Smith was once asked how to start a revival. He answered: "Go home, lock yourself in your room, kneel down in the middle of your floor. Draw a chalk mark all around yourself and ask God to start the revival inside that chalk mark. When He has answered your prayer, the revival will be on."[3]

19

Homeward Bound
Ezra 2

Almost two centuries before the events of this book, the Lord punished the ten tribes of the Northern Kingdom through Assyrian invasion and exile (2 Kgs. 17:23). Isaiah, Amos, and Hosea had each warned Israel that God would judge their deep-seated idolatry, but they did not heed God's call to repentance. A century later Jeremiah, Habakkuk, and Zephaniah warned the Southern Kingdom of military invasion, slaughter, and exile if they did not repent of their idolatry. Again these warnings were dismissed and God used the Babylonians to severely chasten His people. This history explains why the first returning captives from Babylon, mentioned in this chapter, were primarily from two tribes, Judah and Benjamin, and those descendants of the priests and Levites who were in Jerusalem and the Levitical cities of the Southern Kingdom at the time of its downfall (Josh. 21:4). However, Jewish descendants from the Northern Kingdom who had been exiled in the region for two centuries were also permitted to return to their homeland at this time.

Ezra supplies a roster of the Jews who were willing to take advantage of Cyrus' offer. He begins by listing the key civil and religious leaders. The appointed governor of the province of Judah, Zerubbabel, is listed first and Jeshua (or Joshua; see Zech. 3:1) the High Priest is referenced next (v. 2). Also mentioned in verse 2 is Seraiah, the High Priest whom Nebuchadnezzar killed at Riblah after Jerusalem fell in 586 BC (1 Chron. 6:14; 2 Kgs. 25:18-21). Nehemiah and Mordecai are also listed, but these are not the two men mentioned in the books of Nehemiah and Esther, respectively. Nehemiah did not leave Babylon until 90 years later to rebuild the wall around Jerusalem and it would still be 60 years until Mordecai was honored by the Persian King Ahasuerus (Xerxes).

In all, eleven names appear in verse 2. It is suggested that each of these men represent one of the twelve Jewish tribes (i.e. with one name being omitted). These same individuals are listed later by Nehemiah (with some spelling variations) and with the twelfth representative (Neh. 7:7).

After recognizing the tribal leaders, Ezra notes eighteen specific families and clans (2:3-20), inhabitants from twenty-one towns and villages (2:21-35), the priests and the Levites (2:36-42), which included singers and gatekeepers, the descendants of temple and royal servants (2:43-58), and, finally, 652 returnees who could not prove their ancestry (2:59-63). Verses 40-41 record that in Zerubbabel's returning contingency there were more children of Asaph, who were temple singers (128), than Levites (74). Because of the Levites' faithfulness at Sinai to stand with the Lord, they had been promised no inheritance other than the Lord Himself (Num. 18:20). They had the great privilege of serving before God and being ministered to by Him; their smallness in number probably indicates that they had lost their special identity among the Jewish tribes.

Ezra provides a tally of persons associated with each of the above groups which totals 29,829. Yet, the total number of Jews returning home is stated to be 49,897 (2:64-65). The latter number is referred to as "the whole company," which probably included women and children, and descendants from the ten northern tribes. Nehemiah records that 49,942 Jews returned to Israel at this time, which is a slightly different number than Ezra's total, the difference being that Nehemiah includes forty-five additional singers (Neh. 7:66-67). This discrepancy is probably best explained as a scribal error in copying the Hebrew number accurately. The original writings of Scripture were inspired, but the copyists were not inspired and they made errors. Through textual criticism, we can affirm that the Hebrew manuscript is very close to the original autograph with a very high degree of confidence. In fact, ninety percent of the existing Old Testament manuscripts are without variance and nearly all of the remaining ten percent can be attributed to stylistic, spelling, or word order differences. The Jews took great care in copying the manuscripts accurately, but no amount of carefulness is going to prevent mistakes from happening when a text is hand-copied dozens of times.

Numbers presented particular difficulties for Jewish scribes. The Hebrew system of numbers was somewhat like the Roman in that they used letters for numbers. Some of the Hebrew letters were quite similar to one another, making the job of copying numbers even more difficult. However, Hebrew numbering errors are often obvious as such when compared to parallel Bible passages or by using common sense. For example, how many men from the small town of Beth-shemesh died for looking into the Ark of the Covenant: 50,070 (1 Sam. 6:19), or is it more likely the number was 70? The answer is obvious. In a similar fashion, the scribe copying the book of Nehemiah may have picked up the number of mules traveling to Jerusalem in verse 68 (245) and accidently placed that number in verse 67. Accordingly, 245 singers are noted in Nehemiah, in contrast to the 200 singers that Ezra describes. In all, about 50,000 Jews would make the arduous 900-mile trip from Babylon to Israel, and we need not lose any sleep over the trivial difference of numbers in the text.

Among the returnees were *"the men of Anathoth"* (v. 23). About fifty years earlier, while Jerusalem was besieged by the Babylonians, King Zedekiah put the prophet Jeremiah in prison to keep him from discouraging the people with Jehovah's messages (Jer. 32). While a prisoner, the Lord informed Jeremiah that his cousin Hanamel would soon come to visit him and request that he purchase family property located in Anathoth, which was already under Babylonian control. Jeremiah was told to purchase the land to ensure it remained in the family (Lev. 25:25-28). The deed was signed and sealed to protect it until a lawful claimant returning from Babylon years later could possess the land again. It seemed like utter folly to purchase a field in conquered territory, but Jeremiah's faith reached beyond the doom and gloom of the nation's circumstances to the long-expected day of restoration. Now descendants from his hometown, perhaps kin, were returning to reclaim their inheritance – Jeremiah's prophetic message had come true.

It is hard to imagine what those first Jewish pilgrims were pondering as they crested the Mount of Olives and looked down upon the utter devastation of their beloved city and of the temple where their forefathers had worshipped Jehovah. Edward Dennett speculates that God used this particular moment to motivate His people to surrender their time and resources for the rebuilding of the temple (vv. 68-69):

"When they came to the house of the Lord at Jerusalem," showing that the house, whatever its outward condition, and razed to the ground as it had been, still existed before the eye of God. ... God would seem to have used the desolations of His sanctuary to touch the hearts of these chief of the fathers. When they came to Jehovah's house — when they saw, as it were, its condition — they were moved, and they "offered freely" of their substance; and, as the Spirit of God is careful to notice, thus setting the seal of His approval upon the act, "they gave after their ability." In this they are surely examples for all time for those of the Lord's people who have the privilege of ministering to the Lord, whether in having fellowship with His necessitous saints, or with the needs of His service.[1]

After arriving in Palestine, some Jews took up residence in Jerusalem, but many returned to the cities of their ancestors. Verse 70 reads, *"So the priests, and the Levites, and some of the people, and the singers, and the porters, and the Nethinims, dwelt in their cities, and all Israel in their cities."* The latter phrase is astounding; how could a feeble remnant of Jews sparsely spread throughout the land be considered a nation? Yet, this is how God thought of them. His people were home again and occupying the land He had bestowed to them; thus, He refused to consider them in any other way than in their unity and completeness. The same blessed truth can be noticed in our generation, says H. A. Ironside:

So today, it is not possible to re-gather the whole Church of God in one outward visible unity. But it is possible for a feeble few to meet on the ground of the Church of God, refusing all sectarian names and ways, "endeavoring to keep the unity of the Spirit in the bond of peace." The last phrase must never be forgotten. When strife and discord come in, the unity of the Spirit is at once violated. It can never be forced. It is a practical thing, maintained alone as believers walk in the Spirit and recognize in each other all that is of God, while each one individually seeks to "follow peace with all men, and holiness, without which no man shall see the Lord."[2]

The Jews were unified as a people and in purpose – they were going to build God a temple. However, not all of Ezra 2 is festive; there are two sad affairs noted. First, 652 returnees could not verify their Jewish ancestry (vv. 59-60). This would be a hardship, for without genealogies, no legal claim to property previously held by clansmen could be verified. Many professing Christians today suffer from a similar difficulty; though often having zeal, they are unable to provide a clear scriptural response to the hope that is supposedly within them. These Christ-namers praise Him with their lips on Sunday, but deny Him in word and deed throughout the remainder of the week. Are these individuals really children of God? As shown in Ezra 2, we need to be careful in passing judgment, for only the Lord knows who are His and who are the counterfeits – His registry of holy priests is perfect (Rev. 20:15).

The second matter is that the Persian governor, perhaps Sheshbazzar or Zerubbabel, decreed that any priest who could not prove their Aaronic ancestry would be removed from the priesthood. This meant that they could not officiate worship on behalf of the nation at the temple or eat the most sacred foods offered at the temple (v. 63). Unfortunately, the children of Barzillai were removed from the priesthood because no genealogy was found for them (vv. 61-62). The situation could still be rectified by the High Priest after arriving back in Jerusalem through the use of the Urim and Thummim. The Urim and Thummim were held in the High Priest's breastplate and in some way were used to determine the will of God. Supposedly, the High Priest would then be able to determine the legitimacy of the children of Barzillai as priests.

In the former case, where 652 Jews could not verify their ancestry, the application for the Church is not to judge an individual's salvation: only the Lord knows who are His and He is quite capable of separating the sheep and the goats. However, the matter of the children of Barzillai is more profound; they were forbidden to function as priests on behalf of the nation because they could not prove that they were descendants of Aaron, as the Law required. What application can we draw for the Church from this situation?

While it is true that the Lord Jesus invites all believers to participate in the Lord's Supper, a local assembly of God's people should not welcome just anyone into their midst to break bread. In my opinion, it is not that the Lord's Supper needs to be protected, but rather that we do not want to grieve the Holy Spirit by allowing the unregenerate, those in sin, or those who are embracing false doctrines to participate as if they were sanctified believer-priests fit for worship (1 Pet. 2:5, 9).

Only those who have a sound profession of Christ should participate; the Lord's Supper was given by the Lord to His disciples as a memorial feast (Luke 22:19; Acts 2:41-42, 20:7). Those who partake must be doctrinally sound (2 Thess. 2:6, 3:14; 2 Jn. 9-10) and morally sound (1 Cor. 5:1-5, 11, 13). If these aspects are not met, those individuals are welcome to observe, but they should not partake of the bread and wine, nor participate audibly in worship. Letters of reception were used by the early church to validate these priestly qualities in believers journeying from one assembly to another (Acts 18:26-27; Rom. 16:1; Col. 4:7-8). These letters enabled visiting believers to be received into another local church fellowship with joy and all the privileges and responsibilities of a believer-priest (Rom. 15:7). When it comes to participating in corporate worship or the work of God, only those believer-priests who exhibit the life of Christ within should engage in these. For God's holy character cannot be separated from what He accomplishes in His people, and any attempt to do otherwise on our part will surely bring His condemnation. The unqualified priests of Ezra 2 had no testimony of who they were and thus were declared unfit for service.

In addition to the free-will offering taken for the construction of the temple, Cyrus had commanded the people of his empire to personally assist the Jews on their way by giving them gold, silver, goods, and animals. God not only ended the captivity of His people, but also compensated them liberally for their previous suffering. Like their ancestors who departed a millennium earlier from Egypt, their sudden wealth could serve two possible purposes: it could be used to worship Jehovah or for idolatry. In the Sinai wilderness all the Hebrews' basic necessities of life were provided by God; thus, the spoils of Egypt served as a test of their allegiance to Jehovah. Unfortunately, before Moses could bring the commands of Jehovah down from Mount Sinai, the Jews had already used their provision to worship God to form an Egyptian god – the golden calf. However, this was not to be the case with the refined Jewish nation returning from Babylonian captivity.

Ezra records that many leaders among the people contributed to the treasury willingly and as liberally as each was able (vv. 69-70). Unlike their forefathers, the Jews who returned from Babylon understood the importance of supporting the work of the Lord and experienced the joy of doing so. Joy in life is not achieved through things, but in knowing and living for Christ. Consequently, Paul instructed his spiritual son Timothy on how to maintain contentment in life:

> *Now godliness with contentment is great gain. For we brought nothing into this world, and it is certain we can carry nothing out. And having food and clothing, with these we shall be content. But those who desire to be rich fall into temptation and a snare, and into many foolish and harmful lusts which drown men in destruction and perdition. For the love of money is a root of all kinds of evil, for which some have strayed from the faith in their greediness, and pierced themselves through with many sorrows* (1 Tim. 6:6-10).

It is not a sin to be rich, for such things are bestowed by God alone, but to trust in one's wealth to fix personal problems or to indulge in worldliness is sin (1 Tim. 6:17-19). What we have is exactly what God wants us to have and is for the purpose of serving Him, helping others, and providing for our basic necessities. If our necessities are satisfied, Paul exhorts that we should keep working in order to have a provision to help those in need (Eph. 4:28). As the Israelites learned in Moses' day, wealth not consecrated to God soon leads to idolatry. As an idol is anything that draws our affection from God, the warning could never be more relevant than it is today. The western culture is immersed in "too much stuff" and it is strangling the life out of the Church.

In order to ensure that believers did not neglect personal giving, Paul exhorted the Church at Corinth, *"On the first day of the week **let each one of you** lay something aside, storing up as he may prosper, that there be no collections when I come"* (1 Cor. 16:2). All believers are to regularly give to the work of the Lord, as they have been prospered by God (i.e. as God has provided the wherewithal to give back to Him). Believers are not instructed how much to return to the Lord, nor will believers contribute the same amount, but they all should give to the work of the Lord willingly and regularly. God had financially enabled the Jews to give generously to the building of the temple and they willingly chose to do just that.

A Revival Meditation

From the books alone John Wesley gave away between £30,000 and £40,000. He told preacher Samuel Bradburn, in 1787, that he never gave away anything less than £1,000 a year, and yet, when he died, his personal estate amounted to only a few pounds. When earning £30 a year, he lived on £28 and gave the remaining £2 to the Lord. Next year his salary was doubled. He found that he lived comfortably on £28 a year, so, instead of raising his standard of living, he continued to live on £28 a year and gave the whole of his increase to God. So later God entrusted him with larger and larger amounts.[3]

The Foundation Laid
Ezra 3

Some seventy years later, Ezra would make the same 900-mile journey from Babylon to Jerusalem that the first group of returnees trekked in Ezra 2; his journey took four months (Ezra 7:8-9). The edict of Cyrus was issued in 538 BC and the Jews disembarked for Israel sometime afterwards in several groups, mostly arriving in their homeland during the first half of 536 BC. A few months after reoccupying various cities throughout Judah, the Jewish returnees *"gathered together as one man to Jerusalem"* to set up an altar on the first day of the seventh month of the same year (v. 1); this would be early September 536 BC. The altar was erected among the remains of the previous temple. The high priest Jeshua and the governor Zerubbabel, who was a descendant of David, led the effort (v. 2).

About sixteen years later, after the work on the temple had ceased for some fifteen years, God would raise up the prophets Haggai and Zechariah to motivate the Jews to finish the work. This time frame marks the *First Jewish Awakening* in the post-exile period. In Zechariah's fifth vision (520 BC), he describes two olive trees that supplied oil to a lampstand; the Holy Spirit is depicted in the pure oil and the lampstand represents the testimony of God. Speaking of the oil, the Lord told Zechariah: *"Not by might nor by power, but by My Spirit"* (Zech. 4:6). God was confirming that it would be His Spirit working in Joshua (Jeshua) and Zerubbabel (the two olive trees) to accomplish His will and provide a testimony of Himself in Jerusalem, for Jehovah was *"jealous for Jerusalem"* (Zech. 1:14).

Though the opposition would momentarily cause the Jews to stop building the temple, God would use Jeshua and Zerubbabel, who started the project, to also complete the task. Satan was directly opposing Jeshua's efforts at this time, but the Lord enabled the work to continue by rebuking Satan: *"The Lord rebuke you, Satan! The Lord*

28

who has chosen Jerusalem rebuke you! Is this not a brand plucked from the fire?" (Zech. 3:2). When it is the Lord who opens a door of ministry, the enemy cannot prevail: *"I have set before you an open door, and no man can shut it; for you have a little strength"* (Rev. 3:8). Ministry enabled by the Holy Spirit will affect the glory of God and accomplish the purposes of God. Jeshua and Zerubbabel, being void of personal ambition and secret agendas, were empowered by the Holy Spirit to inspire the people to rebuild the temple.

> Until self-effacing men return again to spiritual leadership, we may expect a progressive deterioration in the quality of popular Christianity year after year till we reach the point where the grieved Holy Spirit withdraws – like the Shekinah from the Temple.
>
> — A. W. Tozer

Before the work on the temple could commence, God's sacrificial system for atoning for His people's sins had to be reinstated. The altar and its sacrifices at Jerusalem marked the Jews as a distinctive people among the nations. God's chastening had estranged them from their homeland, but now that they were back in Jerusalem, they were quite willing to identify with Jehovah, and none else. But how should they proceed in this matter? They simply searched the Scripture, and when *"they found it written,"* that was their answer – end of discussion. Scripture comes from God and is all-sufficient; *"is profitable for doctrine, for reproof, for correction, for instruction in righteousness, that the man of God may be complete, thoroughly equipped for every good work"* (2 Tim. 3:16-17). The Jews were unified in purpose and separated from defilement; they had the Word of God to guide them and the Spirit of God to enable them, which meant the nation was primed to experience the greatness of God!

What is the lesson for the Church? Unless what we say and do is true, (that is, based on Scripture), and Spirit-led, it does not honor God; it is mere religious form, without eternal value. This fact is in opposition to the thinking of some that doctrine should be compromised for the sake of unifying Christians together. In the practical sense, Christian fellowship (i.e. what we share together in the commonwealth of Christ), is dependent on how much we determine we have in common with other believers. While it is true that we will not be able to have the same degree of fellowship with all believers, we should strive to walk as far as we can with all those who have been redeemed by the precious blood of Christ. In glory all true believers will come into the unity of the faith (Eph. 4:13), but until that time each believer is personally accountable to God to study His Word and establish his or her faith upon it.

Spiritual battles must be fought with spiritual weapons and the Word of God is an offensive and defensive weapon that a believer must master to be effective in conflict: *"The Sword of the Spirit is the Word of God"* (Eph. 6:17); *"The Word of God is living and powerful, and sharper than any two-edged sword"* (Heb. 4:12). God's Word divides out of the believer what is not sound in life and doctrine to establish that which pleases God (2 Tim. 2:15). The Lord Jesus also used the Sword of the Spirit to confront and defeat the solicitations of Satan to do evil (Matt. 4:1-11). When rightly applied (i.e. guided by the Spirit of God), nothing can stand against the Word of God. How then were the Jews able to stand against and defeat their enemies? The Jews were unified and in fellowship with God because they, as a nation, were being led by the Holy Spirit and in sound doctrine together. If the Church is to be victorious against the gates of hell today, she must follow this example.

The Jews understood from the Law that they were required to offer morning and evening sacrifices on God's altar (Ex. 29:38-46) and to keep the Feasts of Jehovah (vv. 3, 6). The first feast to be nationally commemorated after the return of the captives was the Feast of Tabernacles (v. 4), which began on the 15th day of the seventh month of the Jewish calendar (Lev. 23:34). They did not have a temple, but the Jews understood that it was through the daily offerings that God had been able to dwell in the midst of His people previously. Even if there was neither temple nor mercy-seat for God to dwell above and between the cherubim, the efficacy of the burnt offerings still remained as long the Jews continued to offer by faith as the Law demanded.

As the Jews were surrounded by enemies in their own homeland, it took great courage to raise an altar and begin sacrificing on it after fifty years. Militarily speaking, they were unarmed and outnumbered; their only defense was Jehovah. It is during this time frame (the third year of Cyrus) that Daniel is made aware of the intense angelic battle raging beyond what is seen, the outcome of which would determine the affairs of men (Dan. 10). Indeed, an intense battle for the control of Jerusalem, the place where Jehovah had chosen to place His name, commenced when the Jews began offering sacrifices to Him again. Surely God's people were far safer then, than when Jerusalem in her glory was surrounded by her fortified walls. On this point Edward Dennett writes:

> One of their motives in the erection of the altar would seem to have been their felt need of the protection of their God, and faith discerned that this protection would be ensured on the ground of the efficacy of the sacrifices. And what could be more beautiful than this exhibition of confidence in God? They were but a feeble remnant, having no outward means of defense, and surrounded by enemies of every kind; but their very weakness and peril had taught them the precious lesson, that God was their refuge and strength. The setting up of the altar was therefore their first object; and as soon as the sweet savor of the burnt offerings ascended up to God, all that He was, as then revealed, was engaged on their behalf.[1]

Despite the hostile environment, many Jews offered freewill offerings in addition to the daily sacrifices (v. 5). Having been purged of their idols, God's people were rejoicing in Him again and, thus, were generous in their giving. They donated money to pay the masons and carpenters who would work on the temple foundation and to purchase building materials, such as lumber from Lebanon (v. 7).

Some of the building materials would require significant time to acquire. For example, the cedar logs had to be cut in Lebanon, hauled to the sea coast, shipped to Joppa, then carried overland to Jerusalem. But after seven months the necessary materials were obtained and construction of the temple foundation commenced (v. 8). Zerrubbabel appointed the Levites to oversee the building project. Jeshua, Kadmiel, and Henadad, along with their families, were specifically tasked with supervising the effort. We are not told how long it took to complete the foundation, but it was likely finished later that same year (i.e. 535 BC).

The Jews then paused from their labors to dedicate the temple foundation to the Lord. As John A. Martin notes, God's covenant people were careful to follow the traditions of their forefathers in this matter:

As the priests and the Levites led the dedication service for the temple's foundation, they did the things that were prescribed by David. The order followed was the same as when David brought the ark to Jerusalem. At that time priests blew trumpets and sons (descendants) of Asaph played the cymbals. The order was also similar to the time when the ark was brought to the temple in Solomon's day (2 Chron. 5:12-13), when Asaph and others played cymbals, harps, and lyres; and the priests blew trumpets. In this rebuilding service the priests and Levites sang, *"He is good; His love to Israel endures forever,"* words almost identical to the song of praise in 2 Chronicles 5:13. This song of praise is highly significant for by it the religious leaders were acknowledging that Yahweh had again established His loving protection over the nation.[2]

For most of the Jews this was a festive event, but for the ancients of the people, the smaller foundation before them was a bitter reminder of what had been lost fifty-two years earlier. So while the majority shouted for joy and praised God for this accomplishment, others wept with loud voices (vv. 11-13). Solomon's temple was enormous and had stood for over four centuries. The temple to be erected on the new foundation was in its shadow; it would suffice as a place to worship Jehovah, but in their estimation the new temple would never hold the grandeur of Solomon's temple. But according to the prophet Haggai, the new temple, as yet unfinished, would have a glory beyond that of the previous temple: *"'The glory of this latter temple shall be greater than the former,' says the Lord of hosts. 'And in this place I will give peace,' says the Lord of hosts"* (Hag. 2:9). What would make it great was that the Jewish Messiah, the Prince of Peace, would present Himself in the temple that the Jews had just begun to build. This prophecy was fulfilled 2000 years ago by the Lord Jesus Christ; then, about 38 years after His coming, that temple was destroyed, meaning that no one else claiming to be Messiah could ever fulfill Haggai's prophecy. With surety, then, we can proclaim to every Jew, "Your Messiah has already been in Jerusalem."

In retrospect, it was probably best that the Jews did not think too highly of the temple they were erecting, for earlier generations of Jews had become "temple-worshippers," instead of honoring the One who resided there. In Jeremiah's day, the Jews had the notion that they were invincible because they had the temple (Jer. 7:4, 14); it was viewed as a "good luck charm" which would protect the nation. Apparently, the structure, having been disassociated from Jehovah, was itself regarded as a bastion of safety (i.e. the people trusted in a man-made building to protect them rather than the One it honored). Jeremiah set the matter straight: God valued obedience more than the temple, a fact He demonstrated by destroying it. A half-century later, the Jews had learned this important lesson: They were now trusting in Jehovah to protect them from their enemies, not the temple.

The Jewish nation was enjoying a state of spiritual renewal. As a nation, they would never return to the blatant idolatry of their forefathers; Jehovah had purged them of it. However, another form of religion just as deplorable to God would in time settle into their hearts and minds. H. A. Ironside comments on this spiritual condition, which still plagues many Jews today:

> Their experiences in this stronghold of paganistic corruption [Babylon] cured them effectually of the worship of images, and resulted in a gracious revival under God's good hand which gave to His word a place of importance in their souls that it had not previously held. Unhappily, this blessed work of God's Spirit soon lost its power and degenerated into a mere cold intellectual bibliolatry, in which the letter of the Word was clung to tenaciously while the spirit was quite ignored. So devoted were the Pharisaic successors of "the men of the great synagogue" (as Ezra and his companions were afterwards called) to the study of the sacred Letters of the law. While a great body of expository literature was produced, most of it pedantic and imaginative in the extreme, but all testifying to the veneration in which the Scriptures were held. Yet when He who is Himself the Spirit of the entire Old Testament, and of whom Moses and all the prophets wrote, appeared in their midst, He was not discerned by faith and was rejected and crucified by the descendants of the very remnant whose zeal for God is commended in the book of Ezra.[3]

As a result of this colossal blunder, the Jewish nation was given over to spiritual blindness (Rom. 11:7), and in a day soon coming will decline into a lower form of idolatry than previously committed; during the Tribulation Period they will receive the Antichrist as their long-awaited Messiah. The Lord's Second Advent to the earth will conclude

33

the period of time the Gentiles are allowed to rule over Israel (Rom. 11:25). This event also coincides with the end of Israel's spiritual blindness (Rom. 11:7-14). When Christ came to the earth two thousand years ago, He removed the veil God had put over the Law (i.e. its full purpose was not disclosed until after Christ's ascension into heaven), but the Jews picked the veil back up and blindfolded themselves from the truth (2 Cor. 3:6-18). The purpose of the Mosaic Law was to show the Jews their sin (Rom. 3:20), and to point them to the solution – Christ (Gal. 3:24). At Calvary, Christ satisfied all of the judicial claims of the Law by substitutionally dying in the place of sinners. By rejecting His kingdom gospel message, the Jews became locked into a state of blindness, a condition that Satan has worked to maintain (2 Cor. 4:4).

However, at Christ's Second Advent to the earth, the Hebrew nation will recognize Him as their Messiah (Zech. 12:10). During the Tribulation Period, a Jewish remnant shall be refined and restored to God at its conclusion (Rom. 9:27, 11:26-32). God will protect this remnant from the Antichrist's assault (Rev. 12:6-17), but during the refining process two-thirds of all Jews will be massacred (Zech. 13:7-8). With this said, it must be pointed out that the greatest revival of all time will occur during the Tribulation Period. Walter K. Price comments to this fact:

> One hundred forty-four thousand Jews saved, plus a multitude which no man can number out of all the nations who have been washed in the blood of the Lamb! And all this within the limits of the tribulation period. What a revival! Neither Pentecost in the first century, nor the Reformation on the Continent, nor the evangelical revival in England, nor the Great Awakening in the Colonies, could match this spiritual awakening. Neither Luther, Wesley, Whitefield, Finney, Moody, Sunday, nor Billy Graham, individually or collectively, could muster such statistics as these. The world is yet in store for its greatest spiritual revival in which vast multitudes beyond comprehension, will be saved. ... Emphasis has been put upon the horror of the tribulation that we have lost sight of the fact that it will also be a time of unprecedented revival.[4]

Until the Jewish nation receives the benefits of the New Covenant during the Tribulation Period, the Lord Jesus Christ is building His

Church, which, although it includes both Jews and Gentiles, is chiefly composed of Gentiles. Moreover, God is bestowing blessings on Gentile believers to provoke the Jews to jealousy; this will ultimately result in their return to Him (Rom. 11:11-15). The Jews stumbled over Christ at His First Advent, and the blessing He offered them instead fell into the laps of the Gentiles, who were not expecting it (Luke 20:9-16; Rom. 9:32). Thus, God would call a people that were not His covenant people to be His children, and He would bring them (the Gentiles) into the good of the New Covenant also (Hos. 1:10, 2:23; Rom. 9:25-26).

There are those who teach that God is done with the nation of Israel, and that the Church has replaced the nation of Israel in God's plan of blessing. However, it is emphasized that the New Covenant, sealed by Christ's own blood, was not confirmed with Gentiles, but with the houses of Israel and Judah (Heb. 8:8). Gentiles became a second benefactor to this covenant, by which God was able to fulfill His promise to Abraham that in him all families of the earth would be blessed (Gen. 12:3). This was only possible through Christ's redemptive work at Calvary.

In the days of Zerubbabel, Ezra, and Nehemiah, revival repeatedly swept through the nation because the Jews were willing to obey their God and exercise faith in Him, no matter what the cost. This lesson the Church must learn also, for to follow the letter of the Law, without being guided in grace and love by the Holy Spirit, leads to spiritual decline and eventually legalism. Legalism is none the less idolatrous, for by the traditions of men and "feel good" theology the gospel of Jesus Christ is replaced with a vile form of humanism.

A Revival Meditation

R. A. Torrey was a nineteenth-century evangelist; this is his prescription for revival:

> I can give a prescription that will bring a revival to any church or community or any city on earth. First, let a few Christians (they need not be many) get thoroughly right with God themselves. This is the prime essential. If this is not done, the rest that I am to say will come to nothing. Second, let them bind themselves together in a prayer group to pray for a revival until God opens the heavens and comes down. Third, let them put themselves at the disposal of God for Him

to use as He sees fit in winning others to Christ. That is all! This is sure to bring a revival to any church or community. I have given this prescription around the world. It has been taken by many churches and many communities, and in no instance has it ever failed; and it cannot fail![5]

Progress Invites Attack
Ezra 4:1-5, 24

When God's people are working in unity and for His glory, the enemy of God is sure to take notice and oppose their efforts. This was apparent in Zerubbabel's day, as it was in New Testament times, for wherever the apostles went, laying the foundation of Church truth, the activity of the enemy was prompted. This is evident in our times as well. Paul reminded the believers at Ephesus that their real battle was not with flesh and blood (i.e. people in the world), but rather *"against principalities, against powers, against the rulers of the darkness of this age, against spiritual hosts of wickedness in the heavenly places"* (Eph. 6:12-13). The leader of the powers of darkness is Satan.

Satan consistently opposed the Lord Jesus Christ throughout His ministry on earth, and today he continues to oppose Jesus Christ, His gospel message, and those who would spread it. Satan despises Christ and those who identify with Him and works to manipulate various world systems of thinking to exclude Christ from consideration. Paul identifies Satan as *"the god of this age"* (2 Cor. 4:4), and *"the prince of the power of the air"* (Eph. 2:2). On three occasions the Lord Jesus said that Satan is *"the prince of this world"* (John 12:31, 14:30, 16:11). The world is Satan's delegated domain, but he must function within divine boundaries. God is holy, and He cannot tempt anyone to sin (Jas. 1:13), although Satan is allowed to test man's resolve to obey God.

The prophet Ezekiel informs us that before his fall, Lucifer (who is now called Satan or "the accuser"), was a beautiful cherub, sheathed with precious stones and inherently equipped with musical ability (Ezek. 28:11-16). He was likely the most powerful created being that God made and, thus, is a cunning and dangerous enemy that only God controls. Consequently, believers are not commanded to confront Satan, but rather to resist him by submitting to God in faith (Jas. 4:7). Believers are to be knowledgeable of his tactics so that he does not gain an advantage over them through ignorance. Paul reminded the Christians at Corinth of this fact, saying, *"we are not ignorant of his devices"* (2 Cor. 2:11). Because Satan repeatedly uses the same strategies to oppose the things of God, believers are able to become more aware of his confrontational tactics by studying Scripture.

Ezra 4 contains two satanic attack strategies which have been repeatedly used in diverting God's people from accomplishing His revealed will. The first is to corrupt God's people through *unnatural unions* (i.e. through close associations with the children of the devil). The second is to mentally fatigue them through *discouragement*. Paul states that the children of God should not be *"tossed to and fro, and carried about with every wind of doctrine, by the sleight of men, and cunning craftiness, whereby they lie in wait to deceive"* (Eph. 4:14). Through high-minded philosophies, crafty words, or unrelenting cynicism, Satan attempts to undermine the work of God through His people by deceiving or discouraging them.

Scripture represents Satan both as a threatening lion who is ready to devour God's people (1 Pet. 5:8) and as a cunning serpent who endeavors to deceive and trick them (Gen. 3:1). The strong and brutal lion who had captured the Jews had been conquered by Jehovah through the Persians. Defeated, the enemy now slithered along in the shadows of the departing nation; if he cannot keep God's people in Babylon (a picture of the world), he would work to ensure Babylon kept to them. This tactic was used by Satan a thousand years earlier after his defeat in Egypt by the rod of God in the hand of Moses. A *"mixed multitude"* (i.e. an unbelieving contingency) departed with the Israelites from Egypt to corrupt them (Ex. 12:38). Apparently, the supernatural feats of Jehovah inspired many Egyptians to come with the Jews, but these only served to corrupt God's people in the wilderness. Ezra 4 records that the tactic of *unnatural unions* was the first device Satan employed as an attempt to stop the Jews from building the temple.

As soon as the local inhabitants heard about what the Jews were doing (v. 1), they came to Zerubbabel and the other Jewish leaders with a request: *"Let us build with you; for we seek your God"* (v. 2). *"The peoples around them"* were mainly the Samaritans, the descendants of various ethnic groups who had been forcibly transferred to northern Israel after Assyria invaded the land and carried away the ten tribes of

Israel in 722 BC (2 Kgs. 17). The Jews who remained in the land intermarried with these new inhabitants, and thus, their Jewish identification was lost.

The locals presented a twofold appeal to the Jews. First, they claimed commonality with the Jews as a displaced people; they also had been forcibly moved to Palestine. This statement, however, indicates their lack of understanding of God's working in the situation. God had previously given the Jews the land of Palestine as a homeland, but they had been uprooted because of God's chastening hand. Second, the Samaritans claimed to be worshippers of Jehovah, like the Jews. They said that they, as their forefathers before them, had been offering sacrifices to Jehovah since the time of their arrival nearly two centuries earlier. The fact of the matter was that the Northern Kingdom had not worshipped Jehovah, per the Levitical Law, since the time when they followed Jeroboam in rebellion four centuries prior! Jeroboam had introduced a pagan system of worship to prevent the northern tribes from journeying to Jerusalem to worship at the temple as God demanded (1 Kgs. 12). So why should the Jews believe that their descendants, now of mixed ethnicity, were somehow devoted to Him?

What did the enemy hope to accomplish by joining the Jews in the temple construction project? An attack on the Jews with weapons of war would have proven to be a futile endeavor to stop the temple construction, at least for very long, for the Jews were under King Cyrus' authority. There can be little doubt that Cyrus' military resolve would have quickly quelled such a rebellion. In the end, a frontal assault on the Jews would have only strengthened their cause. But, if the enemy could infiltrate and collapse the effort from within through compromise, then the goal of stopping the work could still be achieved without a physical conflict. Paul warned the Corinthians that Satan often transforms himself into an angel of light and his servants into ministers of righteousness, because he knows it is easier to deceive God's people than it is to deter them from a purpose (2 Cor. 11:14-15). Therefore, Paul's warning to the Corinthians to not be yoked with non-believers is appropriate for God's people in any age, including Zerubbabel and Jeshua:

Do not be unequally yoked together with unbelievers. For what fellowship has righteousness with lawlessness? And what communion

39

has light with darkness? And what accord has Christ with Belial? Or what part has a believer with an unbeliever? And what agreement has the temple of God with idols? For you are the temple of the living God (2 Cor. 6:14-16).

The strategy of *unnatural unions* would not be successful against the Jews. Zerubbabel and Jeshua, with other leaders throughout Israel, knew that their enemies did not worship Jehovah and, thus, would not allow them to have any part of the work which they themselves had been charged to do. Their response was curt and to the point, *"You may do nothing with us to build a house for our God; but we alone will build to the Lord God of Israel, as King Cyrus the king of Persia has commanded us"* (v. 3). The Jews alone were God's covenant people and no outsiders would work alongside them to accomplish what they alone had been given to do.

Satan often uses the device of *unnatural unions* to cripple or terminate what often starts out as a good ministry. The solution to this tactic is to completely avoid any associations with the children of the devil while accomplishing the Lord's business. The Jews did not need the help of their enemies to build the temple. The apostles in the early Church demonstrated the same resolve in fulfilling the Lord's command to spread the gospel message among the nations: *"They went forth, taking nothing of the Gentiles"* (3 Jn. 7).

It is a human tendency to forge unions for the sake of acquiring more strength and resources to accomplish some desired end result. But God does not typically use amassed human wherewithal to work His will; rather, He uses simple and foolish things, so that in every miraculous feat, He alone will be honored by men. Paul reminds the Christians at Corinth of this important fact:

For you see your calling, brethren, that not many wise according to the flesh, not many mighty, not many noble, are called. But God has chosen the foolish things of the world to put to shame the wise, and God has chosen the weak things of the world to put to shame the things which are mighty; and the base things of the world and the things which are despised God has chosen, and the things which are not, to bring to nothing the things that are, that no flesh should glory in His presence (1 Cor. 1:26-29).

40

Strength of the flesh is not the means in which God glorifies Himself, unless it is to show the futility of such unionization. Pharaoh collected all the vigor of Egypt against Moses, yet this only served to prove Jehovah's greatness in the end (Rom. 9:17).

Satan has used this tactic of *unnatural unions* on many throughout Biblical history. Joshua fell prey to the Gibeonites' trickery in Canaan: "we are your servants ... we know your God ... make a peace treaty with us" (Josh. 9). He listened to the enemy, did not seek God's counsel on the matter, and paid a high price for submitting to the deception.

Ahab, the king of Israel, suckered Jehoshaphat, the king of Judah, into forging an alliance with him in order to pool their resources and retake Ramoth-gilead, a city of refuge thirty miles east of the Jordan River. The Syrians controlled and inhabited this city. Ahab was an evil king and godly Jehoshaphat should have known better than to unite with Ahab, especially in a meaningless religious cause that God had not sanctioned. The result of this union nearly cost Jehoshaphat his life, and it would have if he had not cried out for God to save him (2 Chron. 18). After Jehoshaphat returned to Jerusalem, the prophet Hanani rebuked the king, *"Should you help the wicked, and love them who hate the Lord?"* (2 Chron. 19:2). Though Jehoshaphat had done many good things for the Lord, God would punish him for aligning with wicked Ahab (2 Chron. 19:2-3).

Certainly, one of Satan's most successful strategies to confront God's people throughout time is the use of "unnatural unions." C. H. Mackintosh wrote regarding this in the mid-19th century:

There is great danger, at the present day, of compromising truth for the sake of union. This should be carefully guarded against. There can be no true union attained at the expense of truth. The true Christian's motto should be, "Maintain truth at all cost, if union can be promoted in this way, so much the better, but maintain the truth." The principle of expediency, on the contrary, may be thus enunciated: "Promote union at all cost; if truth can be maintained as well, so much the better, but promote union." This latter principle can only be carried out at the expense of all that is divine in the way of testimony.[1]

How many Christians today are reaping God's judgment for teaming up with the unregenerate to accomplish some religious cause or support some charitable activity? If children of God and children of the devil are working together harmoniously, it is not God who is glorified in the endeavor, but the one who has wanted God's glory and station from the beginning (Isa. 14:12-15).

The second tactic the enemy used on the Jews was to discourage them, or as the King James Version puts it, to *"frustrate their purpose"* (v. 4). The enemy hired counselors to harass the Jews in threatening or meaningless dialogue. We are not told what was said, but no doubt a volley of fanciful words was used to undermine the authorization of the work, to make the Jews fearful, or to cast doubt on its progress or success. Although this tactic by itself did not stop the work, it effectively slowed its progress. Mind-games and word-wars waste precious time. These worthless conversations tend to diminish our mental astuteness for doing God's will because we become anxious about things that are not even true.

Instead of fully focusing on building, the Jews would be musing and fretting about what was no threat at all. The enemy thrives when he can pose some virtual reality that has no eternal bearing and then cause us to worry about it. Paul says at such time the believers are to refocus their thinking Godward and concentrate on what is true and real:

> *Be anxious for nothing, but in everything by prayer and supplication, with thanksgiving, let your requests be made known to God; and the peace of God, which surpasses all understanding, will guard your hearts and minds through Christ Jesus. Finally, brethren, whatever things are true, whatever things are noble, whatever things are just, whatever things are pure, whatever things are lovely, whatever things are of good report, if there is any virtue and if there is anything praiseworthy – meditate on these things. The things which you learned and received and heard and saw in me, these do, and the God of peace will be with you* (Phil. 4:6-9).

When Satan cannot stop God's people from serving their Lord, he will be satisfied to distract them through anxiety, so that they cannot serve Him with all their heart, with all their soul, and with all their mind (Matt. 22:37). This device frustrates God's people because it reduces their mental ability to concentrate on what they know God desires them to do. The solution is to train the mind to keep focused on the Lord and His sovereignty in the situation. By allowing Him to resolve what only He can, we mentally relieve ourselves to devote our full attention to what God wants us to do for Him.

The Jews were being obedient to the will of God and opposed by the forces of Satan. Should this be a surprise? The devil wastes no ammunition on those not living for Christ. Satan used the tactic of *unnatural unions*, but the Jews were determined to build the temple without Gentile participation. The devil then used the device of *discouragement* to frustrate the Jews and slow their progress, and in time stop it altogether. The proper defense against this tactic is to ignore what the enemy says altogether and just focus on the Lord and His Word. This strategy precludes God's people from getting mentally sidetracked by both vain intellectual arguments and unjust criticism.

Verse 24 is one of the saddest portions of the entire book: *"Thus the work of the house of God which is at Jerusalem ceased, and it was discontinued until the second year of the reign of Darius king of Persia."* Apparently, the hired counselors were relentless in their opposition even after the Jews ceased working on the temple. The onslaught of discouraging words continued throughout the reign of King Cyrus and until Darius was the new King of Persia (v. 5). The enemy's tenacity demonstrates how much Satan loathes the worship of God. He was not satisfied with just stopping the work of God; he wanted to ensure that it never started again. But revival among God's people would come, as recorded in the next chapter.

A Revival Meditation

Sometimes revival is associated with blessed reductions. Two church leaders were talking about revival when one said to the other, "We've had a revival in our church." The other man replied, "That's good. How many were added to the congregation?" "None were added, but ten were subtracted."[2] The spiritual oneness of God's people manifests the glory of God to a lost world (John 17:21-23). This reality characterized the early Church and is why it was so successful in reaching the masses for Christ (Acts 2-6). Accordingly, the unconverted and the converted choosing to remain in sin cannot enhance the spiritual vitality of the Church, but rather can only serve to weaken it and degrade its testimony.

Stop Rebuilding Jerusalem
Ezra 4:6-23

A fifty-seven year gap exists between Ezra 6 and 7 (515 to 458 BC); it is during this interim that the events recorded in Ezra 4:6-23 occurred and that the book of Esther was written. Apparently, Ezra stepped out of chronological order to include these later accounts of Jewish opposition in the Ezra 4 narrative to further substantiate his claim made in verse 5 that the rebuilding of Jerusalem was relentlessly opposed (even after the temple was built). Ezra noted that the enemies of God's people continued to oppose the Jews and the rebuilding of the temple until the reign of King Darius (v. 5), a Mede who ruled from 521 to 486 BC.

Verse 6 is a parenthetic note which refers to a letter written from the opposition against the Jews at the beginning of the reign of King Xerxes (Ahasuerus), about thirty years after the temple was completed. Xerxes, the son of Darius, succeeded to the throne of the Medio-Persian Empire after his father's death. He reigned from 486 BC to 465 BC. His son Artaxerxes (Esther's husband) then ruled Persia from 464 to 424 BC. Thus, the approximate date of this accusatory letter would be 485 BC, (shortly after King Xerxes came to power), and would predate the book of Esther.

Ezra supplies more information concerning three additional letters written during the reign of Artaxerxes (vv. 7-23). The first two letters are from the enemies of the Jews to King Artaxerxes. The content of the first letter is not specified, but we know it was written by Bishlam, Mithredath, Tabeel and others to King Artaxerxes. Ezra does include a copy of the second letter to the king in his narrative. It was penned by Rehum, the chancellor, and Shimshai, his secretary, on behalf of a large contingency of various peoples throughout the region who were adamantly opposed to the Jews rebuilding Jerusalem. The third letter is written by King Artaxerxes himself commanding that the reconstruction be stopped.

In short, the opposition did not even mention the temple, for they knew that the Jews had King Cyrus' permission to worship there; rather, they informed Artaxerxes that the Jews were rebuilding Jerusalem as a fortified city (vv. 11-16): *"Let it be known to the king that the Jews who came up from you have come to us at Jerusalem, and are building the rebellious and evil city, and are finishing its walls and repairing the foundations"* (v. 12). This statement was clearly false as the walls of Jerusalem still laid waste when Nehemiah arrived in Jerusalem years later. The Lord Jesus said there is no truth in Satan: *"When he speaks a lie, he speaks from his own resources, for he is a liar and the father of it"* (John 8:44-45). John reminds us that he is the *"accuser of the brethren"* (Rev. 12:10). Lying and accusing is natural to the Father of Lies, and we can see that he was the true author of Rehum's letter.

While it is true that the Jews had previously rebelled against the Babylonians, there was no hint of an uprising against the crown of Persia. Yet, the intent of the letter was to plant suspicion in the king's mind through an exaggerated story and the suggestion that if the Jews had a fortified city, they would cease from paying taxes and tribute money to the empire (v. 13). This, of course, would bring dishonor upon the king's good name (v. 14). Furthermore, with a stronghold in Palestine, the Jews might try to reclaim their land taken by Babylon years earlier. If this occurred, it would weaken the control of the Persian Empire in that region.

After receiving Rehum's letter, King Artaxerxes commanded that the archives be searched for historical information concerning the Jewish people; he wanted to assess whether or not the Jews truly posed a threat to his kingdom. It was learned that Jerusalem had previously been the capital of a powerful kingdom, probably referring to the days of David and Solomon. Artaxerxes decided not to take a chance and wrote the following to the governing authorities in Palestine: *"Now give the command to make these men cease, that this city may not be built until the command is given by me"* (v. 21). Although the work was forcibly stopped, there were two aspects of Artaxerxes's response which must have encouraged the Jews. First, he acknowledged that they indeed had once been a powerful people, and second, the opportunity for the work to continue in the future was still a possibility. In fact, years later Artaxerxes himself would give Nehemiah permission to rebuild the wall of Jerusalem (Neh. 2).

It is noteworthy that the enemies of the Jews used the same tactic of threatening accusations that had failed during the reign of Darius, to stop the work during the reign of his grandson Artaxerxes. Why were the accusations against the Jews effective in stopping the rebuilding of Jerusalem, but not the rebuilding of the temple? Three reasons are suggested. First, the rebuilding of the temple was prophesied in Scripture, and thus, commanded and completed by God in accordance with His sovereign purpose. The following efforts to rebuild Jerusalem, while noble, were not commanded by God; in fact, God planned to accomplish something quite spectacular at a later day through the leadership of Nehemiah. What had been attempted for decades would be completed in only fifty-two days. Even the enemies of the Jews would recognize that by the hand of Jehovah, the God of the Jews, the impossible had been accomplished (Neh. 6:16).

A second possible reason that the tactic of *accusation* worked in the latter case is that the accusers had banded together in greater numbers (v. 9); it was only the local governor and a few of his companions who wrote to Darius in opposition to the reconstruction of the temple (5:6). The appeal to Artaxerxes against the reconstruction of Jerusalem was made by a broad coalition of various people groups throughout the region.

Generally speaking, in most confrontational matters the guilty party is the individual who defends himself or herself by gathering others (often friends and family) to accuse the other party of wrongdoing. On the other hand, the individual who leaves the matter with the Lord to judge is usually the innocent party (1 Pet. 2:19-21). Those who choose this course of action are demonstrating true brokenness before the Lord, writes William MacDonald:

> It is a mark of deepest and truest humility to see ourselves condemned without cause and to be silent under it. To be silent under insult and wrong is a very noble imitation of our Lord. "Oh, my Lord, when I remember in how many ways You did suffer, who in no way deserved it, I know not where my senses are when I am in such haste to defend and excuse myself. Is it possible I should desire anyone to speak any

good of me or to think it, when so many ill things were thought and spoken of You?"[1]

Sometimes even tears, as in the case of profane Esau, can be misleading – embracing an appeal of sympathy apart from reason will often leave us holding hands with the devil. This was certainly the case with the Lord Jesus Christ, who was accused of wrongdoing by an emotionally charged crowd, yet He was completely innocent of the charges against Him (1 Pet. 2:21-23). The one engaged in social politics and soliciting the pity and aid of others is usually the one at the heart of the problem. Satan enjoys using such a one to sow division among the brethren instead of making for peace and allowing the Lord to judge the matter (1 Pet. 2:20-23). God hates *"a false witness who speaks lies, and one who sows discord among brethren"* (Prov. 6:19).

> I fear not the tyranny of man, neither yet what the devil can invent against me.
> — John Knox

The third reason that the enemy's accusations prospered in the days of Artaxerxes is what was said about the Jews' history was partly true, although the projected outcome of their labors was not. Through the power of suggestion, the enemy appealed to the king's imagination as to what might happen if the Jews continued their work. During the days of King Darius, the opposition did not believe that the Jews were telling the truth, and therefore they asked the king to validate their claims. They were hoping that Darius would find that the Jews were lying and did not have authority to rebuild the temple. But this was not the case; the Jews were telling the truth and the construction effort continued. However, in the days of Artaxerxes the enemy drew fragments of the truth and embellished the facts to create a false reality. As Eve learned in the Garden of Eden, Satan is particularly dangerous when he combines some degree of truth within his presentation and then misguides his audience by suggesting an untrue outcome. His attack on her was methodical and deadly.

First, Satan projected doubt on what God actually said, inquiring, *"You shall not eat of every tree of the garden?"* (Gen. 3:1). It was a leading question, for its purpose was not to provoke rational thought but to instill doubt and invoke rebellion. The tactic worked on the woman, who quickly slid from the ground of faith into human reasoning. Satan's question to Eve has a flavor of unfairness: "Could God be good and limit you in such an unfair way? Surely a good God would not keep you from all that is good."

Second, Satan caused the woman to focus on the negative rather than the positive. Man was invited to eat from every tree in the garden, save one. Yet, the serpent beckoned mankind to focus upon the only one off-limits. Satan enjoys sowing dissatisfaction. When embraced, dissatisfaction stirs up doubts concerning God's goodness and wisdom. Dear believer, the next time Satan tempts you not to be content, train your eye upon all the blessings in Christ and not what, in your own mind, you lack or deserve.

Third, notice Satan added to what God had said: *"Then the serpent said to the woman, 'You will not surely die'"* (Gen 3:4). The addition of a single three-letter word changed God's intended meaning completely. God said, *"when you eat you shall surely die,"* but Satan said, *"you will **not** surely die."* Satan was referring to physical death while completely ignoring the subject of spiritual life with God. God warned of immediate spiritual death, though physical death would naturally come to those apart from God. Every cemetery is proof that God told the full truth and that Satan is a liar.

Satan began by questioning God's Word and presenting a half-truth, and mankind acted on the wrong half. Satan is never more dangerous than when he has a Bible in his hands. As the Jews found out in the days of Artaxerxes, accusations partly founded in truth are the most dangerous. This is why Paul exhorts the believers at Colosse to have a faith fully grounded on Christ and His teachings:

> *Now this I say lest anyone should deceive you with persuasive words. For though I am absent in the flesh, yet I am with you in spirit, rejoicing to see your good order and the steadfastness of your faith in Christ. As you therefore have received Christ Jesus the Lord, so walk in Him, rooted and built up in Him and established in the faith, as you have been taught, abounding in it with thanksgiving* (Col. 2:4-7).

God is a God of absolute truth; therefore, let our faith rest on the foundation of biblical truth. If so grounded, we will be less likely to fall prey to threatening accusations and secular reasonings. The value of our service relates directly with having fellowship with God in spirit and in truth. If we become satisfied with the goodness of God's blessings and yet lose sight of what He desires for us, we will become feeble and powerless – God strengthens those who want to be guided into the knowledge of Himself and the purposes of His grace.

Believers will experience the most satisfaction and joy in life when they are fully resting in God's grace and obeying His Word. In the eternal purposes of God, the accusations of the devil cannot overcome those who abide in the Lord Jesus Christ!

The Jews were spiritually hamstrung and no significant effort to rebuild Jerusalem occurred for many years. They dwelled among the ruins – a constant reminder that the wages of sin is death (i.e. separation from God). But God would summon two men to do the spectacular. Ezra would win Artaxerxes's favor and return to Jerusalem in 458 BC to spiritually rebuild the people; then, thirteen years later, Nehemiah, Artaxerxes' cupbearer, would receive his approval to return to Jerusalem to rebuild the wall about the city. God was using men who sought His honor alone to accomplish great things for His people, but on His own timetable.

A Revival Meditation

Harry Moorehouse, while still a young man, was conducting evangelistic services in a certain city, but there was no revival; it was as though he were beating against a stone wall. Day and night he was on his knees searching his heart and crying out, "O God, why is there no revival?"

One day he was walking along the street, and the Holy Spirit showed him a large placard on which appeared these words: "Harry Moorehouse, the most famous of all British preachers!" At once he said to himself, "That is why there is no revival!"

He went to the campaign committee, and said, "Brethren, now I know why there is no revival. See how you have advertised me as the greatest of this and the greatest of that! No wonder the Holy Spirit cannot work! He is grieved and quenched because you haven't magnified the Lord Jesus Christ. He is the wonderful One. I'm just a poor, simple, humble servant, preaching the glorious Gospel, and saying, 'Behold the Lamb of God that taketh away the sins of the world'."[2]

The Work Resumes
Ezra 5:1-2

We leave Ezra's parenthetical explanation of future opposition to the rebuilding of Jerusalem to the matter at hand, the building of the temple. Preparations for this project had begun in 536 BC after the Jews had arrived in Jerusalem and erected an altar. The temple foundation was completed and dedicated in 535 BC, but the building program ceased sometime after that due to the efforts of the enemy to discourage and break down the resolve of God's people. At the outset, the Jews rested solely on God's authority. The sufficiency of His Word was their battle-axe against opposition when they first arrived in Jerusalem; that focus needed to be regained. What was God's solution to this situation? He called two prophets, Haggai and Zechariah, to reprove His people of sin and to motivate them to again begin the temple construction (v. 1).

Haggai was first to speak for the Lord. On August 29, 520 BC he delivered his first message to his countrymen. He confronted their spiritual complacency (Hag. 1:2) and their comfortable standard of living (Hag. 1:4-6). Apparently, materials earlier donated to build the temple had been used by the Jews to build themselves nice paneled houses, while God's house was in ruins: *"'Is it time for you yourselves to dwell in your paneled houses, and this temple to lie in ruins?' Now therefore, thus says the Lord of hosts: 'Consider your ways!'"* (Hag. 1:4-5). The prophet went on to inform the Jews that they were being economically punished by God for their lethargic attitudes towards Him (Hag. 1:6). After revealing this reality, he again appealed to them to consider their ways (Hag. 1:7).

Besides the enemy's tactics of *unnatural unions, discouragement,* and *accusations* discussed in Ezra 4, another device Satan uses to confront the will of God is to promote ease and comfort among God's people. Our flesh craves comfort and lusts for pleasure. Christians

52

rarely fall into sin, but rather step down into it (1 Tim. 6:9-10). First, they enjoy **comfort**, an environment void of biblical exhortation and reproof. Over time they become **complacent** to the things of God. The next downward step is **compromise**, which finally leads to **carnality** – willful sin and an appetite for worldliness.

> When is a revival needed? When carelessness and unconcern keep the people asleep.
> — Billy Sunday

Although in many parts of the world today the Church is vibrant and growing, often because of the purifying and strengthening effect of persecution, this is generally not the case in the post-modern world. The "pampered Church" today is weak and highly susceptible to worldliness. Why should the hordes of lost souls seriously consider the claims of Christ when many Christians do not? Why should the unregenerate fear hell and the eternal judgment when the Christians they associate with are quite satisfied with the temporary thrills and the sensual trinkets of the world?

> The problem is not hostility to the church; it is indifference. For many the church is simply irrelevant; it is not even worth criticizing, it is simply to be ignored.
> — William Barclay

If the Church is to witness revival again, she must awaken from her spiritual slumber. The modern Church may be likened to the Shulamite bride of old, who after bathing and retiring for the night failed to rise from her comfortable bed even when her beloved came to her chamber: *"I have taken off my robe; how can I put it on again? I have washed my feet; how can I defile them?"* (Song 5:3). Later, she loathed her complacency, hurriedly arose, only to find that her beloved was no longer at her door; the time of intimacy which her beloved sought with her was lost. Today, many who have been redeemed and cleansed by the blood of Christ remain in their comfortable beds of complacency, and never experience the passion of knowing Christ and living for Him. The words of the beloved to the Shulamite ring true today: *"Rise up, my love"* (Song 2:10).

As long as we are content to live without revival, we will.

— Leonard Ravenhill

What effect did Haggai's pungent preaching have on a comfortably slumbering nation?

> *Then Zerubbabel the son of Shealtiel, and Joshua the son of Jehozadak, the high priest, with all the remnant of the people, obeyed the voice of the Lord their God, and the words of Haggai the prophet, as the Lord their God had sent him; and the people feared the presence of the Lord. Then Haggai, the Lord's messenger, spoke the Lord's message to the people, saying, "I am with you, says the Lord." So the Lord stirred up the spirit of Zerubbabel the son of Shealtiel, governor of Judah, and the spirit of Joshua the son of Jehozadak, the high priest, and the spirit of all the remnant of the people; and they came and worked on the house of the Lord of hosts, their God, on the twenty-fourth day of the sixth month, in the second year of King Darius* (Hag. 1:12-15).

On September 21, 520 BC, after 15 years of inactivity, the Jews began again to build God a house. Although the labor had commenced, the Lord moved Haggai to deliver three more messages and Zechariah to deliver his first message before the end of the year. Haggai's confrontational ministry abruptly ended in December of 520 BC, but Zechariah, who motivated the Jews with hope for the future, continued prophesying for two more years. Why did God's prophets keep preaching even after the Jews started rebuilding the temple? Because service for Jehovah was not enough; He also required a spiritual transformation of attitudes and behavior. Otherwise, His people would fail to properly represent Him among the nations after the temple was completed (Rom. 2:23-24). In his initial message, Zechariah pleads with the people, *"Turn now from your evil ways"* (Zech. 1:4). Confronting sin among God's people is the first step towards spiritual revival. The effect of these messages caused the Jews to understand that God had justly chastened them in love and that they deserved it.

True repentance has a double aspect; it looks upon things past with a weeping eye, and upon the future with a watchful eye.

— Robert Smith

Haggai's first message began with rebuke, but ended with encouragement. He pleaded with them to consider their ways, but also reminded them of God's abiding presence. He also announced that the temple they were erecting would have a future glory associated with it – Messiah would come and purify it and offer peace in it (Hag. 1:7-9). He would use a similar format in his final two messages, where Haggai reminded the Jews that no amount of obedience can undo one act of disobedience (Hag. 2:13), that God's seventy-year-rest judgment on the land had ended (Hag. 2:18-19), and that in a future day, Gentile oppression would come to an end forever (Hag. 2:22). This message format dealt with their sin, which hindered them from living for God, and also inspired the people with hope (i.e. to anticipate what great things God would accomplish through them and for them).

Revival is a renewed conviction of sin and repentance, followed by an intense desire to live in obedience to God. It is giving up one's will to God in deep humility.
— Charles Finney

Apparently, God knew His people needed constant encouragement and exhortation from His prophets to preserve them in the midst of immense opposition. This reality is still true today. In Acts 18:27 the Greek word *protrepomai* is rendered "encouraged" in the RV and NASV: *"The brethren encouraged him* [Apollos]*."* The meaning of this word is "to turn forward for oneself." The first portion of this word, *protrepo,* literally implies "to urge forward." In Acts 18:27, the verb is in the middle voice which indicates the brethren's particular interest to propel Apollos forward in ministry at Corinth. When God's people do well, especially in areas in which they tend to struggle, believers should add energy to the right behavior with praise and encouragement in order to reinforce it.

According to the writer of Hebrews, believers also need constant exhortation to serve the Lord properly: we are instructed, *"Exhort one another daily"* (Heb. 3:13). "To exhort" is translated from the Greek word *parakaleo*, which means "to call near and invoke." If a child of God has lost his or her direction, those with maturity are to draw near and direct his or her path. Perhaps someone who is lost has asked the reader for directions. Normally, you would draw near to the inquiring individual and then point out the way. Both encouragement and exhortation are necessary tools for assisting God's people to live for Him.

Revival was spreading among the Jewish nation; it had started with its leaders, Zerubbabel and Jeshua. Ezra records one other detail that Haggai does not mention: *"So Zerubbabel the son of Shealtiel and Jeshua the son of Jozadak rose up and began to build the house of God which is in Jerusalem; and the prophets of God were with them, helping them"* (Ezra 5:2). The prophets of God were not just preachers; they practiced what they preached. National revival meant that all would take part in the work, so even God's messengers and leaders labored alongside their brethren. It is a good reminder that no child of God should be above doing any task for the Lord, no matter how mundane. God's prophets were preaching divine truth, God's leaders were proactive with divine vision, and God's people were divinely awakened from their spiritual slumber – revival had come again to Israel.

A Revival Meditation

I read of the revivals of the past, great sweeping revivals where thousands of men were swept into the Kingdom of God. I read about Charles G. Finney winning his thousands and his hundreds of thousands of souls to Christ. Then I picked up a book and read the messages of Charles G. Finney and the message of Jonathan Edwards on *Sinners in the Hands of an Angry God*, and I said, "No wonder men trembled; no wonder they ... cried out in repentance and sobbed their way to the throne of grace!"

— Leonard Ravenhill

Threatening Accusations
Ezra 5:3-17

Ezra was not an eye-witness to the events of Ezra 1-6; he wrote this passage from a historical perspective. His vantage point is interesting in that he does not mention the disobedience of the nation in ceasing to build the temple, but rather details how the opposition slowed its construction to a grinding halt. Haggai and Zechariah are forthright in confronting the sins of the people, and announcing their divine chastening and the necessity of their repentance. Ezra, however, informs us of the techniques used by the enemy and how God, in His timing, overcame the opposition. Jehovah's prophets were required to reprove wrong attitudes and behaviors among the Jews, but Ezra writes to show how God uses weak things to accomplish the impossible, thus displaying His greatness. Certainly, calls to repentance are a necessary part of the Christian living, but if believers better understood the futility of Satan's devices in respect to God's omnipotence, the need for corrective ministry would be significantly diminished.

The paramount reason to study Scripture is to learn what God reveals about Himself – to know the One who is all-knowing. Knowledge that "puffs up" is not the goal, but rather awareness of God's greatness which prompts us to fall on our faces in wonder and awe before Him. The reason Paul prayed that the Colossian believers would be *"increasing in the knowledge of God"* is that he knew such knowledge would lead them into spiritual wisdom, strength, and fruitfulness (Col. 1:9-11). Whenever a believer's understanding of God slips, or his or her desire to know God more intimately wanes, something has gone very wrong. Understanding who God is, and what He has done and will do, promotes our spiritual vitality. Most of our doubts and anxieties arise from a diminished view of God's true nature and of the power of His gospel message centered in the Lord Jesus Christ.

Consequently, those with a degraded estimation of God will usually live defeated lives because they also underestimate the strength of the devil and the danger his cunning devices pose. These spiritually despondent souls fall prey to the whims of the enemy, and then fail to learn from their disappointing experiences and rise in grace to victory. Whether we tumble or stumble, it is wise to learn from our mistakes, but past failures should not hinder Christians from pressing onward in their heavenly calling. Falling is a normal part of learning to walk properly; it is not falling that makes us a failure, but rather, it is remaining down after the fall: *"A righteous man may fall seven times and rise again, but the wicked shall fall by calamity"* (Prov. 24:16). Dear believer, when you fall, learn from your mistake, get back up in the strength of the Lord, and keep running! There are just consequences for falling, but there are even more for wallowing in self-pity and rejecting God's grace in time of need.

> God's compassion flows out of His goodness, and goodness without justice is not goodness. God spares us because He is good, but He could not be good if He were not just.
>
> — A. W. Tozer

By this point in the book of Ezra, the Jews had learned from experience that their enemies were strong and relentless, but now the Jews possessed a new resolve to obey the Lord no matter what the cost – revival was sweeping through their ranks. Of course, this meant there would be more attacks from the opposition. So far, the tactics of *unnatural unions, discouragement, accusations,* and *comfort* had been levied against the Jews. After the successful preaching of Haggai the work on the temple progressed expediently. This, of course, was noticed by the enemy who quickly tried to counter the work (v. 8). The temple would stand for a testimony of God in the region, and Satan hates such things. He chose to reuse the device of *threatening accusations,* and these would come from the top political figure of the region, Tattenai (v. 3). A cuneiform tablet, dated 502 BC, has been unearthed which refers to a slave of Tatutanni (i.e. same ruler, but with a slightly different spelling). This ancient Babylonian document not only confirms the existence of this man, but also the fact that he was the governor of the Trans-Euphrates region (which included Syria and Palestine). Shethar-Bozenai was likely Tattenai's assistant. He and other officials approached Zerubbabel and Jeshua to ask who had authorized the temple building project and request a list of names of those chiefly responsible for the effort (v. 4).

History records that there was unrest throughout the Persian Empire at the time Darius took the throne. Perhaps Tattenai thought that the Jews would, by building their temple, incite rebellion in his region. How did the Jews respond to this attack? They stated a pure testimony of the truth, including the reason the temple had been destroyed in the first place, and they continued working:

We are the servants of the God of heaven and earth, and we are rebuilding the temple that was built many years ago, which a great king of Israel built and completed. But because our fathers provoked the God of heaven to wrath, He gave them into the hand of Nebuchadnezzar king of Babylon, the Chaldean, who destroyed this temple and carried the people away to Babylon. However, in the first year of Cyrus king of Babylon, King Cyrus issued a decree to build this house of God (Ezra 5:11-13).

After hearing this response, governor Tattenai and key political figures drafted a letter to King Darius, informing him of the situation and the Jewish answer, and requesting him to search the Babylonian archives to confirm whether the Jews were indeed finishing the task originally authorized by King Cyrus some eighteen years earlier. Under Persian law the decrees of kings could not be reversed (Dan. 6:12), meaning that if the Jews were telling the truth, their opposition could not force the Jews to stop building the temple. It would take several months to receive a response from King Darius; in the meantime, the Jews continued erecting God's house in Jerusalem.

Threatening accusations are like shifting shadows; they can scare you, but they cannot hurt you. The Jews knew *"that the eye of their God was watching over them"* (v. 5) and by His enablement their enemies would not prevail against them. Their authority came from One who was higher than Tattenai, as validated by the phrase *"the God of Israel, who was over them"* (v. 1). This expression and others, such as *"the hand of the Lord was on him,"* are found often in the books of

Ezra and Nehemiah to confirm that God was present among and co-laboring with His people. Paul reminds the believers at Corinth of this same truth (1 Cor. 3:9). It is one thing to know God is omnipresent; it is quite another to have His abiding presence and to appreciate His handiwork in all that you do – this realization is a distinguishing characteristic of a true revival.

> Revival is the manifestation of the glory, power, and blessing of the Son of God among His people. Revival is ultimately Christ Himself, seen, felt, heard, living, active, moving in and through His body on earth. Revival is not some emotion or worked-up excitement; it is rather an invasion from heaven which brings to man a conscious awareness of God.
>
> — Stephen Olford

If the Jews had continued working from the onset, the temple would have been finished and no accusations would have even been raised against them. But, since they had stopped building for fifteen years, and begun again, it seemed like the Jews were acting on their own authority, not a Persian decree. The lesson to learn from this is to keep busy in the Lord's work. Believers who faithfully co-labor with the Lord will find that they have little time available for the "fluff of life" or for compromising situations which tempt them to sin. It is good for us to remember that His eye is upon us also; may we continue to co-labor with Him.

Meaningless accusations or unjust criticisms have keenly wounded many Christians and neutralized many profitable ministries. Remembering that Satan has used these previously to oppose God's work is helpful. It is noted that the enemy also used unfounded accusations in an attempt to prevent Nehemiah from building the wall around Jerusalem some seventy-five years later.

> If what they are saying about you is true, mend your ways. If it isn't true, forget it, and go on and serve the Lord.
>
> — H. A. Ironside

If you are doing anything for the Lord, expect to be criticized. Evaluate criticism for potential constructive benefits, especially when it comes from those who love you unquestionably, and then cast the rest aside and forget about it. And if you yourself are prompted to critique another, know that if it pains you to do it, then you have the right attitude, but if you have even a hint of pleasure in it, then it would be best to keep still. Why? This is because our flesh naturally opposes the things of God (Gal. 5:17), and *"the wrath of man does not produce the righteousness of God"* (Jas. 1:20). Paul did not even judge the value of his own ministry because he knew his flesh was biased (1 Cor. 4:2-4). A spiritual person wants to edify others, not hurt them for the sake of personal vindication or self-justification.

> Abraham Lincoln once said, "If I tried to read, much less answer, all the criticisms made of me, and all the attacks leveled against me, this office would have to be closed for all other business. I do the best I know how, the very best I can. And I mean to keep on doing this, down to the very end. If the end brings me out all wrong, ten angels swearing I had been right would make no difference. If the end brings me out all right, then what is said against me now will not amount to anything."[1]

As the Jews soon learned, living for God and doing what pleases Him has consequences – suffering. Paul reminded his spiritual son Timothy of this important fact: *"Yes, and all who desire to live godly in Christ Jesus will suffer persecution"* (2 Tim. 3:12). This is a facet of the Christian experience for which all believers need to be mentally prepared (1 Pet. 1:13), and in which they ought to rejoice (Acts 5:40-42, 16:23-25). Paul told the saints at both Philippi and Thessalonica, who were being persecuted for their faith, that suffering patiently was evidence (a proof) of their salvation. The Jews who returned from captivity were suffering patiently in the will of God and He was blessing their work in a tremendous way. When living for Christ becomes arduous, let us remember that it is God and not our accusers who control the worth of our service!

61

A Revival Meditation

John Wesley rode tens of thousands of miles on horseback to carry the gospel message from town to town and house to house some 250 years ago in the United Kingdom. According to his journal, he often preached two or three messages a day. He was often persecuted for his work; in fact, to Wesley the lack of persecution was a troubling sign of broken fellowship with God. On one occasion, John Wesley was riding along a road when it dawned on him that three whole days had passed in which he had suffered no persecution. No brick or even an egg had been thrown at him for three days! Alarmed, he stopped his horse and exclaimed, "Can it be that I have sinned, and am backslidden?" Slipping from his horse, Wesley went down on his knees and began interceding with God to show him where, if any, there had been a fault. A rough fellow on the other side of the hedge, upon hearing the prayer, looked across and recognized the preacher. "I'll fix that Methodist preacher," he said, and then he proceeded to pick up a brick and hurl it at John Wesley. It missed its mark and fell harmlessly beside Wesley, whereupon he leaped to his feet joyfully exclaiming, "Thank God, it's all right. I still have His presence."[2]

The Temple Completed
Ezra 6

In response to governor Tattenai's letter requesting verification of the Jewish claim, King Darius ordered a search of historical scrolls, which were stored in various treasuries throughout the kingdom. Indeed, a record of Cyrus's decree was found *"at Achmetha, in the palace that is in the province of Media"* (v. 2). Achmetha (or Echatana) was the capital city of Media located about 300 miles northeast of Babylon. The royal document read as follows:

> *In the first year of King Cyrus, King Cyrus issued a decree concerning the house of God at Jerusalem: "Let the house be rebuilt, the place where they offered sacrifices; and let the foundations of it be firmly laid, its height sixty cubits and its width sixty cubits, with three rows of heavy stones and one row of new timber. Let the expenses be paid from the king's treasury. Also let the gold and silver articles of the house of God, which Nebuchadnezzar took from the temple which is in Jerusalem and brought to Babylon, be restored and taken back to the temple which is in Jerusalem, each to its place; and deposit them in the house of God"* (vv. 3-5).

The royal document not only granted the Jews permission to build the temple, but it also provided a general description of what should be built (e.g. its dimensions and how many rows of stones it should have). Original temple vessels and articles confiscated by Nebuchadnezzar were to be returned and building expenses were to be provided for from the king's treasury. Having validated the Jewish claim, Darius wrote Tattenai of his findings and told him to allow the Jews to continue building the temple at its present location (v. 7). He also passed along two royal decrees of his own:

The First Decree: *Moreover I issue a decree as to what you shall do for the elders of these Jews, for the building of this house of God: Let the cost be paid at the king's expense from taxes on the region beyond the River; this is to be given immediately to these men, so that they are not hindered. And whatever they need – young bulls, rams, and lambs for the burnt offerings of the God of heaven, wheat, salt, wine, and oil, according to the request of the priests who are in Jerusalem – let it be given them day by day without fail, that they may offer sacrifices of sweet aroma to the God of heaven, and pray for the life of the king and his sons* (vv. 6:8-10).

The Second Decree: *Also I issue a decree that whoever alters this edict, let a timber be pulled from his house and erected, and let him be hanged on it; and let his house be made a refuse heap because of this. And may the God who causes His name to dwell there destroy any king or people who put their hand to alter it, or to destroy this house of God which is in Jerusalem. I Darius issue a decree; let it be done diligently* (vv. 6:11-12).

One can only imagine the looks of dismay on the oppressors' faces when this letter was read. The elite political figures of the region were hoping that King Darius would scrap the construction project altogether. Instead, Darius commanded that the work should continue unhindered, that it be funded by the region's taxpayers, and that the government sustain the labor force and supply animals and other provisions such as wheat, salt, oil, and wine for the daily Jewish sacrifices. Furthermore, anyone opposing the Jews would have their house demolished and be hung on scaffolding erected from its debris. Darius closed his decree by acknowledging that the God of the Jews would destroy any nation which tried to damage His house. Instead of opposing them, now the enemies of the Jews had to pay for the building of God's temple. What a sense of humor God has! What poetic justice! God had worked a miracle and the Jews had one more story to pass down for generations to come.

The Jews had continued to build the temple while the appeal to Darius was being considered. Now that Darius had sided with them, Tattenai and his companions did what any veteran politician would do who wants to stay in office after losing in the courtroom – they swiftly changed their platform (v. 13). With the resistance stymied, the holy prophets motivating the people, and the financial support of the government, the temple was quickly finished (v. 14). Ezra notes that the Jews had obeyed the commandment of the God of Israel, and also those of the earthly kings, Cyrus and Darius, whom God had moved to accomplish His will (vv. 14, 22).

The temple was joyfully dedicated by all of Israel on March 12, 515 BC, approximately four and a half years after they had resumed construction (vv. 15-16). As none of these Jews would have been personally familiar with the Levitical system of offerings practiced by their forefathers, one may well wonder how they would go about worshipping Jehovah. The priests were set in their divisions and the Levites in their courses, *"as it is written in the book of Moses"* (v. 18). They were content to follow the commands of Scripture. How many needless controversies in the Church today would be resolved if believers agreed to abide by Scripture alone in all matters of Church doctrine and practice? How many customs, traditions, observances, rites, and ceremonies would be removed today from Churchianity, if Scripture alone was used to guide all meetings and ministries of the Church?

God is a God of order and not confusion (1 Cor. 14:33). He is also a communicating God, who has never, in any era of human existence, left His people ignorant of how to worship Him. For example, the Lord Jesus informed the Samaritan woman that there was a time coming in which those who would worship God would be able to do so in spirit and truth: *"But the hour is coming, and now is, when the true worshipers will worship the Father in spirit and truth; for the Father is seeking such to worship Him. God is Spirit, and those who worship Him must worship in spirit and truth"* (John 4:23-24). The Lord was speaking of the Church Age. Those who have been born again through the gospel message have the Holy Spirit within them and are thus able to worship God through their human spirit according to the truth of Scripture.

The Holy Spirit guides believers into a deeper understanding of truth concerning the Lord Jesus and the overall greatness and goodness of God (John 16:13-14). Only through Spirit-led worship, which will be completely founded in divine truth, can the believer offer any acceptable sacrifice of praise unto God. Thus, the words of John the Baptizer ring true: *"A man can receive nothing, except it be given him from heaven"* (John 3:27). Thankfully, the Jews of Ezra's day had received God's written Law through Moses to guide their worship. Therefore, they *"set the priests to their divisions and the Levites to their divisions, over the service of God in Jerusalem, as it is written in the Book of Moses"* (Ezra 6:18). Whatever their religious practices might have been in Babylon, those traditions and rites were left in the scene of their captivity; they had been delivered and brought back, and nothing could satisfy them short of the authority of God's written Word.

With the priestly order in place, sacrifices were then offered to dedicate the house of God: *"one hundred bulls, two hundred rams, four hundred lambs, and as a sin offering for all Israel twelve male goats, according to the number of the tribes of Israel"* (v. 17). Shortly after the temple dedication, the Passover and the Feast of Unleavened Bread were commemorated, again with joy (vv. 20-22). Not only had the Jews obeyed the Lord's command to build Him a house, but also they were ordering their worship in accordance with His Word.

The priests and Levites went through ceremonial cleansing in order to kill the Passover lambs on behalf of all the families desiring to celebrate the Passover Feast. But beyond what the Law ritually demanded, the nation had a great awareness of God's holiness and knew that, as His special people, they must be holy too: *"Then the children of Israel who had returned from the captivity ate together with all who had separated themselves from the filth of the nations of the land in order to seek the Lord God of Israel"* (v. 21). Who were these people who separated themselves from the filth of the nations to join the children of Israel in celebrating the Passover? Were they the Jews who had been left in the land after the Babylonian deportations, or were they perhaps converted Gentiles? In pondering this question Edward Dennett offers an important observation for us to consider:

> There were others besides themselves who united with them in this observance — those who had "separated themselves unto them from the filthiness of the heathen of the land, to seek the Lord God of Israel." Whether these were of the few Israelites who had been left behind in the land, when their brethren were carried away captive, or whether they were of the heathen, is not mentioned. In Exodus 12 it is said, *"There shall no stranger eat thereof;"* but it is added, *"When a*

stranger shall sojourn with thee, and will keep the Passover to the Lord, let all his males be circumcised, and then let him come near and keep it.'' (See also Num. 9:14). They were probably therefore "strangers;" and if so, they had been attracted to the children of the captivity by witnessing the divine power that was seen in their separation from evil. Alas! We do not read of any more being thus drawn; rather the children of Israel were drawn afterwards to the heathen. It is ever the same with the people of God. When the Spirit of God works in their midst, and when, as a consequence, they walk, in any measure, according to the nature of their calling, there will always be numbers, constrained by what they behold, seeking their company and fellowship. When, on the other hand, life and power vanish, and are succeeded by coldness and indifference, it is the world that attracts, and not the Church. Hence it is that every movement in the Church of God is most influential at the outset, because then the display of the Spirit's power is more manifest.[1]

Whoever these "separated strangers" were, they were compelled to worship Jehovah by keeping the Passover because of the power He had displayed to them through His people. The Lord Jesus reminds us that all who seek God through revealed truth will be divinely welcomed: *"All that the Father gives Me will come to Me, and the one who comes to Me I will by no means cast out"* (John 6:37). The final invitation in the Bible expresses this same reality: *"And the Spirit and the bride say, 'Come!' And let him who hears say, 'Come!' And let him who thirsts come. Whoever desires, let him take the water of life freely"* (Rev. 22:17). God does exclude the proud and vain from His heavenly abode, but those heeding and trusting in His Word will always be welcome. Thus, the consecrated "strangers" in Ezra 6 were permitted to worship God also.

The Passover Feast was of great importance to the Jewish nation. It was instituted by God to remind them they had been slaves in Egypt, but that by His great power He had delivered them from bondage and from the impurities of Egypt (i.e. worldliness). On the eve of the Exodus, God gave instructions to Moses concerning the Passover lamb. On the fourteenth day of the first month, the young, tested, unblemished lamb was to be killed in the evening. For the initial Passover, the lamb's blood was to be applied to the doorpost and lintel of the offerer's home in order to spare the life of the firstborn living there. The sprinkling of blood was the visible expression of one's faith and thus averted God's judgment. But this action occurred only because the sprinkler reckoned that Jehovah had spoken the truth and that He could not lie. Jehovah had promised not to judge the firstborn within the houses marked by lamb's blood, but rather to pass over them.

Some 1500 years later, John the Baptist declared that Jesus Christ was *"the Lamb of God which takes away the sin of the world"* (John 1:29). Paul taught that Christ was the literal fulfillment of the Passover lamb: *"For indeed Christ, our Passover, was sacrificed for us"* (1 Cor. 5:7). The millions of lambs previously slaughtered by the Jews served as a constant reminder of their sin, and a testimony that animal blood could never cleanse the stain of sin. The Jewish animal sacrifices merely atoned for sin and pointed to God's once-for-all sacrifice – Christ! Today, the Church is to remember Christ and proclaim the value of His sacrifice through *"the breaking of the bread"* (1 Cor. 11:23-27). The Lord Jesus said to keep the His Supper often (Luke 22:19-20). The practice of the early Church was to meet weekly on the Lord's Day in obedience to the Lord's command to remember Him (Acts 20:7). It is a blessed privilege of the Church to honor the Lord in this way until He returns to take His beloved home.

Likewise, obedience to Scripture caused the Jews of Zerubbabel's day to remember their past deliverance and redemption by blood and to look to the future with hope and expectation. To be overwhelmed by the goodness of God, to be self-driven to obey His commands, and to be joyful in His presence are clear signs of spiritual revival. The Jews were joyful, because *"the Lord made them joyful;"* He had done a work of grace in their hearts (v. 22). They had yielded to His will and He responded by transforming them. In every respect, God was being honored by His people – this is clearly a high-water mark in Israel's history.

A Revival Meditation

In the Irish Revival of 1859, people became so weak that they could not get back to their homes. Men and women would fall by the wayside and would be found hours later pleading with God to save their souls. They felt that they were slipping into hell and that nothing else in life mattered but to get right with God... To them eternity meant everything. Nothing else was of any consequence. They felt that if God did not have mercy on them and save them, they were doomed for all time to come.

— Oswald Smith

Prepared Hearts
Ezra 7

As mentioned previously, there is a significant chronological gap between Ezra 6 and 7; it is during this interim that the events recorded in Ezra 4:6-23 and in the book of Esther occurred. Artaxerxes ruled Persia from 464 to 424 BC and the narrative in Ezra 7 commences in the seventh year of his reign (i.e. 458 BC), meaning fifty-seven years had passed since the completion of the temple in 515 BC.

In 458 BC, the scribe Ezra led a second group of Jews, numbering about 5,000 souls in all, from Babylon to Jerusalem. Under Zerubbabel's leadership a great post-exile revival had occurred among God's people – the *First Jewish Awakening*, per se. By God's help they had overcome immense opposition to erect His temple in Jerusalem. However, during the interim between Ezra 6 and 7 the Jews had become secular in thinking and worldly in practice. This can happen to God's people in any era when their love for the Lord wanes.

The Jews were no longer a consecrated people and they needed to be bluntly told so. This would be Ezra's calling as a teacher; he would use God's Word to confront, instruct, and encourage his fellow countrymen. Whereas Zerubbabel rebuilt the temple, Ezra would strive to spiritually rebuild the people. The Jews had lost their way and Ezra would reacquaint them with Jehovah and His Law. The outcome of his ministry would be the *Second Jewish Awakening* (Ezra 7-10).

The events Ezra detailed in the first six chapters of his book occurred long before Ezra's own journey to Palestine. However, the remainder of this book relates his personal experiences in Jerusalem; accordingly, references to himself are made in the first person (i.e. he uses pronouns such as "I" and "we"). Ezra was a priest and had an authentic lineage to Aaron, though for the sake of space not every generation in his ancestry is mentioned in verses 1-5. He is mentioned as being a descendant (i.e. "the son") of Seraiah, who was the High

Priest when Jerusalem fell in 586 BC (2 Kgs. 25:18). Given that 128 years had passed since that event, Ezra was likely the great-grandson of Seraiah. What is evident is that Ezra rejoiced in his priestly descent and longed to fulfill his calling to serve God. We too must be settled and committed to our calling in Christ if we are going to do anything meaningful for God. Each believer has been given some specific spiritual gift(s) and a calling within the body of Christ to accomplish (1 Cor. 14; Eph. 2:10, 4:11-12).

The fact that King Artaxerxes granted all that Ezra requested of him, though no details are given, indicates that Ezra was a man well-respected in Persia (v. 6). Further evidence of this point is affirmed by the king's charge to Ezra. He was not only to return to Jerusalem, but the king entrusted him with the transfer of riches from his own treasury and bestowed to him royal privileges and liberties while in Jerusalem. No doubt Ezra could have petitioned the king for wealth and status in Persia, but instead he used his influence and opportunity to bless his countrymen back in their homeland. His trip from Babylon to Jerusalem took exactly four months (v. 6). He arrived in Jerusalem mid-summer of 586 BC, on the first day of the fifth month (v. 7).

From the Jewish perspective, Ezra was a priest and a skilled scribe (v. 6). He is referred to as a "teacher" four times in Ezra and as a "scribe" six times in Nehemiah. Ezra was not just a teacher of God's Word, but he was a pursuer of truth and was committed to living out what he knew to be true: *"For Ezra had prepared his heart to seek the Law of the Lord, and to do it, and to teach statutes and ordinances in Israel"* (v. 7). Ezra studied God's Word and then practiced and taught what he knew to be true – these are exemplary marks of a good teacher. How did God respond to Ezra's prepared heart? We repeatedly read that *"God's hand was upon him"* (vv. 6, 9, 28, 8:18, 22, 31). When God empowers a believer who is earnestly determined to know, to do, and to teach others God's Word, great things are bound to happen for the glory of God. Ezra would be privileged to experience this honor.

Artaxerxes' decree, which Ezra was given a written copy of, bestowed several beneficial provisions to Ezra's expedition to Palestine, but also commissioned Ezra to do something for Artaxerxes. On the receiving side, Ezra was given leave and allowed to take any Jews who were willing to uproot back to Israel. Over 5000 men, women, and children took advantage of this liberty (Ezra 8). Artaxerxes was quite generous: he entrusted Ezra with precious vessels, silver, and gold for the temple and allowed him to receive more Babylonian riches while journeying back to Jerusalem (vv. 15-16, 20). The Jews were permitted certain freedoms, including offering at the temple (vv. 17-18). Beyond this, they could receive from the state whatever wheat, oil, salt, and wine was needed for meal and drink offerings at the temple, up to a certain limit (vv. 21-22).

What did King Artaxerxes want from Ezra in return? He asked Ezra to prevent Jewish uprisings and the development of bad attitudes towards the king (v. 23), and to keep order in that part of the empire by teaching the people the laws of the God of Heaven and administering justice among them (vv. 25-26). Ezra had Artaxerxes' authority to judge the people and to punish the guilty (v. 26). King Artaxerxes was the son of King Xerxes, who made the Jewish woman Esther his queen. Ezra arrived in Jerusalem some 15 to 20 years after Haman's plot to exterminate the Jews failed and ultimately led to the slaughter of 76,000 of their enemies. As a young man, Artaxerxes would have witnessed this miraculous event, and apparently he had concluded it was a better ruling strategy to extend favors to the Jews, rather than to oppress them.

Ezra's prayer of thanksgiving in response to Artaxerxes' decree is admirable (vv. 27-28). First, he praises the Lord for what God was accomplishing through him, knowing the Lord had strengthened him. Second, he acknowledges that it was God who had put the matter into the king's heart to bless the Jews. It was not Ezra's political influence that moved Artaxerxes to be gracious, but God moving in the king's heart. Third, he states that God was acting to bring honor to Himself and glory to His house. Fourth, Ezra tells Artaxerxes' advisors and officials that his God had shown favor to him by the king's response to his request. Ezra's response to the goodness of God is indeed an honorable pattern for us to follow. Let us be careful not to steal from God what He alone deserves – the praise of men!

Though Artaxerxes had spoken in favor of the Jews, his pride is still apparent in his reference to himself as *"the king of kings"* (v. 12), a title that Scripture reserves for the Lord Jesus Christ alone (Rev. 19:16). Ezra, on the other hand, takes no title other than what his Levitical heritage bestowed to him as a servant of God (i.e. "a priest"), and as a servant of the people (i.e. "a scribe"). Ezra functioned as a priest and a teacher, but had no formal title associated with those ministries. Men covet titles so that they might be honored by others – it is a natural pull of our fallen nature. But those who worship Christ must not dishonor Him by stealing His glory. Listen to the solemn words of the Lord Jesus on this very matter:

> *But you, do not be called 'Rabbi'; for one is your Teacher, the Christ, and you are all brethren. Do not call anyone on earth your father; for one is your Father, He who is in heaven. And do not be called teachers; for one is your Teacher, the Christ. But he who is greatest among you shall be your servant. And whoever exalts himself will be humbled, and he who humbles himself will be exalted* (Matt. 23:8-12).

Disciples of Christ seek neither the praise of men nor titles of position – all titles of status and all praise are reserved for the Lord Jesus Christ. Men love titles; yet, no disciple of Christ has any title of position before his or her name in Scripture; all such titles are reserved for the Lord Jesus Christ.

In a spirit of humility, Ezra prepared his heart to follow God (v. 10) and God stirred Artaxerxes' heart and moved his tongue to ensure all that Ezra desired to do and more was made possible (v. 27). *"The preparations of the heart belong to man, but the answer of the tongue is from the Lord"* (Prov. 16:1). Ezra understood this, but do we? Is there any adversary, any political figure, or any earthly authority that can move against the will of God? Why then do we fret and worry about what only God can control? Ezra, recognizing that God was with him, thus steps forward in faith: *"So I was encouraged, as the hand of the Lord my God was upon me; and I gathered leading men of Israel to go up with me"* (v. 28). Edward Dennett encourages all God's people to follow Ezra's humble attitude:

> It was thus not his request (v. 6) that induced the king to act, but it was God who put the thing into the king's heart; it was not Ezra's influence that commended him to the king and his princes, but it was God that extended mercy to him in their presence; it was not in his own power that he assembled the chief men to go up with him, but it was God who strengthened him with His own hand upon him. In all this he is a striking example to every believer; and happy is he who, like Ezra, has learned to live in the presence of God, to look beyond

the actions of men to the power that controls them all, and to receive all, favor or persecution, aids or hindrances, from the Lord. That soul has acquired the secret of perfect peace amid the confusion and turmoil of the world, as well as in the presence of Satan's power.[1]

Ezra sets forth a great example to follow; he acknowledges God's goodness in all that has happened, he thanks the Lord for what He has done, and then he steps forward in faith anticipating what marvelous things God will yet do through him. When our gracious God does bless our endeavors, may we be careful to bestow all the glory to Him, in whom all things depend. May the psalmist's prayer be our own: *"Let Your work appear to Your servants, and Your glory to their children"* (Ps. 90:16); this lost and wicked world desperately needs to see the glory of God through His people!

A Revival Meditation

Perhaps the greatest barrier to revival on a large scale is the fact that we are too interested in a great display. We want an exhibition; God is looking for a man who will throw himself entirely on God. Whenever self-effort, self-glory, self-seeking or self-promotion enters into the work of revival, then God leaves us to ourselves.

— Ted Rendall

Seeking the Right Way
Ezra 8

This chapter begins with a roster of names of those who voluntarily take advantage of the royal decree allowing them to leave Babylon. This group departs with Ezra on the first day of the first month (7:9). After traveling for nine days the entourage comes to *"the river that flowed to Ahava and camped there three days;"* during this time Ezra familiarizes himself with those returning to their homeland and discovers that there were no Levites in their midst (vv. 15-16). Ezra, being alarmed that there were no *"ministers for the house of our God"* among them, works to resolve the limitation (vv. 15-20).

Per the Law of Moses, only the priests (descendants of Aaron) were permitted access to the holy places within God's house, and only the Levites were to be the ministers in what pertained to its service. While some priests did respond to the king's proclamation, the Levites were not moved to resume the privileges of their calling; they had become indifferent and calloused to the things of God. Evidently, it was harder for the Levites to leave established homes in Babylon and journey to a place where their whole portion must be in God, than it was for those who expected to reclaim their former inheritance.

The very place that their forefathers had loathed as forced captives had now become a comfortable abode for the Levites – they did not want to leave; they were content to live in the pagan capital of the world. When the Lord's people become absorbed with earthly things, it will be impossible for them to be heavenly-minded. Thus, Paul reminds the believers at Colossae: *"Seek those things which are above, where Christ is, sitting at the right hand of God. Set your mind on things above, not on things on the earth"* (Col 3:1-2). Ezra, knowing that the Jews needed Levite teachers of the Law and that the temple could not function without the Levites, consequently is not willing to leave them behind; without the Levites the journey would be futile.

75

Ezra sends for a number of chief men among the people and also for two *"men of understanding,"* Joiarib and Elnathan, with whom to take counsel (v. 16). Thank the Lord for men of understanding who can appeal to the consciences of God's people to avert them from experiencing further spiritual decline! Ezra knew where some Levites could be found, Casiphia, and he commissions the above men to deliver his appeal to Iddo, the clan leader of the Levites. In it, Ezra requests that the Levites and the Nethinims (temple servants of non-Jewish descent) fulfill their divine calling as ministers in God's house and join the Jewish expedition bound for Jerusalem (v. 17). Ezra's zeal for the Lord and His house is honorable, but the matter would now solely depend on God's work within the hearts of men. What would the outcome be?

> *Then, by the good hand of our God upon us, they brought us a man of understanding, of the sons of Mahli the son of Levi, the son of Israel, namely Sherebiah, with his sons and brothers, eighteen men; and Hashabiah, and with him Jeshaiah of the sons of Merari, his brothers and their sons, twenty men; also of the Nethinim, whom David and the leaders had appointed for the service of the Levites, two hundred and twenty Nethinim* (vv. 18-20).

Thankfully, thirty-eight Levites from two families and two hundred and twenty Nethinims respond to Ezra's request. That so few Levites would answer Ezra's call is another proof of the carnal ease which plagued God's people in Babylon. Most of the Jews no longer identified with Jehovah, nor with the tremendous privileges that were theirs as His covenant people. However, Ezra determined that there were now enough Levites and Nethinims to disembark for Jerusalem. Their contingency now numbered 1,772 men (258 of these were Levites and Nethinims), plus their families: perhaps 5,000 people in total.

Now that the appropriate people and provisions had been obtained for the trip, there was one remaining concern, spiritual preparation for the journey:

> *Then I proclaimed a fast there at the river of Ahava, that we might humble ourselves before our God, to seek from Him the right way for*

us and our little ones and all our possessions. For I was ashamed to request of the king an escort of soldiers and horsemen to help us against the enemy on the road, because we had spoken to the king, saying, "The hand of our God is upon all those for good who seek Him, but His power and His wrath are against all those who forsake Him." So we fasted and entreated our God for this, and He answered our prayer (vv. 21-23).

The work of God is precious to the Lord and, therefore, His people should never enter into it flippantly. We need the Lord's discernment and blessing to accomplish His purposes. If we lack knowledge, then we need to pause from our labors and ask the Lord to direct us in *the right way*. Ezra is not wanting to proceed to Jerusalem in the power of the flesh (v. 21) or by reliance on the king's protection (v. 22); accordingly, the entire camp is instructed to fast and pray for God's direction and protection. This scene is one of the best pictures of sincere humility in Scripture – separated from the world, with personal ambition set aside, the Jews completely and willingly cast themselves upon Jehovah. Although they would soon learn that the previous group of returnees had suffered spiritual failure, both groups, as H. A. Ironside notes, shared a common focus and goal:

Albeit the movement in which Ezra and his company were participants was distinct from that of Zerubbabel, Jeshua and their brethren, there were no new principles involved than those the former company had already learned from the word of God. No new center was ever thought of. No new place to gather was suggested. Jerusalem was the one only place and Jehovah the one only Name. He had set His name at Jerusalem; consequently thitherward were the faces of all Ezra's company turned. They were soon to learn that those who had preceded them had made a mess and a failure of the whole thing; but that did not set them inquiring if it would not be wise to gather elsewhere, to give up the principle of separation, to step aside from the movement and contentedly go back to Babylon. Not at all. God's word remained, God's center remained. God's Spirit remained. And for this fresh company there was nothing to do, as guided by that Spirit, but to return to and continue to own the one center in accordance with the unchanging Word.[1]

With one heart, in one place, they afflicted their souls before the Lord for the furtherance of His glory in Jerusalem. The Spirit of God longs to act upon such demonstrations of contriteness, as testified by all the great revivals throughout Church history.

The Great Awakening occurred in England during the early part of the 18th century under the zealous preaching of Whitefield, Wesley, and others. When John Wesley was asked from where he drew the strength and inspiration for his work, he responded, "I resolve to devote an hour each morning and evening to private prayer, no pretense or excuse whatsoever."[2] Why did George Whitefield have such a powerful gospel ministry? Here is his response: "Whole days and weeks have I spent prostrate on the ground in silent or vocal prayer."[3] These two men knew that if God did not move in the hearts of men to bring conviction and repentance, all their persuasive preaching would be in vain. It is absolutely necessary for the lost to hear the gospel message to experience rebirth, for *"faith comes by hearing, and hearing by the word of God"* (Rom. 10:17). But only the Holy Spirit can enlighten the unregenerate soul to the truth and power of the gospel message (1 Cor. 2:9-14). The earnest prayers of those with clean hands and pure hearts then become the stimulus for revival among God's people and the unregenerate.

> I have said, more than once, that the spirit of prayer that prevailed in those revivals was a very marked feature of them. It was common for young converts to be freely exercised in prayer; and in some instances so much so, that they were constrained to pray whole nights, and until their bodily strength was quite exhausted, for the conversion of souls around them.
>
> — Charles Finney

Before starting for Jerusalem, Ezra had entrusted twelve leaders from among the priests with the care of the holy vessels, and the silver and gold which had been donated for the temple (vv. 24-30). Ezra charges them to watch over these things until each item would be weighed in Jerusalem before the leaders of the priests, Levites, and Israel (v. 29). Where God places responsibility, there is also accountability, and the auditing procedures would not only ensure that what had been given to the Lord would not be pilfered, but it also more importantly would keep honest men from being accused of wrongdoing. On this point, Edward Dennett elaborates:

> It was not that Ezra doubted the fidelity of the priests he had selected; but even as the apostle of a later age, he would *"provide for honest things, not only in the sight of the Lord, but also in the sight of men."* (2 Cor. 8:21). The people might have had full confidence in the integrity both of Ezra and of the priests; but Ezra would remove all occasion for the enemy's work by having the vessels, and the silver and the gold, weighed when put into the priest's hands, and again weighed when delivered. He thus proved his and their fidelity. And surely this is a godly, a scriptural example to be followed by those who in any way have charge of the offerings of the Lord's people. Such should be careful to render an account of their stewardship, and not wait to be pressed to give it. Many a difficulty in the Church of God might have been obviated if this practice had been adopted. It may further be noted that on reaching Jerusalem the weighing was done by others than Ezra, *"and all the weight was written at that time"* (vv. 33, 34). In modern language, the accounts of Ezra were checked and audited, and this was done on the fourth day after the completion of their journey. [4]

The journey to Jerusalem required four months and God protected His people through its entirety (vv. 31-32). We read that after three days of rest, and with the accounting process complete, the returning Jews bless God by offering burnt sacrifices (v. 35). As in Ezra 3, the Jews are again establishing a proper connection with Jehovah through the sacrifices He had specified in the Law of Moses; in this they are demonstrating their desire for His continued favor and protection. Having put themselves under the efficacy of the sacrifices, and having been brought into the proper fellowship with God through these, the Jews then deliver the king's decree to the local governing authorities (v. 36). In Babylon they had prayed for the right way to be known to them, and God's hand had both directed their path and protected them from those lying in wait to harm them. Jehovah had proven to be a much better Guide and Guardian than any armed Persian escort that could have accompanied them.

A Revival Meditation

Oh! men and brethren, what would this heart feel if I could but believe that there were some among you who would go home and pray for a revival – men whose faith is large enough, and their love fiery enough to lead them from this moment to exercise unceasing intercessions that God would appear among us and do wondrous things here, as in the times of former generations.

— Charles Spurgeon

"Give Us a Reviving"
Ezra 9

Shortly after delivering the king's decree to the governors, some of the leaders from among the Jews paid a visit to Ezra, informing him that: *"The people of Israel and the priests and the Levites have not separated themselves from the peoples of the lands, with respect to the abominations of the Canaanites, the Hittites, the Perizzites, the Jebusites, the Ammonites, the Moabites, the Egyptians, and the Amorites"* (v. 1). Even some of the Jewish leaders had married local pagans. This was forbidden, as it normally resulted in the corruption of idolatry, the very sin for which the nation had been exiled to Babylon.

The sin of spiritual adultery is hideous to God at any time, but it would be especially so when He had just purged it from His people through severe chastening. How could the people so quickly forget this painful lesson? This is a good example of just how powerful our lusting flesh can be. To willingly do what causes both us and God pain is not a rational or spiritual choice. Yet, thankfully, there were still some Jewish leaders who were keenly aware of the consequences of *unnatural unions*, and were moved to help in order to deliver and to restore their brethren from what God abhors.

We see that Ezra, having departed from the heart of the pagan world, and having just experienced four months of God's wherewithal through separation and faith, is exceedingly appalled at the pitiful condition of his Jewish brethren. H. A. Ironside explains why Ezra is overcome by sorrow and anguish at this juncture:

> There is perhaps no greater trial a man can be called upon to face, than to take, through grace, a position he has seen from the word of God to be scriptural, and then to be rudely awakened to the realization that the people who were in that position before him, are not what he had hoped to find them. Yea, that they are even less spiritual, less

devoted, less zealous for God, than some he has left behind him in systems where quasi-darkness prevailed. Then indeed one needs to be firmly held by the truth, or he is likely to be altogether overcome and completely disheartened. Many an unstable soul has, by such a test, been utterly swept away from his moorings. Such often go back in despair to the unscriptural positions they had abandoned, and give out a bad report of the land, thus hindering others from following the light vouchsafed to them.[1]

Ezra does not pull away from his spiritual moorings; rather, being immensely vexed, he tears his clothes and mantle, pulls hair from his head and beard, and sets down in the dirt. He remains in the dust of the earth until the evening sacrifice (vv. 3-4). What type of man or woman bends the ear of God? Isaiah informs us: *"But on this one will I look: On him who is poor and of a contrite spirit, and who trembles at My word"* (Isa. 66:2). James puts the matter this way: *"The effective, fervent prayer of a righteous man avails much"* (Jas. 5:16). Thankfully, there were still such men among the remnant, and upon them the Lord would bestow His blessing. Though these were few in number, these men acting with Jehovah for the good of the nation would be a majority.

How did God's people slide into such a dire spiritual condition in such a short period of time? William Kelly comments on the enemy's successful campaign against the Jews through the use of *unnatural unions*:

> When people are walking hand in hand with the world, Satan can leave them. He knows where the world will lead them, and if flesh and spirit are joined hand in hand it is always flesh that gets the uppermost. The only way to walk in the Spirit is to judge the flesh — to have nothing to do with it, but denounce it — to mortify our members that are upon the earth. But all attempts to have a friendly harmony between the flesh and the Spirit is vain. Therefore Satan can leave that harmony to take its course. He knows right well that that which is fleshly will always break down in the things of God, whatever there may be of the Spirit connected with it.[2]

Satan had again ensnared God's covenant people in *unnatural unions*. These forbidden marital relationships were eroding the Jews' affection for Jehovah, who was jealous of them. He yearned to commune with them, but that obviously required their fidelity. The situation was bleak and swift action was required to avert God's judgment on them. Indeed, others *"who trembled at the words of the God of Israel"* were dismayed also and gathered with Ezra to pray. At such desperate times as this, the words of the prophet Isaiah are worthy of meditation:

> For thus says the High and Lofty One who inhabits eternity, whose name is Holy: "I dwell in the high and holy place, with him who has a contrite and humble spirit, **to revive** the spirit of the humble, and **to revive** the heart of the contrite ones" (Isa. 57:15).

Most, if not all, of the great revivals of the Church Age have begun with the same two realities that we have before us now. First, God's people were spiritually lethargic and pathetically settled in the world and a remnant of consecrated, God-fearing, Christ-loving, Bible-believing Christians earnestly sought the Lord for a miraculous solution – revival. With this being the case, the modern Church is ripe for revival. What is needed now is for the latter condition to be satisfied. In 1740, when God began to move through New England it was called "The Great Awakening." Before The Great Awakening, Christianity had sadly declined. Unitarianism had gained much ground, and pagan philosophy was poisoning the minds of millions of people; there was much indifference to the things of God. J.C. Ryle writes, speaking of England prior to the Methodist Revival, "These times were the darkest age that England has passed through in the last 300 years. Anything more deplorable than the condition of the country, as to religion, morality, and high principle, it is very difficult to conceive."[3]

The Church today is in much the same condition as it was when The Great Awakening took place over two centuries ago. Christians today know the Word of God better than those before us, but few know the God of the Word. Our pulpits are filled with more highly-degreed men than ever before, yet we have little knowledge of the true God. We study rather than pray, plan rather than trust, boast rather than weep. The modern Church has gone from experiencing and expecting the supernatural to being choked to death by the superficial. As in the days of Ezra, we desperately need revival and the conditions are ripe for it in the Church. What would happen if a few believers desperate for change would separate themselves from the world and consecrate themselves to God in prayer? Might God again shake and shift the earth for His glory? Might the Spirit of God again wring out the arrogance and tawdriness from our calloused hearts and cause them to beat spontaneously for Him? Might the masses be converted to Christ as in past times?

> Revival is that strange and sovereign work of God in which He visits His own people – restoring, reanimating, and releasing them into the fullness of His blessing.
>
> — Stephen Olford

> Evangelism affects the other fellow; revival affects me.
>
> — Leonard Ravenhill

The remainder of Ezra 9 records the prayer of Ezra. With his companions, he bows before His Creator and, being fully identified with his countrymen, takes their place before God. He proceeds to confess the nation's past and present sins as his own.

> When God intends a great mercy for His people, the first thing He does is to set them a-praying.
>
> — Matthew Henry

Given recent events, the Jews deserved instant reprisal for their offenses, but Jehovah again demonstrated His long-suffering and forbearing nature to them. Speaking to God, Ezra proclaims: *"You our God have punished us less than our iniquities deserve, and have given us such deliverance as this"* (v. 13). Ezra was affirming that all God's judgments were righteous and that He had extended to them much undeserved mercy. Even though His people were not faithful to Him, God was ever faithful to them, unchanging in mercy and grace.

Paul reminded his spiritual son Timothy that the Lord's faithfulness was not dependent on the behavior of men: *"If we are faithless, He remains faithful; He cannot deny Himself"* (2 Tim. 2:13). God is a covenant-keeping God; His blessings and purposes are without repentance; and therein lies the reason for His patience and the sustenance of His people in the presence of their enemies. In confession to God, Ezra speaks as if he were among the guilty and pleads with God to revive them again:

> *O my God, I am too ashamed and humiliated to lift up my face to You, my God; for our iniquities have risen higher than our heads, and our guilt has grown up to the heavens. Since the days of our fathers to this day we have been very guilty, and for our iniquities we, our kings, and our priests have been delivered into the hand of the kings of the lands, to the sword, to captivity, to plunder, and to humiliation, as it is this day. And now for a little while grace has been shown from the Lord our God, to leave us a remnant to escape, and to give us a peg in His holy place, that our God may enlighten our eyes and **give us a measure of revival in our bondage**. For we were slaves; yet our God did not forsake us in our bondage; but He extended mercy to us in the sight of the kings of Persia, **to revive us**, to repair the house of our God, to rebuild its ruins, and to give us a wall in Judah and Jerusalem* (Ezra 9:6-9).

Continuing in the attitude of prayer, Ezra acknowledges to God the very command of Moses that many of the Jews had broken (i.e. not to intermarry with pagans). God wanted a "holy seed" that would represent Him among the nations – a pure people that would cleave to Him alone. Just as the wives of Solomon turned his heart after false gods, the foreign wives of the Jews in Ezra's time had corrupted their pureness and singleness of heart to follow Jehovah. This sinful practice must stop! They had already learned through experience that the severity of their chastening only increased the further they drifted from the Lord. It was time to act, which meant God's Word must be declared with authority and power (and it was, as we will see in the next chapter). Even those with the dullest ears and most seared consciences were swayed Godward by the Spirit of Truth. He alone can revive what is near death.

Revival is the visitation of God which brings to life Christians who have been sleeping and restores a deep sense of God's near presence and holiness. Thence springs a vivid sense of sin and a profound exercise of heart in repentance, praise, and love, with an evangelistic outflow.

— J. I. Packer

After fully identifying with his countrymen and acknowledging their sin as a nation, Ezra pleads for mercy on behalf of the people, though they are undeserving of it. Ezra's behavior is a sign of deep brokenness before the Lord, says William MacDonald:

> We need to be so broken that we will confess the sins of God's people as our own. This is what Daniel did (Dan. 9:3-19). He was not personally guilty of most of the sins he catalogued. But he identified himself so closely with the nation of Israel that their sins became his sin. In this he reminds us, of course, of the One who "took our sins and our sorrows and made them His very own." And the lesson for us is that instead of criticizing other believers and pointing the accusing finger, we should confess their sins as if they were our own.[4]

Having completed the preparatory work of prayer with his companions and having completely entrusted God with the outcome, Ezra is now ready to gather the nation. He is emboldened to preach the Word of God and to confront the sins of the people without regard to religious status or social rank. God is no respecter of persons, nor should His people be. Sin is sin regardless of who the guilty party is, and it must be confronted with the authority of God's Word.

A Revival Meditation

Ezra and his companions' anguish and concern for the spiritually despondent, and their intercession to God to bring an awakening, preceded the revival that would come. Jonathan Edwards noticed the same exercise of God's people prior to the great revival in America two centuries ago:

> The spirit of those that have been in distress for the souls of others, so far as I can discern, seems not to be different from that of the apostle who travailed for souls. On the evening of the day preceding the outbreak of the revival, some Christians met, and spent the whole night in prayer. There was scarcely a person in the town (Northampton), old or young, left unconcerned about the great things

of the eternal world. The work of conversion was carried on in a most astonishing manner, and increased more and more; souls did as it were come by flocks to Jesus Christ. This work of God soon made a glorious alteration in the town; so that in the spring and summer following, the town seemed to be full of the presence of God; it was never so full of love, nor of joy, and yet so full of distress, as it was then.[5]

Edwards also acknowledged that testimonials of God's grace at work in other places had a positive effect on those who had experienced revival in Northampton. May the Lord's people encourage each other by acknowledging the legitimate exercises of divine grace witnessed among us.

Nothing tends more to promote the work of grace among his [Edward's] people at Northampton, than to tell them what God was doing in other places.[6]

Confession and Separation
Ezra 10

As recorded in Ezra 9, certain unnamed leaders of the people, perhaps being motivated to action by Ezra's arrival, visited Ezra and informed him of the spiritual decline of the people, chiefly brought about through the intermarrying of foreign women. In response to this news, Ezra tears his garments, plucks out his hair, and sits appalled until the evening sacrifice (i.e. 3 PM). In Ezra 9:5, we see Ezra fallen on his knees, spreading out his hands to God and praying as he sobbed aloud. But it is not until Ezra 10 that we discover the location of these exploits; Ezra cast himself down in front of the temple. This action showed everyone that, on behalf of the nation, he was throwing himself on the mercy of God. The entire scene, lasting for hours, was completely public. He was not telling the others what to do, but rather he was showing them the path of righteousness, the whereabouts of which they had long forgotten.

At first, those who feared the Word of God gathered with him, but as Ezra wept and confessed the sins of nations, a great congregation of men and women assembled about him. The Lord used the deep sorrow of His servant for the sins of his fellow countrymen to pierce through their dull consciences. Many of the Jewish leaders seemed to be aware of how far the people had slipped from holy ground. The Jews did not feel the guilt of their own sin until they had witnessed how deeply it grieved a righteous man who, now prostrate before the Lord, openly mourned for them. The people also began to weep with Ezra, some for contrition and perhaps others in fear of the consequences of their offenses, for Ezra had the authority of the crown to judge them as he deemed appropriate.

It would have been far easier for Ezra to withdraw from those in sin and just let them go their own way, or perhaps preach against them from a lofty pulpit; instead, he personally identified himself with his brethren, demonstrated deep interest and concern for their sorry state, and through personal faithfulness to God lifted the entire company to a higher spiritual plane. God is glorified by the recovery of failing saints and Ezra wanted to reach more than the few who might have responded to direct public reproof. Ezra wanted all to come to repentance, both those in sin and those who had winked at it.

Just as God had used one consecrated man, Ezra, to arouse the entire congregation to feel the guilt of breaking God's Law, He would use the zeal of one man, Shechaniah, to speak for the congregation and motivate them to confession and repentance. Shechaniah responds to Ezra's zeal with this statement:

> *We have trespassed against our God, and have taken pagan wives from the peoples of the land; yet now there is hope in Israel in spite of this. Now therefore, let us make a covenant with our God to put away all these wives and those who have been born to them, according to the advice of my master and of those who tremble at the commandment of our God; and let it be done according to the law. Arise, for this matter is your responsibility. We also are with you. Be of good courage, and do it* (Ezra 10:2-4).

Shechaniah is a man in touch with the character of His God. He boldly stands and speaks to the congregation about the mercy of God: *"Yet now there is hope in Israel in spite of this"* (v. 2). All was not lost – there was still a way of escape and recovery! He, like Ezra, owns the people's sins, and acknowledges their failures as a nation. The Jews had been commanded by Moses not to marry outside of the Jewish community (Ex. 34:11-16; Deut. 7:1-4); in fact, they were to marry from within their respective tribes to maintain their own tribal distinction and inheritance (Num. 36:6). Under the Law, the taking of a foreign wife was forbidden because they were considered unclean, and their children were also regarded as unclean. Shechaniah encourages the people to not only repent, but to take responsibility for their sin and put away their foreign wives and the children born to them. God wanted a holy nation, not a double-minded, semi-pagan people. Remember the command, *"Be ye holy; for I am holy"* (Lev. 11:44). This certainly was a difficult thing to do: families were divided and relationships severed, but the Mosaic Law demanded this action. There would, however, be another set of laws, *the laws of the harvest*, which would dictate the consequences for their disobedience.

Paul explains that what *"a man sows, that he will also reap; for he who sows to his flesh will of the flesh reap corruption"* (Gal. 6:7-8). As the Jews were learning, the "sowing and reaping" principles of the harvest also applied to sin. The three laws of the harvest are as follows. First, you reap what you sow. Second, you reap more than what you sow. Third, you reap later than you sow. All the personal pain and suffering that they were now experiencing was the result of sinful behavior rendered long ago. The consequences of their sin were much more than they could have ever imagined at the time of the initial sin. Some sins can be hidden from others, but not the marrying of foreign wives. Although others may not know of our secret sins, God knows all about it and we also have to bear its burden; the enjoinder rings true, *"be sure your sin will find you out"* (Num. 32:23). Whether others know of our sins or not, the laws of the harvest still apply and it is better to repent, come clean, and suffer the consequences willingly than to continue in sin.

The Law was given to teach the Jews about sin (Rom. 3:20), and to point them to the solution – Christ alone (Gal. 3:24). Therefore, the Law allowed no wiggle room on this matter of being unequally yoked in marriage. However, in the Church Age, a measure of grace is permitted. Although Christians are not to marry non-believers (2 Cor. 6:14), a believer, after his or her conversion, is encouraged to remain with his or her unbelieving spouse. The believer provides a unique testimony of God's grace to the family (1 Cor. 7:14-16). In fact, Paul says that the lost spouse and children in that family are "sanctified" by the believer, meaning that they have been *set apart* in a special way to hear the gospel message.

Immediately following Shechaniah's confession on behalf of the people, and sensing God's work among His people, Ezra seizes the opportunity and he makes *"the leaders of the priests, the Levites, and all Israel swear an oath that they would do according to this word. So they swore an oath"* (v. 5). The spiritual power of one consecrated person to God is thus demonstrated – a huge crowd is propelled Godward in action. However, at this point there is still an entire nation that needs to be influenced for the glory of God. A proclamation is made *"throughout Judah and Jerusalem to all the descendants of the captivity, that they must gather at Jerusalem, and that whoever would not come within three days, according to the instructions of the leaders and elders, all his property would be confiscated, and he himself would be separated from the assembly of those from the captivity"* (vv. 7-8). Verse 9 records that *"all the men of Judah and Benjamin"* gathered at Jerusalem on the twentieth day of the month in response to this decree.

Ezra, having witnessed the hand of God upon His people, does not celebrate, but rather continues to mourn for the people and fast and pray for the conversion of the entire nation. He is not satisfied with the spiritual renewal of a mere remnant; he longs for national revival in which all Jews would revere and live for Jehovah.

The scene that unfolds at the temple is striking: *"all the people sat in the open square of the house of God, trembling because of this matter and because of heavy rain"* (v. 9). Ezra stands and addresses them. He first charges them with their sin (v. 10), and then insists that they *"make confession to the Lord God of your fathers, and do His will; separate yourselves from the peoples of the land, and from the pagan wives"* (v. 11). God had been offended by their sin, and Ezra was pleading with them to confess to Him their wrongdoings and to submit themselves to His will. True confession of sin is not just saying you are sorry about what you have done, but that you are sorry enough not to do it again (2 Cor. 7:10). This is what Ezra was determined that the people realize; only then could restoration with God be possible.

A revival is nothing else than a new beginning of obedience to God.

— Charles Finney

This event was the crescendo in Ezra's ministry: he was a spiritually-empowered man with a special calling for a unique situation. Although he continued to labor among God's people, he was no longer the prominent figure, nor did he desire to be, as Edward Dennett remarks:

Ezra, as may be seen from Nehemiah (Neh. 8:1), continued to labor in the midst of his people, [though] he no longer appears as the prominent figure – as the leader. Together with this chapter his special work was done, and he discerns it. For this great grace is

91

needed. The temptation, when the Lord uses one of His servants for some particular and public service, is to think that he must continue in a foremost place. If he yields to the temptation, it brings sorrow to himself, and failure for the people. The Lord who uses one today, may send another tomorrow; and blessed is that servant who can recognize, as Ezra did, when his special mission is ended, and who is willing, like John the Baptist, to be anything or nothing if so be his Lord may be exalted.[1]

Ezra was God's man of the hour! He had been bold for the Lord and God had rewarded Ezra's tears and dedication, but now the nation was in revival and it was time for the people to take charge of their own doings. Ezra was God's stimulus to point the nation in the way it should go, but only the Spirit of God could sway them to walk upon that straight and narrow path.

> Only one life will soon be past; only what's done for Christ will last.
> And when I am dying, how happy I'll be, if the lamp of my life has
> been burned out for Thee.
> — C. T. Studd

The congregation responded well to Ezra's rebuke and petition. With one accord they said, *"Yes! As you have said, so we must do"* (v. 12). However, the leaders realized the logistical difficulties in resolving the problem, for it was widespread. Time would be required to perform the investigations, to summon guilty parties, and to write bills of divorcement to properly separate foreign wives and their mixed children. It was also the rainy season; women and children could not be expected to stand in foul weather for days while the proceedings were ongoing (v. 13). Although four leaders opposed the plan (one, Meshullam, being guilty himself), it was agreed to allow local governments to investigate and execute judgments in the matter. This would be best, as each community would be the most familiar with each family situation, thus ensuring a thorough and just conclusion (vv. 14-15). It is noted that the King James Version of the Bible identifies these four men as supports of the investigation plan, but the context of the passage does not give credence to this understanding.

The investigations began eleven days later and were completed in three months (vv. 16-17). The results of the investigation are recorded in verses 18-44. In all, 114 families were impacted: 17 priests, 10 Levites, 3 gatekeepers, and 84 others had married foreign wives; some of these families had children (10:44). The separations were no doubt quite distressing for all involved. Ezra does not mention what happened to the foreign women and children; it is likely that they returned to the people groups from which they came. The priest, in accordance with the Law, offered rams for guilt offerings (Lev. 5:14-15). Unfortunately, the people did not abide by these painful reforms; when Nehemiah would arrive in Jerusalem about thirteen years later, he would find that many of the Jewish men had again taken foreign women as wives (Neh. 13:23-28).

It is here that the narrative abruptly concludes, having sufficiently pressed three main points. First, God's covenant people could not be in right fellowship with Him without a temple to offer sacrifices in – the temple, therefore, needed to be built (Ezra 1-6). Second, the enemy of God will consistently oppose His people through various tactics when they desire to serve Him in truth. Third, restoration with God is not possible until His people confess their offenses, turn from sin, and obey His Word. Today, in this dispensation, God is building a spiritual temple on earth which cannot be destroyed. We have the Lord Jesus Christ, who is the Altar in heaven (Heb. 13:10) and the unchanging heavenly High Priest who never sleeps (Heb. 4:14, 7:23-28). So, unlike the Jews, we are not required to rebuild a temple to have fellowship with God, but we would do well to heed the latter two principles, for the wiles of the devil and the nature of depraved flesh have not changed since the days of Ezra!

A Revival Meditation

Duncan Campbell, an evangelist and preacher of the Word, was an eyewitness to the great revival in the Hebrides (isles of northwestern Scotland) in the fall of 1949 through 1950. He documented the happenings of that revival in a book entitled *The Lewis Awakening*. Lewis was one of the larger isles in the Hebrides. In reflection, he suggests that revival in the Hebrides was marked by three clear characteristics: an awareness of God, deep conviction of sin, and physical manifestations and prostrations. The following are two excerpts from *The Lewis Awakening*:

In writing of the movement, I would like first to state what I mean by revival as witnessed in the Hebrides. I do not mean a time of religious entertainment, with crowds gathering to enjoy an evening of bright gospel singing; I do not mean sensational or spectacular advertising — in a God-sent revival you do not need to spend money on advertising. I do not mean high-pressure methods to get men to an inquiry room — in revival every service is an inquiry room; the road and hillside become sacred spots to many when the winds of God blow. Revival is a going of God among His people, and an awareness of God laying hold of the community. Here we see the difference between a successful campaign and revival; in the former we may see many brought to a saving knowledge of the truth, and the church or mission experience a time of quickening, but so far as the town or district is concerned no real change is visible; the world goes on its way and the dance and picture-shows are still crowded: but in revival the fear of God lays hold upon the community, moving men and women, who until then had no concern for spiritual things, to seek after God.[2]

Here is a scene witnessed during the first days of the movement: a crowded church, the service is over: the congregation, reluctant to disperse, stand outside the church in a silence that is tense. Suddenly a cry is heard within: a young man, burdened for the souls of his fellow men, is pouring out his soul in intercession. He prays until he falls into a trance and lies prostrate on the floor of the church. But Heaven had heard, and the congregation, moved by a power that they could not resist, came back into the church, and a wave of conviction of sin swept over the gathering, moving strong men to cry to God for mercy. This service continued until the small hours of the morning, but so great was the distress and so deep the hunger which gripped men and women, that they refused to go home, and already were assembling in another part of the parish. An interesting and amazing feature of this early morning visitation was the number who made their way to the church, moved by a power they had not experienced before: others were deeply convicted of their sin and crying for mercy, in their homes, before ever coming near the church.[3]

Will You not revive us again, that Your people may rejoice in You?
Show us Your mercy, Lord, and grant us Your salvation (Ps. 85:6-7).

94

Nehemiah

Overview of Nehemiah

The Author

It is generally agreed that Nehemiah is the author of the book that bears his name; nearly all the account is written in the first-person perspective. Not much is known about Nehemiah. His father was Hacaliah (1:1) and he had a brother named Hanani (1:2). He was likely born in Babylon some twenty to forty years after the building of the temple in Jerusalem was completed (520 BC). That Nehemiah had risen to a place of prominence in King Artaxerxes' court is evident by the fact that he was his cupbearer. Certainly the king would only entrust the most wise, honest, and loyal of his subjects with such a vital role and position.

Nehemiah's name means "comfort (or consolation) of Jehovah;" both his name and his occupation confirm Nehemiah to be a man of good character. Harry Ironside likens Nehemiah's ministry of leadership and comfort to that of Paul's:

> Like Paul, he [Nehemiah] was to comfort others with the comfort wherewith he himself was comforted of God (2 Cor. 1:4). This is a weighty principle in God's ways with His servants. Many a saint is permitted to go through deep waters, to pass through severe trial both of body and mind, not only for his own profit, but that he may be the better fitted to be a channel of blessing to his brethren when cast down and in distress. Happy is the saint who is thus subject to the will of God and enabled to be His agent in consoling his discouraged fellows and restoring them, through a ministry received in times of sorrow.[1]

Nehemiah held various jobs throughout the course of the book: he begins as the king's cupbearer (chps. 1-2); he becomes the king's wall-builder (chps. 3-6); and finally, he is seen as the king's governor (chps.

7-12). Nehemiah is a man of integrity, who, with God's help, accomplishes the seemingly impossible with exceeding proficiency.

The Date

Nehemiah returned to Jerusalem in 444 BC and spent twelve years in Jerusalem before returning to Babylon. He later revisited Jerusalem for a brief time to rebuke certain Jews who had regressed back into forbidden habits. Nehemiah mentions Darius the Persian (12:22), a reference to Darius II who reigned from 423-404 BC and was the successor of Artaxerxes Longimanus. It is likely that Nehemiah completed his book in the early part of Darius II's reign. Thus, an approximate date for the book would be 423-420 BC. It is quite likely that Malachi penned God's final Old Testament message to the Jewish nation shortly after Nehemiah completed his written work.

The Setting

Although Ezekiel, Daniel, and Jeremiah vividly describe the destruction of Jerusalem and how the Jews were uprooted to Babylon as captives, little is known about their time there. Other than the brief view of Jewish life in Babylon afforded by the book of Esther, the biblical narrative is mostly silent until the Jews return home.

There were three major groups of Jews who returned from their Babylonian captivity. Zerubbabel, under King Cyrus' decree, led approximately 50,000 Jews back to Jerusalem in 537-536 BC to rebuild the temple (Ezra 2:64-70). Although opponents were able to delay the work, the temple was finished in 515 BC. The *First Jewish Awakening* occurred during this time.

The second group of Jews was led from Babylon to Jerusalem by the scribe Ezra in 458 BC. This was a smaller contingency, numbering between 5,000 and 10,000 people in total. Whereas Zerubbabel had been charged with rebuilding the temple, Ezra's duty was to spiritually rebuild the people. The Jews had lost their way and Ezra would reacquaint them with Jehovah and His Law; this was the stimulus for the *Second Jewish Awakening*. A fifty-seven year gap exists between the sixth and seventh chapters of Ezra; it is during this interim that the events recorded in the book of Esther occurred; King Xerxes (Ahasuerus), Esther's husband, reigned from 486-465 BC.

Thirteen years after Ezra departed for Jerusalem, a third group of approximately 2,000 Jewish captives were led home by Nehemiah in 445-444 BC. Nehemiah, the cupbearer for King Artaxerxes, requested leave to rebuild the wall around Jerusalem, as his countrymen had no protection against raiding marauders. Since its destruction 140 years earlier by Nebuchadnezzar, the walls of Jerusalem remained broken down and its gates burned. Now, ninety years after Zerubbabel had first returned to Jerusalem, God raised up Nehemiah to lead more Jews home and to rebuild the wall and gates of the city.

Nehemiah was granted a twelve-year leave from his palace duties and was granted resources to assist in the monumental task of rebuilding the wall around Jerusalem. The wall was miraculously built in fifty-two days; this occurred during the *Third Jewish Awakening*. Nehemiah remained as governor of the region until the appointed time he was to return to Shushan (Neh. 6:15, 13:6).

Outline
Chapters 1-6: The Rebuilding of the Wall
Chapters 7-13: The Reviving of the People

Historicity
The historicity of Nehemiah has been well established by the discovery of the Elephantine papyri, which substantiates the roles of various key characters in the Biblical narrative. These papyri refer to Johanan as the high priest in Jerusalem and the sons of Sanballat (Nehemiah's great enemy) as the governors of Samaria in 408 B.C. Johanan is referred to in Nehemiah 12:22-23 and Sanballat throughout the book (2:10, 2:19, 4:1...). We also learn from these papyri that Nehemiah had ceased to be the governor of Judea before the same year, as a man named Bagoas is mentioned as holding that position.[2]

The Vision
The earlier revivals in the days of Zerubbabel and Ezra had passed; now apathy and despair again gripped the Jewish nation. Thirteen years earlier, God had used the prayers and preaching of the scribe Ezra to awaken the Jews to their pitiful spiritual condition and to seek the Lord. In an oath, the people pledged their loyalty to God and His Word. Thus, 114 Jewish men put away their foreign wives in an effort to reestablish

99

the purity of the people. The books of Ezra and Nehemiah deal with the vital issue of rebuilding a testimony of God when it has been ruined by sin. God's people must first feel the shame and reproach of God's tarnished testimony; only then will they be motivated to rise up and build.

This is the message of Nehemiah; God's people must rise up and build a lasting testimony of God's greatness. The effort will be labor-intensive and require much tenacity and wisdom to withstand the opposition, but with the Lord's help, it can be done. In Nehemiah's time, there was a lot of rubble to remove before the wall could be rebuilt. Likewise, today the Church's testimony of Jesus Christ is in ruins in much of the world. May God's people feel remorse over this tragedy and be spiritually revitalized to rise up, remove the rubble of religious pride and stifling traditions, and build again on the foundation of the Lord Jesus Christ (1 Cor. 3:10-11). Time is in short supply, for the days are wicked and the Lord's return for His Church is imminent. Let us pray for revival and then do our part to be a part of it!

Revival Meditation

The Puritan Richard Sibbes (1577-1635) preached Christ to the students and townsmen at Cambridge with much success until his death. He acknowledges that Christ through the gospel message is the One who has the power to revive all nations, including the Jews:

> Let no man therefore despair; nor, as I said before, let us despair of the conversion of those that are savages in other parts. How bad so ever they be, they are of the world, and if the gospel be preached to them, Christ will be "believed on in the world". Christ's almighty power goes with His own ordinance to make it effectual.... And when the fullness of the Gentiles is come in, then comes the conversion of the Jews. Why may we not expect it? They were the people of God. We see "Christ believed on in the world." We may therefore expect that they shall also be called, there being many of them, and keeping their nation distinct from others.[3]

Nehemiah Devotions

The Cupbearer
Nehemiah 1

The book commences with Nehemiah, the son of Hacaliah, serving in the winter headquarters of the Persian Empire located at Shushan, also called Susa (v. 1; Est. 1:2; Dan. 8:2). It is the month of Chislev and the twentieth year of Artaxerxes' rule (i.e. November-December 445 BC). Nehemiah was the king's cupbearer, meaning that he had the important task of ensuring that the king's wine and perhaps his food had not been poisoned: "Now, it is a well-known fact that the king's cupbearers, when they proffer the cup, draw off some of it with the ladle, pour it into their left hand, and swallow it down—so that, if they should put poison in, they may not profit by it."[1]

Extra-biblical references indicate that the office of cupbearer in the Persian court was a position second only in authority to the king.[2] Accordingly, Nehemiah may have been the chief treasurer and the keeper of the king's signet ring. A. T. Olmstead encapsulates Nehemiah's influence: "The cupbearer... in later Achaemenid times was to exercise even more influence than the commander-in-chief."[3] As this service required frequent access to the king, it is likely that Nehemiah enjoyed a favorable and influential relationship with Artaxerxes. The palace at Shushan was a place of splendor and extravagance; it is doubtful that any Jew could have risen to a higher position than this.

Being in the king's court had its privileges; Nehemiah would have certainly known of Chancellor Rehum's letter to Artaxerxes on behalf of a large contingency of various people adamantly opposed to the Jews rebuilding Jerusalem. The letter stated that the Jews had been a powerful and rebellious people previously and that if they were allowed again to fortify the city's defenses, they would again rebel and refuse to pay the king's taxes (Ezra 4). Artaxerxes decided not to take a chance and wrote the following to the governing authorities in Palestine: *"Now give the command to make these men cease, that this city may not be built until the command is given by me"* (Ezra 4:21). Although the work was forcibly stopped, the opportunity for rebuilding Jerusalem in the future was still a possibility. Nehemiah was anxious to hear news of how this decree affected his countrymen and, in time, he did.

A group of Jews, Nehemiah's brother Hanani being among them, had just returned from visiting Jerusalem. A concerned Nehemiah immediately inquired about the welfare of God's people and about the place where God had placed His name – Jerusalem. The report was not favorable; 140 years after Nebuchadnezzar's successful invasion, the wall around Jerusalem and, indeed, much of the city lay in ruins, and the burned gates had not been replaced. Though the temple had been built, and sacrifices were being offered to Jehovah, the people themselves were *"in great distress and reproach"* (v. 3).

We read of Nehemiah's response to this report: *"So it was, when I heard these words, that I sat down and wept, and mourned for many days; I was fasting and praying before the God of heaven"* (v. 4). The Law did not require the Jews to fast, except on the Day of Atonement, but Nehemiah was deeply affected by the dismal report and immediately petitioned the Lord for help while fasting *"day and night"* (v. 6). This does not mean Nehemiah prayed every moment of every day, but rather that he engaged in the type of prayer Paul exhorts the believers at Thessalonica to engage in: *"Pray without ceasing"* (1 Thess. 5:17).

The Greek word *adialeiptos*, which is rendered "without ceasing" implies that our prayers should be "constantly recurring" rather than "continuously occurring." It would be impossible to pray twenty-four hours a day, seven days a week. But it is possible to have an actively recurring prayer life. To "pray without ceasing" means to stay in contact with God in such a way that our praying is like a long conversation with short pauses: we never sense a break in communion. The believer should pray at regular times and as exercised when needs arise (to confess sin, to make intercession, to seek grace in a time of need). The Lord should never be far from our thoughts, for He is always willing to bend His ear to the pangs of a humble heart: *"Lord,*

You have heard the desire of the humble; You will prepare their heart; You will cause Your ear to hear" (Ps. 10:17). The Lord knows the desire of our hearts and grants the humble that desire. For example, Paul prayed for the souls of the nation of Israel – that they might be saved (Rom. 9:1-3, 10:1). Paul also informed the Gentiles that they came to Christ as a result of God answering the prayers of Jewish Christians (2 Cor. 9:14). Hudson Taylor, who labored for the Lord as a missionary in China, had three important principles concerning prayer:

1. You can work without praying, but it is a bad plan.
2. You cannot pray in earnest without working.
3. Do not be so busy with work for Christ that you have no strength left for praying. True praying requires strength.[4]

Warren Wiersbe writes, "Prayer is not an escape from responsibility; it is our *response* to God's *ability*. True prayer energizes us for service and battle."[5] Nehemiah knew that the situation was impossible without God's help, so he committed himself to the only course of action available to him – ongoing prayer until God answered the burden of his heart. We learn in the next chapter that the door of opportunity occurred four months after he had begun to pray. Why was Nehemiah so deeply exercised to pray about horrid conditions in Jerusalem? H. A. Ironside supplies an answer to this question:

> That Hanani felt this keenly there can be no doubt, but that he or his companions were before God about it, as was Nehemiah, seems scarcely probable. It is one thing to shake the head and sigh over the vicissitudes of the congregation of the Lord, it is quite another to look up to Him to give deliverance, and to put His truth and testimony above every other interest. This latter Nehemiah did.[6]

Like Moses a millennium before him, Nehemiah was concerned for his suffering brethren to the jeopardy of his social rank. The book of Hebrews provides insight as to why Moses chose to identify with God's covenant people instead of with the Egyptian royalty:

> *By faith Moses, when he became of age, refused to be called the son of Pharaoh's daughter, choosing rather to suffer affliction with the*

people of God than to enjoy the passing pleasures of sin, esteeming **the reproach of Christ** *greater riches than the treasures in Egypt; for he looked to the reward. By faith he forsook Egypt, not fearing the wrath of the king; for he endured as seeing Him who is invisible* (Heb. 11:24-27).

Moses understood who he was and he chose to identify with God's people. Moses was willing to forsake great riches and high status to suffer *the reproach of Christ* in the world. Moses didn't suffer because of his testimony for Christ, for Moses did not know the Lord at that time, but rather for foreshadowing Christ's suffering for identifying with God's covenant people. Somehow he understood that there was a day of reckoning with God, and he determined that it would be better for him to identify with God's people and forsake the splendor of Egypt rather than to be associated with a dismal system of rule which brutalized God's people.

Nehemiah enjoyed a position of prominence and social security, but his heart was with his people and he was zealous for God's testimony in the world. Jerusalem should be a city of glory and praise, rather than a reproach to God's name. Nehemiah knew that a wall around Jerusalem would serve both for protection and for exclusion. Once erected, the wall would provide defense against their enemy and also bind the Jews in a spiritual safe haven, exclusive of heathen ways. Thus, Nehemiah poured out his heart in prayer before the Lord. In fact, he is a man of prayer; 46 of the 406 verses (or 11 percent) of his book are recorded prayers. Nehemiah's reaction was evidence of his great concern for the Lord's work and His people. Do we feel the same sense of desperation today that Nehemiah felt long ago? Do we mourn over the Church's indifference, moral failures, and lack of commitment to the Lord Jesus Christ and His Word? What might God do today, if believers were broken over the Church's ruined testimony of Christ, and in prayer and fasting pleaded with the Lord to revive His Church?

Nehemiah would be called to build the wall, but first he had to weep over the ruins. The rubble had to be first watered with tears before a new wall could arise out of the ashes.

— Mike Attwood

The remainder of the chapter records Nehemiah's prayer and response to the dire situation in Jerusalem. One of the fundamental principles of problem resolution is this: If you are not part of the problem or part of the solution, don't get involved. Although Nehemiah was not part of the enormous problem at Jerusalem, he did desire to be a part of God's solution. Nehemiah's situation is similar to the time when the Lord told the disciples to pray for laborers for the mission field, and in the next verse they discovered that they were the answer to their own prayers: *"Therefore pray the Lord of the harvest to send out laborers into His harvest. And when He had called His twelve disciples to Him, He gave them power over unclean spirits, to cast them out, and to heal all kinds of sickness and all kinds of disease"* (Matt. 9:38-10:2). Be careful dear believer that you do not fail to pray for the miraculous, and when you pray, do not forget that you may be God's answer to your own prayers!

If a believer fails to pray, he in fact fails in everything!

— Watchman Nee

The Lord Jesus taught His disciples to pray through His personal example and by providing them with a model prayer, but not one to be repetitiously prayed (Matt. 6:7-9). The Lord began, *"Our Father in heaven, Hallowed be Your name"* (Matt. 6:9). Nehemiah's prayer also commences with expressions of worship and wonder: *"Lord God of heaven, O great and awesome God, You who keep Your covenant and mercy with those who love You and observe Your commandments"* (v. 5). Both the Lord Jesus and Nehemiah compel us to first ponder the character and attributes of God when approaching Him in prayer. Why? The more we understand of our God's awesome nature, the faster the enormity of our problems diminish by comparison.

Like his predecessors, Moses, Daniel, and Ezra (Ex. 34:9; Dan. 9:5; Ezra 9:10), Nehemiah owns the sins of the nation and confesses them as his own. The horrific conditions at Jerusalem were not the consequences of the Persian Empire, but rather of their own disobedience to God's Word. However, Nehemiah also realizes that God is a covenant-keeping God and that despite human failure, God is obligated to keep His Word: *"For what if some did not believe? Will their unbelief make the faithfulness of God without effect? Certainly not! Indeed, let God be true but every man a liar"* (Rom. 3:3-4). Consequently, in times of persecution and failure, it would be profitable for Christians to remember and proclaim the promise of the Lord Jesus: *"I will build My church, and the gates of Hades shall not prevail against it"* (Matt. 16:18).

Nehemiah concludes his prayer by specifically requesting that God's grace would uphold His people for His glory (v. 11). Being the king's cupbearer, Nehemiah feared the king's response if he told him the burden of his heart; so, he prays for the king's mercy. How would he be able to get Artaxerxes' permission to obtain a long leave of absence to rebuild Jerusalem's wall? What motivated Nehemiah to risk his own life and get involved? He wanted to be a part of God's solution because he feared God's name (v. 11). Dear believer, do you fear God and the power of His name? Do you want to be a part of the solution of restoring and rebuilding the testimony of Jesus Christ today? It is easy to possess a bit of discernment about a problem, remain at arm's length, and criticize others who are getting their hands dirty trying to fix it; it is entirely another thing to want to be part of God's solution no matter what others say or the personal sacrifice involved. For the praise and glory of God, Nehemiah was compelled to do something for the Lord, though he didn't know how to go about it. Although God's people had failed Him, Nehemiah would not falter with them; he was determined to re-establish God's testimony in Jerusalem no matter what the cost.

In the next chapter, we discover that God will present Nehemiah with the opportunity he has been praying for. In unwavering faith, Nehemiah will step forward in fear and trembling to make a bold request of the king.

A Revival Meditation

David Brainerd struggled with poor health for years while laboring among the Delaware Indians in Pennsylvania and New Jersey during the early eighteenth century. At the age of twenty-nine, he ultimately succumbed to consumption (tuberculosis). Brainerd was a man of prayer, sometimes venturing out into the forest on winter nights and kneeling in snow a foot deep to petition God. Even after being in the cold for hours, he would often become wringing wet with perspiration as he labored in prayer. After some years of difficult and almost fruitless work among the Indians, God responded to Brainerd's agonizing prayers. A powerful revival commenced in July, 1745. This revival was beyond anything that anyone could have imagined at that time and continued for some years with lasting results. Brainerd wrote:

July 26th. In the evening, God was pleased to help me in prayer, beyond what I have experienced for some time. My soul was especially drawn out for the enlargement of Christ's kingdom; and for the conversion of my poor people; and I relied on God for the accomplishment of that great work. My soul, my very soul longed for the ingathering of the poor heathen; and I cried to God for them most willingly and heartily, and yet because I could not but cry. I longed that the remaining part of my life might be filled up with more fervency and activity in things of God.

August 3rd. Having visited the Indians in these parts in June last, and tarried with them some considerable time preaching almost daily, I now found them serious, and a number of them under deep concern for an interest in Christ. I preached to them this day, 'Whosoever will, let him take the water of life freely.' The Lord, I am persuaded, enabled me, in a manner somewhat uncommon, to set before them the Lord Jesus Christ as kind and compassionate Savior, inviting distressed and perishing sinners to accept everlasting mercy, and a surprising concern soon became apparent among them. There were about 20 adult persons together, and not above two that I could see with dry eyes.

August 6th. In the morning I discoursed to the Indians at the house where we lodged. Many of them were tenderly affected, so that a few words about their souls would cause the tears to flow freely, and produce many sobs and groans. In the afternoon I again discoursed to them. They seemed eager to hear; but there appeared nothing very remarkable, till near the close of my discourse; and then divine truths were attended with a surprising influence, and produced a great concern among them. All seemed in an agony to obtain an interest in Christ. It was surprising to see how their hearts seemed to be pierced with the tender and melting invitations of the Gospel, when there was not a word of terror spoken to them.

August 8th. In the afternoon I preached to about sixty-five persons, and was favored with uncommon freedom. There was much visible concern among them; but when I spoke to one and another more particularly, the power of God seemed to descend upon the assembly 'like a rushing mighty wind,' and with an astonishing energy bore down all before it. I stood amazed at the influence which seized the audience: old men and women, and some children, as well as persons of middle age. I never saw a day like it in all respects: it was a day wherein I am persuaded the Lord did much to destroy the kingdom of darkness among this people.[7]

The Petition
Nehemiah 2

Nehemiah 2 commences approximately four months after the events of the previous chapter. Nehemiah did not know what to do about the situation in Jerusalem, so he committed himself to prayer and waited for the Lord to open the door of opportunity. In the meantime, he faithfully continued to fulfill his responsibilities to Artaxerxes. The king's court was to be an oasis from personal threats and political criticism; thus, only the most loyal and jovial of his subjects would be permitted there. One day, while Nehemiah was performing his duty, the king noticed Nehemiah's glum disposition. Heathen kings often considered themselves as gods, and felt that their very presence should dispel gloom from their subjects. Accordingly, anyone with a downcast demeanor before the king was in danger of insulting him and reaping his wrath.

This particular occasion may have been a private meeting, for the queen was sitting with Artaxerxes (v. 6), and Persian queens did not normally attend formal affairs unless summoned to do so (Est. 1:10-11, 5:1-2). The king knew Nehemiah well and rightly discerned that he was not ill, but rather heartsick with sorrow. The king inquired of Nehemiah what was bothering him. Nehemiah knew that his was not an acceptable disposition for the king's cupbearer to have and thus became anxious for his life (v. 2).

Rather than answering presumptuously, Nehemiah breathes out a quick prayer to heaven before making his bold request. These unuttered words from his heart resounded before the throne of grace and prompted an immediate response from heaven. In the Church Age, all who are born again become temples of the living God and are indwelt with the Spirit of God (1 Cor. 6:19-20). This allows the human spirit to directly commune with God the Father; this is accomplished through the intercession of His indwelling Spirit (Rom. 8:26) and through the mediation of His Son (1 Tim. 2:5). Although Nehemiah was not indwelt by the Holy Spirit, as Christians are today, God knew of his purity and his heart's burden and was prompted to act in the same way He does for believers today. It is comforting to know that when we do not know what to pray, or are so downhearted we are incapable of forming words in prayer, the Spirit of God intercedes perfectly on our behalf.

The Lord Jesus told His disciples: *"Your Father knows the things you have need of before you ask Him"* (Matt. 6:8). And John reminded the church at Philadelphia that it is the Lord alone who opens and closes doors of opportunity: *"These things says He who is holy, He who is true, 'He who has the key of David, He who opens and no one shuts, and shuts and no one opens'"* (Rev. 3:7). Nehemiah did not rush ahead of the Lord to try to fix the problem as soon as he became aware of it; rather, he waited for the Lord's timing and solution to become apparent – then he took action. God's blessing is often forfeited because Christians impetuously run ahead of the Lord to engage in some religious cause or some seemingly good deed which the Lord does not endorse. Nehemiah had been praying and fasting for four months, patiently waiting for God's answer; it had now arrived. He had probably been contemplating how he could approach the subject with the king, but God's solution was better: He moved the king to question Nehemiah about the matter. Nehemiah's situation teaches us how utterly defenseless the enemy is against the power of earnest praying.

> The habit of regular, lingering prayer, more than anything else, makes any Christian a dangerous holy weapon in the hand of God.
>
> — J. Sidlow Baxter

Before informing the king of why he is sorrowful, Nehemiah is careful to honor the king with the expression, *"Let the king live forever"* (v. 3). No doubt Nehemiah had a gained a good report with the king, but this gesture affirms Nehemiah's subjection to and respect for him. Then, as concisely as possible, Nehemiah expresses the reason for his grief: *"Why should my face not be sad, when the city, the place of my fathers' tombs, lies waste, and its gates are burned with fire?"* (v. 3). Without hesitation the king responds, *"What do you request?"* (v.

4). Although Nehemiah had been in steadfast prayer, he probably felt like the brethren who prayed for Peter's release from prison in Acts 12: when Peter, who had been sentenced to death, arrived to knock at the door of the very house in which they were engaged in prayer on his behalf, they were so astounded that they initially doubted his identity (Acts 12:15). When God is in a matter, we should expect the answer to our prayers to be beyond anything that we could have mentally conceived. This was Nehemiah's experience. Although he may have been astonished by the king's *carte blanche*, he proceeded (after another quick prayer) to make his request.

Nehemiah asked the king to send him to Judah to oversee the reconstruction of Jerusalem (v. 5). Artaxerxes inquired about the duration of the task. There was obviously some private discussion that followed but was not recorded in the narrative; however, Nehemiah concludes, *"So it pleased the king to send me; and I set him a time"* (v. 6). We later learn that Nehemiah would honor the king's request and return to Babylon after completing his twelve-year stint in Jerusalem (5:14).

Having secured the favor of the king, Nehemiah further requested royal documents to allow unhindered passage to Jerusalem and a supply of free lumber from the king's forest. A vast amount of timber would be required to reconstruct the wall and the city's gates, and to build Nehemiah a house while he sojourned in Jerusalem. This the king granted and the letters were written. This is a valuable lesson for the believer: not only do we need the Lord to open the doors of opportunity, but He also must supply the resources to accomplish the work. It is quite possible that God's timing may be correct for us to proceed in a matter, but if we do so in the power of the flesh or in human wisdom, the blessing of God will be lost none the same.

Having both the Lord's direction and resources, Nehemiah ventured to Jerusalem in confidence that he had the mind of the Lord. When we wait on the Lord to open doors of ministry for us, we become more sure of our specific calling to accomplish something for the Lord. Because Nehemiah had witnessed God's working in the king's heart, he knew that God had endorsed his ministry. This fact would gird his mind against discouragement in the difficult days ahead; the Lord was indeed with him! If we are walking with God, we will be encouraged to continue to step forward in faith because of the sure footing of grace

111

realized in the previous step. To rise up and build effectively, the work must be done God's way, in God's timing, and with God's resources.

To ensure the protection of his cupbearer, the king provided Nehemiah with a military escort to Jerusalem. It is unknown if Nehemiah asked for the escort or if the king assigned it to him on his own initiative. Certainly the king knew the political landscape in Jerusalem and the intense opposition Nehemiah would face when he began to rebuild the city. Likewise, today we should expect that no true work of God will ever go unopposed.

There were two men in particular that were grieved that Nehemiah had come to Jerusalem to seek the welfare of the Jews: Sanballat, the Horonite, and Tobiah, his servant and an Ammonite (v. 10). Archeological evidence has confirmed the existence of Sanballat: the Elephantine papyri written in 407 BC (37 years after this event) names Sanballat as the governor of Samaria.[1] Whenever God lifts someone up to accomplish His will who is without personal ambition, is void of selfish interests, and has no desire for personal glory, the enemy will try to stop that person. Regardless, Nehemiah rallied the Jews with the call, *"Let us rise and build"* (v. 18). In response, the enemy also organized themselves to stop the work, even if it meant murdering Nehemiah and those laboring with him (4:11, 6:1-12). The enemy of God knows no mercy; he will do anything, no matter how ghastly, to prevent a testimony of God's goodness from being realized or to degrade one that already exists.

Although Jews had lived in Jerusalem for several generations, they did not seem concerned about God's ruined testimony among the nations. Though some had started to rebuild the city during Artaxerxes' reign, they had been stopped by the king in response to Chancellor Rehum's accusatory letter a few years before Nehemiah's arrival. The Jews were apparently content to let the matter be, as Scripture does not record any appeal to the king to reconsider the decree. A great revival had occurred under Ezra thirteen years previous, but now the people had grown spiritually complacent again. In this spiritual condition, God's people are no threat to the devil in any age. But when a man zealous for the Lord arrived in Jerusalem, the enemy quickly noticed, sounded the alarm, and summoned its forces for war. Nehemiah was a man whose zealous attitude declared war against things as they were. It was high time for God's people to rise up and to retake the ground captured by the enemy.

> Satan wastes no ammunitions on those who are dead in trespasses and sins.
> — Corrie Ten Boom

Nehemiah had heard reports about the condition of the city, but after being in Jerusalem three days he investigated the matter for himself. He took a few trusted men with him and inconspicuously slipped out at night to examine what remained of the wall of the city. Departing from the Valley Gate on the west side of the city, he headed south, and then turned north again after rounding the southern edge of the city at the Dung Gate (also possibly called the Potshard Gate in Jer. 19:2). The rubble on the east side of the city was so immense north of the Fountain Gate that he could not pass on horseback and so instead he ventured up the Kidron Valley (v. 14). The fact that Nehemiah "turned back" would seem to indicate that he did not encircle the entire city, but rather retraced his route back to the Valley Gate.

The entire investigation was accomplished in secret; neither the Jews nor the rulers knew about Nehemiah's nighttime sally (v. 16). Nehemiah teaches us an important principle to consider before we rise and build for the Lord. It is vitally important to understand the facts in order to correctly diagnose and address the problem. Nehemiah now understood the scope of the work and could better formulate a plan to accomplish it efficiently. If we want to witness the type of revival that occurred under Nehemiah's leadership, we too must face the cold, hard facts of the condition of the Church, of our indifference, and of our ruined testimony of Christ.

After investigating the walls and obtaining a correct understanding of their condition, Nehemiah then rallied the Jews to rebuild the wall: *"Come and let us build the wall of Jerusalem, that we may no longer be a reproach"* (Neh. 2:17). Mike Attwood states, "Agonizing and organizing go together in Christian work. Nehemiah agonized first and then he organized." Nehemiah realized the necessity of involving all the people in the work, for the task was enormous. So he sought the cooperation of the people and committed himself to co-labor with them: *"Let us rise up and build"* (v. 18). Unity of vision must mean unity of purpose for God's people to stand as one with Him and be unconquerable. Moses highlighted the importance of unity and working with God: *"How could one chase a thousand, and two put ten thousand to flight, unless their Rock had sold them, and the Lord had surrendered them?"* (Deut. 32:30). God can use one man to defeat a thousand foes, but two men fighting as one with the Lord can defeat ten thousand! God's people have greater wherewithal when they work together, rather than as individuals, for the cause of Christ.

> Cooperation increases efficiency in amazing proportions. Two working together in perfect agreement have fivefold the efficiency of the same two working separately.
> — S. D. Gordon

The first six chapters of Acts indicate that the early Church was successful in evangelism when there was unity and Christ-mindedness among the disciples. When there were divisions and factions within the church, their testimony was marred, the Spirit was quenched, and fruitfulness ceased. The lesson for us all is to lay hold of the mind of Christ. This will bring unity to the Church, which will then have only one goal: *"that all things be unto the glory of God."* On the eve of His suffering, the Lord repeatedly acknowledged in His prayer in John 17 the inseparable link between unity and the display of the glory of God:

> *I do not pray for these alone, but also for those who will believe in Me through their word; that they all may be one, as You, Father, are in Me, and I in You; that they also may be one in Us, that the world may believe that You sent Me. And the glory which You gave Me I have given them, that they may be one just as We are one: I in them, and You in Me; that they may be made perfect in one, and that the world may know that You have sent Me, and have loved them as You have loved Me* (John 17:20-23).

When the Church is unified, the glory of God is displayed in it for all to see. Peaceful unity among men is not a naturally occurring phenomenon, so when it does occur the world takes notice. The lost are prompted to consider what they see and by the grace of God some will be won to Christ! It is absolutely necessary for a local assembly to be of one accord before they can properly exhibit Christ to their neighborhoods. If there is disunity in the church, the work of the Holy Spirit is concentrated within the house of God in order to remove the rubble of pride, hypocrisy, willful sin, and doctrinal error. Only when the flesh-made rubble is removed from the local assembly can Spirit-controlled saints rise up and build as one for the glory of God.

> It is my conviction that we are never going to have a revival until God has brought the church of Jesus Christ to the point of desperation.
>
> — Stephen Olford

Nehemiah informed the people of how God had blessed his concern over the state of Jerusalem, and also of the king's decree to rebuild it. Understanding that both God and king were on their side, the Jews respond favorably to Nehemiah's rallying cry: *"So they said, 'Let us rise up and build.' Then they set their hands to this good work"* (v. 18). This oneness of purpose and excitement for the things of God immediate drew the attention and condemnation of Sanballat, Tobiah, and Geshem, the devil's agents. These men would use a variety of tactics over the course of the next few chapters in an attempt to stop the building of the wall. As one tactic fails, the next will become more aggressive than the previous, until finally the enemy, in utter desperation, seeks Nehemiah's life. But God was with His people and they were determined to build.

The first strategy the enemy used to stop the work was to *sidetrack* the Jews from the work through harassment, demeaning jokes, scorn, planting doubts, etc. Nehemiah just ignored the enemy's bantering and declared: *"The God of heaven Himself will prosper us; therefore we His servants will arise and build, but you have no heritage or right or memorial in Jerusalem"* (v. 20). Harry Ironside provides the following helpful insight concerning Nehemiah's response:

> He has thrown down the gauntlet and declares his uncompromising attitude in a manner not to be misunderstood. Henceforth he will be hated as only those can hate who resent having their false religious claims made nothing of! The out-and-out worldling does not hate what is truly of God so bitterly as the Christless professor who has a name that he lives but is dead. Such an one cannot bear spiritual realities; for when confronted with them the hollowness of his

profession is exposed, like Dagon when the ark of Jehovah was set down before it. This explains the bitterness with which these adversaries opposed the work of God going on at Jerusalem.[2]

Dear believer, if you are walking with the Lord, and understand His calling for your life, there is no need to listen to the enemy at all, for he despises the things of God. Don't let the devil play mind-games with you; rather, be given to prayer and be diligent in the work at hand. May the Church awake from her despondency, rise up in unity and consecration, and build with undistracted resolve for the glory and honor of the Lord Jesus Christ.

A Revival Meditation

The conversion of Hudson Taylor demonstrates the power of effectual and fervent prayer.

> Hudson Taylor, founder of China Inland Mission, says that about 1830 his father became so interested in the spiritual condition of China, that he was led to pray that if God ever gave him a son, he might be privileged to labor as a missionary there; a prayer unknown to the son until after seven years of service in that mission field. Though carefully trained to the study of God's word and a life of devotion, yet at the age of fifteen the lad was a skeptic.

> Of his conversion he says: "One day, which I shall never forget, when I was about fifteen years old, my dear mother being absent from home some eighty miles away, I had a holiday. I searched through the library for a book to while away time. I selected a gospel tract which looked unattractive, saying, there will be an interesting story at the commencement, and a sermon or moral at the end; I will take the former, and leave the latter for those who like it. I little knew what was going on in the heart of my dear mother. She arose from the dinner-table with an intense yearning for the conversion of her boy, and feeling that, being from home, and having more leisure than she otherwise would, there was a special opportunity afforded her of pleading with God for me. She went to her bedroom, and turned the key in the door, and resolved not to leave the room until her prayers were answered. Hour after hour did that dear mother plead for me, until she could only praise God for the conversion of her son. In the meantime, as I was reading the tract, 'The Finished Work of Christ,' a light was flashed into my soul by the Holy Spirit, that there was

nothing to be done, but to fall 'on my knees and accept this Savior and his salvation, and praise God forevermore. While my mother was praising God in her closet, I was praising Him in the old warehouse where I had retired to read my book. When I met mother at the door on her return with the glad news, she said: "I know, my boy; I have been rejoicing for a fortnight in the glad tidings you have to tell me!"

Many souls are lost for want of persistent pleading with God in their behalf. Time that might be used in prayer is consumed in other ways, and souls and opportunities pass forever from our reach. For those hours of pleading with God, this faithful mother received not only her son for God, but the great work God put into his hands – China Inland Mission. Hudson Taylor has led out into the heart of China more than one hundred and seventy missionaries, none of whom receive support except through faith in God.[3]

The Wall-Builders (Part 1)
Nehemiah 3:1-14

In the two previous chapters, we learned of the deplorable condition of Jerusalem: its wall lay in ruins, its gates burned, and its people oppressed; in short, the place where God had chosen to declare His name was in a pathetic state. After evaluating the enormous task and developing an executable plan, Nehemiah challenges the people to rise up and build by affirming that both their God and king are with them. The Jews were enthusiastic and a cooperative spirit existed among them to do the work.

This chapter describes the construction of the various sections: the northern wall (vv. 1-5), the western wall (vv. 6-12), the southern wall (vv. 13-14), and the eastern wall (vv. 15-31). Nehemiah divided the Jews into forty-two work groups, each one responsible for their own section; yet, all were working cooperatively with a single objective – to complete the wall. This communal oneness is expressed by the repeated expressions "next to him," "next to them," and "next to that" in Nehemiah 3. Though functioning within distinct work groups, everyone was to have a part in God's work.

The situation in Jerusalem was bleak, but one man, zealous for God, had served as a catalyst for revival. What God would accomplish through His people would be nothing less than a staggering testimony of His eminence among the nations – the entire wall about the city would be finished in only fifty-two days. Even the enemies of the Jews would come to understand that the building of the wall was a supernatural feat accomplished by Jehovah (6:16). The Jews had been spiritually awakened to experience the wonder of their God.

An assortment of people from various occupations and social backgrounds engaged in the rebuilding project: travelers, goldsmiths, perfumers, nobles, priests, young women, civil leaders, etc. Goldsmiths and perfumers performed delicate work – no doubt their hands and bodies were not accustomed to hard manual labor – yet, they happily worked alongside their brethren. Even Jews who were not under Nehemiah's authority as governor traveled from other towns, such as Jericho (v. 2), Tekoa (v. 5), Gibeon (v. 7), and Mizpah (v. 7), to Jerusalem to participate in the work.

Beginning with the Sheep Gate on the north side of Jerusalem, Nehemiah takes us on a counter-clockwise tour of the city so that we might appreciate both the ongoing work and the hands of those engaged in it. Besides noting the various workers and their accomplishments, Nehemiah particularly calls our attention to Jerusalem's ten gates. The life of the city, its goods and people, entered through the fractured gateways in the wall surrounding the city. Once the wall and its gates were rebuilt, the gates would be closed at certain times to secure the city, for if an enemy could breach even one gate, the entire city could fall (7:3).

Nehemiah's wall would feature ten gates; modern Jerusalem today has eight gates. Ezekiel prophesied that the Jewish nation, after being restored to Christ at the onset of the Kingdom Age, will have twelve gates, one for each tribe (Ezek. 48:31-34). Similarly, God's eternal city, the New Jerusalem, which descends out of heaven at the conclusion of Christ's Millennial Kingdom, will have twelve operational gates (Rev. 21:10-12). What message is being conveyed in the number of the gates?

Twelve is the number of *perfect administration* in Scripture; thus, twelve tribes composed the nation of Israel, the Church was founded on the teachings of the twelve apostles. Consequently, the New Jerusalem has twelve gates, one named after each tribe of Israel, and twelve foundations, one named after each apostle (Rev. 21:12-14). The number *ten* is used to represent *responsibility* in Scripture; for example, the Ten Commandments made the Jews directly accountable to God for their behavior. (Before receiving the Law, their sin was not imputed as transgression; Rom. 5:13). Another example of this symbolism is seen again in one of the Lord's parables, where the Jewish nation, just prior to the Lord's Second Advent to the earth, is likened to ten virgins (Matt. 25:1-13): five virgins were genuine followers of Christ and five were not and, consequently, would not enter into His kingdom. Examining the narrative of Nehemiah, the following question comes to mind: If Jerusalem was to have twelve gates, why are only ten mentioned here? Perhaps the message in the numbers provides an explanation: you have not yet reached perfection; therefore, remember that you are directly accountable to God for your actions.

The Sheep Gate (vv. 1-2)

The towers of Hammeah and Hannanel stood on either side of this gate (see illustration on page 135). The first laborer mentioned is Eliashib, the High Priest. No doubt his example of clearing away debris and carrying heavy stones would inspire other priests to join in the work. When a man of status and spiritual maturity chooses to get his hands dirty, it motivates others to do the same. This is a good lesson for the Church: if church elders think that they are above doing the "dirty work" (such as evangelistic outreach work, cleaning the church building, washing the dishes after a fellowship dinner, etc.), then they should not be surprised if the sheep they attend shy away from such tasks also.

This gate was directly north of the temple and was used to bring animals, including sheep, to the temple for sacrifice, hence the name. The Sheep Gate is most likely the gate through which *"the Lamb of God who takes away the sin of the world"* (John 1:29) was led to be crucified. Just as the blood of the sacrificial animals was poured out on the north side of the Bronze Altar, the Lord Jesus shed His blood for sinners at Golgotha, "the place of the skull," just north of Jerusalem (John 19:17). Eliashib's name means "God restores," and it is only through the finished work of His Beloved Son that God can restore man to Himself. As Nehemiah's journey starts and ends at the sheep gate, it would seem that God never wants us to forget His Son, or what He accomplished on a cross outside of the Sheep Gate.

The Fish Gate (vv. 3-5)

As previously mentioned, the phrase *"next to them"* frequently recurs throughout this chapter and confirms that while each group labored on their particular section of the wall, they were conscious of the fact that they were all working together for a common cause. This camaraderie provided not only encouragement to keep working but also the protection of numbers in the case of an attack. It was through the Fish Gate that merchants brought fish caught in the Sea of Galilee to the marketplace to be sold. The Sheep Gate and Fish Gate are rightly connected in application for the believer: let us not forget that those who have been redeemed by the shed blood of the Lamb of God are also called to be "fishers of men" (Mark 1:16-17).

The tranquil scene of God's people working together in harmony is marred by a statement in verse 5: *"Next to them the Tekoites made repairs; but their nobles did not put their shoulders to the work of their Lord."* Despite the spiritual despondency of their nobles, the Tekoites continued to build. However, God's indictment against these slackers was recorded for all to notice, and in a coming day the nobles of the Tekoites shall give account of themselves before the Lord (Rom. 14:14). This serves as a reminder that at the Judgment Seat of Christ each believer will be examined and rewarded for faithful service (1 Cor. 3:11-15; 2 Cor. 5:10). May we be found to be faithful soldiers of the cross having not deserted *the Captain of our Salvation.*

The Old Gate (vv. 6-12)

The Old Gate was located on the northwest portion of the wall and was the main entrance into the city from the north; it later may have been called the Damascus Gate. The Old Gate speaks to us of the old paths of divine truth which do not change and should still be obeyed today. The prophet Jeremiah puts the matter this way: *"Thus says the Lord: 'Stand in the ways and see, and ask for the old paths, where the good way is, and walk in it; then you will find rest for your souls.' But they said, 'We will not walk in it'"* (Jer. 6:16). Thankfully, absolute truth cannot contradict itself. That which is not found consistently accurate cannot be true. It is understood that scientific perception of absolute truth is imperfect, for science is a process of refining understanding of definitive reality. While laboring for God, believers should not abandon the Old Paths of Divine Truth for alternate paths of human reasoning; these will eventually result in shipwrecked lives. God is infallible and unchanging; His paths of truth are eternally faithful. May God's people be guided by the ancient paths of righteousness and enter into His joy and peace through the Old Gate.

Rephaiah (v. 9) and Shallum (v. 12) were each half-rulers of Jerusalem. These men were probably not accustomed to the rigors of construction work, but they happily joined the fellowship of cut and blistered hands. Shallum's daughters labored with their father; it is indeed a lovely sight when families serve the Lord together. Joshua declared to his fellow Jews, *"But as for me and my house, we will serve the Lord"* (Josh. 24:15).

The families of Benjamin and Hasshub (v. 23) and of Meshullam (v. 30) also worked together and opposite their own homes. The home is a great training ground for ministry. Children are prompted to revere and serve the Lord when they witness their parents' unwavering dedication and investment in the things of God. It is important for children to experience the joy and satisfaction which results from serving the Lord. Parents, involve your children directly in the work of the Lord as early as possible. In the future when they reflect back on their childhood, your children should never remember a time when the work of the Lord was not a family pursuit.

The Valley Gate (v. 13)

There was a long stretch of wall between the Old Gate and the Valley Gate, and then another lengthy portion between the Valley Gate and the Dung Gate. Hanun and the inhabitants of Zanoah not only rebuilt the Valley Gate, but also 1,500 feet of wall! Nehemiah's nighttime inspection of the wall three days after arriving at Jerusalem began and ended at this western gate.

In application, new believers are often protected from severe trials until they have sufficiently learned the *"first principles of the oracles of God"* as pictured in the Old Gate (Heb. 5:12). If a believer continues to journey southward from the Old Gate, he or she will eventually reach the Valley Gate which speaks of testing and refinement. The distance between these two gates encloses the longest stretch of the wall, perhaps indicating both the importance of and the time necessary to learn the fundamentals of the faith. The Valley Gate is where we learn humility and experience personal growth. Fruit-bearing trees are not found on mountaintops, but rather in valleys. The same is true for believers when they have, spiritually speaking, experienced brokenness at the Valley Gate.

The Dung Gate (v. 14)

This gate was properly named as it led to the Hinnom Valley just south of Jerusalem, the city's garbage dump. Piles of burning rubbish smoldered there incessantly. The Jews likely thought of this place when the Lord Jesus spoke of hell, a place of eternal fiery judgment (Mark

9:43-47). In Jeremiah's day, the summits surrounding the valley had become the high places of Baal, the scene of intense idolatry. This was where Jewish children were sacrificed on pagan altars and where Jeremiah broke a flask in front of the Jewish leaders to pronounce judgment on them (Jer. 19). According to Jeremiah, the Hinnom Valley would become the *Valley of Slaughter* after the Babylonians conquered Jerusalem. This was God's chastening hand against His idolatrous people. Jeremiah told the people that there would be insufficient tombs to bury them and that many of their bodies would decay on the ground in this valley and wild beasts would devour their flesh.

Given its horrid history and putrid odors, it is no wonder that only one man volunteered to work at this location, Malchijah, a ruler from Beth-haccerem. Scripture does not record that anyone else assisted him to build the Dung Gate, but with the Lord's help he completed the daunting task. Malchijah reminds us that the Lord rewards His people for faithfulness, rather than for spectacular accomplishments. In the parable of the talents, the Lord bestowed two servants with differing quantities of talents (abilities), but each was rewarded exactly the same for their faithfulness (Matt. 25:20-23). Believers will be rewarded for their faithfulness at the Judgment Seat of Christ. It is then that the value of our actions will be made clear. With what motive and in whose strength did we serve the Lord? How did we avail ourselves of the throne of grace and God's Word? How did we use our natural abilities, spiritual gifts, time, finances, and possessions to serve the Lord? Were we faithful to share the gospel message with the lost? May we be found faithful when we stand before the Lord Jesus Christ and give an account of ourselves.

The inhabitants of Jerusalem purged their city of what was corrupt and disgusting through the Dung Gate. The humbling experiences learned at the Valley Gate should prompt believers to clear away all the filth from their lives and the Dung Gate. When believers are willing to abandon that which defiles them, their testimony "turns the corner," just as the Jerusalem wall turns eastward at the Dung Gate.

A Revival Meditation

Revivals begin with God's own people; the Holy Spirit touches their heart anew, and gives them new fervor and compassion, and zeal, new light and life, and when He has thus come to you, He next goes forth to the valley of dry bones…Oh, what responsibility this lays on the Church of God! If you grieve Him away from yourselves, or hinder His visit, then the poor perishing world suffers sorely!

— Andrew A. Bonar

The Wall-Builders (Part 2)
Nehemiah 3:15-32

The Fountain Gate (vv. 15-25)

Shallum, a ruler from the district of Mizpah, built the Fountain Gate, which was located on the east wall just north of the Dung Gate (v. 15). The king's garden was just inside this gate. The man-made pool at this location (v. 16) probably refers to the king's pool (2:14), the "lower pool" spoken of by Isaiah (Isa. 22:9); it is also likely the location of the Pool of Siloam. This was the pool where the blind man was sent by the Lord to wash and to be healed; the journey served as a test of his faith (John 9). It was from here that King Zedekiah unsuccessfully attempted to escape Jerusalem during the last days of the Babylonian siege (Jer. 39:4). He had rebelled against God's command to surrender to the Babylonians and they killed his sons in front of him and then put out his eyes to seal the agonizing memory (Jer. 39:7). These two references in Scripture to this pool provide a valuable lesson: those faithful to God gain greater insight into the things of God, and those who are not, lose sight of what is important.

The tombs of David and his descendants were also located in this area, which centuries earlier had been called "the city of David" after he took Jerusalem from the Jebusites (2 Sam. 5:5-7; 1 Kgs. 2:10). The "house of the mighty men" may be a reference to the barracks of David's elite soldiers (2 Sam. 23:8).

Especially commended here is Baruch who "earnestly" repaired the section of wall assigned to him: *"After him Baruch the son of Zabbai carefully repaired the other section, from the buttress to the door of the house of Eliashib the high priest"* (v. 20). The Hebrew word *charah* is translated "carefully" in the NKJV and "earnestly" in the KJV. The word literally means "to glow or grow warm." Baruch *blazed up* with zeal for the Lord and His work. Baruch's name means "blessed" and it is always a blessing to God's people to have a zealous and enthusiastic

125

worker among them; the disposition tends to be contagious and inspires others to have the same attitude.

This passage demonstrates that the Lord remembers faithfulness to Him; we also see that He takes note of both the quality of work done (e.g. Baruch's zeal) and the quantity of service rendered to Him (e.g. the amount completed by Meremoth and the Tekoites). Meremoth repaired two sections of the wall (vv. 4, 21), as did the Tekoites (vv. 5, 27). It is not the work itself that is most important to God, but rather that His character and attributes are rightly presented in what we do. Wrong motives and attitudes can ruin spectacular feats. Though these men served the Lord with zeal and tenacity some 2500 years ago, the Lord still has not forgotten their efforts, for the Lord *"is a rewarder of those who diligently seek Him"* (Heb. 11:6).

The Dung Gate and the Fountain Gate are located near each other. Likewise, when believers are determined to purge filth from their lives in order to live for the Lord, the fountain of rejuvenation begins to flow. The energizing power of the Holy Spirit is pictured in the flowing water (John 7:37-39) at the Fountain Gate. After His conviction and prompting are heeded, the living waters of the Holy Spirit cleanse and empower a believer to live for Christ.

The Water Gate (vv. 26-27)

The Great Projecting Tower stood out from the wall between the Water Gate and the Horse Gate on the east side of the city. The tower was also near the palace, likely referring to the one Solomon had built (v. 25). The Hill of Ophel was between the old city of David and the temple mount; this is where the Nethinim, the temple servants, lived.

Believers are able to live and grow spiritually as they are watered by the Word (John 15:3, Eph. 5:26). The Fountain Gate and the Water Gate were in close proximity. This illustrates the intimate connection of the Holy Spirit with the cleansing effect of Scripture. Through the illumination of the Holy Spirit believers are able to understand God's Word, which promotes further purification, spiritual growth, encouragement, and fruitfulness. These beneficial aspects of the Water Gate would be later realized by the Jews as a great revival among the people began at this gate after the Word of God was read (8:3).

The Horse Gate (v. 28)

The priests, Levites, and their non-Jewish servants the Nethinim worked on the wall nearest the temple and their own dwelling places. The Horse Gate may have been where the royal horses entered the palace area.

Horsemen are used to symbolize warfare in Scripture (Rev. 6:1-8), with a notable example being the Lord's Second Coming to the earth to battle the Antichrist (Rev. 19:11). Until the Lord's return for the Church, believers are to contend vigorously for the Christian faith. All true believers are presently engaged in spiritual warfare, though some are more cognizant of it than others. The Horse Gate represents the ongoing battle that soldiers of the cross are to maintain until their earthly sojourn has ended (1 Thess. 4:13-18; 2 Tim. 2:3-4).

The East Gate (vv. 29-30)

This gate was located directly east of the temple. Malkijah repaired a lengthy section of wall from the East Gate to the hill of Ophel, where the temple servants lived. This gate faced the rising sun, a powerful reminder of the Lord's return to reign in power and righteousness. As a result of unrepentant Jewish idolatry, the prophet Ezekiel witnessed the glory of the Lord departing from the temple and then Jerusalem by way of the East Gate (Ezek. 10:18-19, 11:23). However, he later describes the return of God's glory to the temple through the same gate at the Second Advent of Christ to the earth (Ezek. 43:4, Zech. 14:4).

The East Gate is thus strongly connected with the glory of God. Today, the gate directly east of the old temple mount, the Golden Gate or Beautiful Gate, is sealed and has been so for nearly five centuries. Jewish tradition holds that the Messiah will come to Jerusalem through the East Gate (this assumption is based on Ezekiel 44:1-3). Ottoman Sultan Suleiman sealed the gate in 1541 and it is suggested that he did so to keep the Jewish Messiah from entering and reclaiming the city. Whether or not the gate will remain sealed until Jesus Christ returns to the earth to establish His kingdom is unknown, but certainly the gate directly east of the temple will be open to receive Him when He does come.

The Miphkad (Inspection) Gate (v. 31)

The Inspection Gate was located in the northeast corner of the city; apparently there was a room located on the wall above the gate. Merchants often lived near the temple and set up their shops near this gate because of the high volume of pedestrian traffic into and out of the temple mount. In conclusion, Nehemiah's tour about the city ends where it started, at the Sheep Gate.

There are many valuable principles to glean from Nehemiah's description of the wall-building effort. First, God is not the author of confusion, but the God of order (1 Cor. 14:33). Before feeding the masses, the Lord Jesus had the people sit down in groups of fifties and hundreds and then they were served by the disciples; this prevented chaos from erupting and ensured that everyone had an opportunity to be filled (Mark 6:39-42). Likewise, Nehemiah had the Lord's people working together in an organized fashion. Order and unity are earmarks of a true work of God.

Second, everyone had a job to do. Paul informs us that all believers have spiritual gifts and are members of the body of Christ and, therefore, each has a calling and purpose to fulfill – every believer is important to the functionality of the Church. No builders, carpenters, stonemasons, etc. were mentioned as being present with Nehemiah. This illustrates a broader realization in Scripture; God normally uses ordinary people to do impossible feats to ensure He receives all the glory. As Paul explains, God uses the weak and foolish things of the world to confound that which is mighty and wise, so *"that no flesh should glory in His presence"* (1 Cor. 1:29); our boasting will be in the Lord alone (1 Cor. 1:31).

Third, a careful record in heaven is being kept of faithful service, and of those slacking off – the Lord Jesus will judge and reward accordingly. Hamilton Smith explains this principle from the text:

> It is noticeable that, from the greatest to the least, all were united in this particular work. ... But while all engaged in this work have honorable mention, yet it is to be noticed that some are *distinguished* in the work above others. Of Baruch we read that he not only repaired the wall but he did so "earnestly" (20). Then some are distinguished for the *quantity* of their work. Of "Hanun and the inhabitants of Zanoah" we read that they not only set up "the valley gate" but they

also built "a thousand cubits of the wall" (13). The Tekoites not only repaired a piece of wall, following Zadok's work, but later we are told that they repaired "another piece" (5, 27). And of others we read that they "repaired a second piece" (11, 19, 30).

Moreover some are distinguished for the *quality* of their work, for God makes a difference between "quantity" and "quality." The quantity of the work accomplished by Eliashib and his brethren exceeds that of the sons of Hassenaah, for whereas the priestly company built a gate and apparently a considerable portion of the wall, the sons of Hassenaah only set up a gate. Nevertheless the quality of the work of the sons of Hassenaah exceeds that of the high priest and his brethren, for they not only built the gate, but they laid the beams thereof, and secured it with locks and bars. Such details are not recorded of the high priest's gate. Again others are distinguished for their *personal faithfulness* in the work. They built over against their own houses (10, 23, 28, 29). God thus marks out for special approval those who are careful to maintain separation within the sphere of their own responsibility.[1]

At His Judgment Seat, Christ will judge each believer's work and reward him or her accordingly. He will consider the quality, quantity, and motivation of the believer's service. The believer's availability and faithfulness to the opportunities afforded him or her will also be considered. Social clout and status, ethnic persuasion, education, profession, etc., do not matter to the Lord, but faithfulness to our calling in Him does. The Lord is not looking for professionalism and programs in the Church today, but rather for believer-priests who are passionate for Him, zealous for truth, broken-hearted over the ruined testimony of our day, and earnest to do something about it.

Fourth, the work of the Lord begins in the home (vv. 23, 28-30). Shallum's daughters labored with their father (v. 12) and the families of Benjamin and Hasshub (v. 23) and of Meshullam (v. 30) worked together and opposite their own homes. Children must develop morally, physically, spiritually, emotionally, and academically to really thrive and reach God's full potential for their lives. When children have a balanced development, they lay hold of self-acceptance and self-awareness of their calling in God's master plan. In so doing, they gain a sense of importance and security, knowing God is in control and has a plan for each one's life.

A Christian family is not a household of Christians, but a Christian household. It is more than Christ dwelling within the hearts of family members; it is a family that is pursuing the heart of God. If the Bible is not at the center of family life and all home affairs, that home cannot be called a true Christian home. The vital focus and end objective of every Christian household is the glory of God! The local assembly is composed of families; when those families are Christian households, the local church will be a strong House of God!

A Revival Meditation

Let us pray for revival, and may it first begin in our homes. It is parents, not the church or Christian schools, who have the primary responsibility to teach their children doctrine and godly conduct. On this point C. H. Spurgeon is quite pungent:

> In this simple way, by God's grace, a living testimony for truth is always to be kept alive in the land –the beloved of the Lord are to hand down their witness for the gospel, and the covenant to their heirs, and these again to their next descendants. This is our first duty; we are to begin at the family hearth: he is a bad preacher who does not commence his ministry at home. The heathen are to be sought by all means, and the highways and hedges are to be searched, but home has a prior claim, and woe unto those who reverse the order of the Lord's arrangements. To teach our children is a personal duty; we cannot delegate it to Sunday school teachers, or other friendly aids; these can assist us, but cannot deliver us from the sacred obligation; proxies and sponsors are wicked devices in this case: mothers and fathers must, like Abraham, command their households in the fear of God, and talk with their offspring concerning the wondrous works of the Most High. Parental teaching is a natural duty – who so fit to look to the child's well-being as those who are the authors of his actual being? To neglect the instruction of our offspring is worse than brutish.[2]

Jerusalem in the Time of Nehemiah[3]

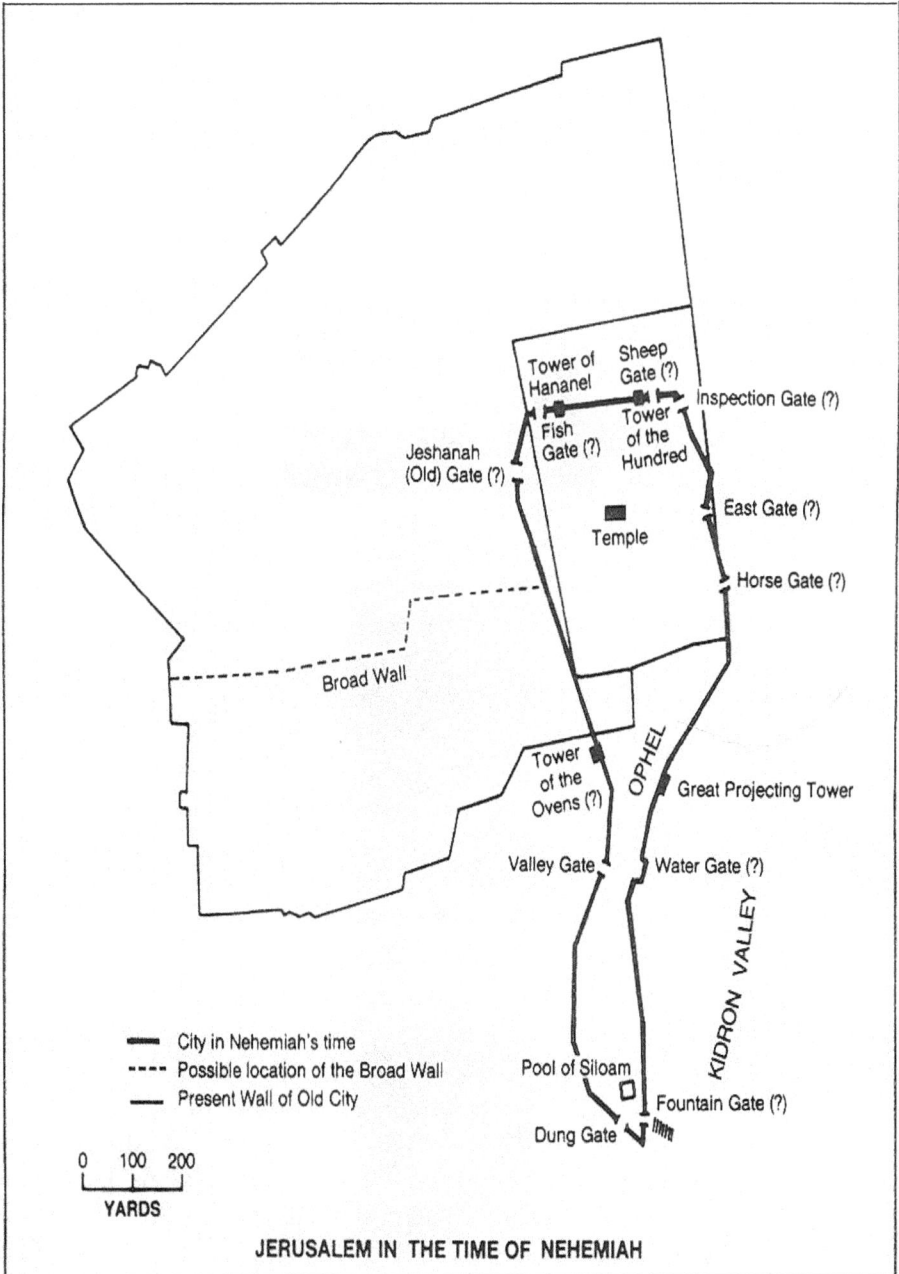

JERUSALEM IN THE TIME OF NEHEMIAH

Opposition
Nehemiah 4

Concerning the exact scope of the project there is much debate among theologians and archeologists as to how long, how high, and how thick the wall that Nehemiah built actually was. The *Maximalist View* of the project asserts that Nehemiah's wall was nearly identical to that which stood at the time of Christ, about 2.5 miles in length and enclosing the Old City and the southwest hill called Mount Zion (about 230 acres in all). King Agrippa built a wall known as the "Third Wall" in 41-44 AD, which was destroyed by the Romans in 70AD. The Jewish historian Josephus states that at that time, the outer wall of Jerusalem was about 4.5 miles in circumference; and that some walls were over 52 feet tall with several high towers positioned on the wall.[1] Josephus also refers to the Broad Wall, presumably the one Nehemiah speaks of (3:8), as being erected by King Hezekiah. Excavations in the Old City have located this wall; it was found to be 23 feet thick.[2]

According to *Minimalist View*, the wall built by Nehemiah would be about two miles long and enclosed a narrow strip of land including the original City of David to the south, the hill of Ophel in the middle, and the temple area to the north (about 90 acres in all). Certainly, this portion of land would be more than sufficient to support 4,500 people, the estimated population of Jerusalem in Nehemiah's day, as compared to 40,000 in Christ's day.[3] It is my opinion that the *Minimalist View* better fits the situation described by Nehemiah. Thus, the wall that Nehemiah repaired would have been about two miles long, some 20 to 25 feet wide, and perhaps fifty feet high. This estimate of the breadth and height is an intuitive correlation with the dimensions given by Josephus around the time of Christ, as new walls usually were made to match existing ones in height so as to not weaken the city's overall defensive posture. The Jews did not have the aid of modern heavy equipment, but rather their God and unity in purpose enabled them to clear away huge amounts of debris and build the entire wall in fifty-two days.

In the previous chapter we witnessed Nehemiah's ability to motivate the Jews to rise up and build, but the enemy quickly noticed and mobilized its forces to hinder them. Despite Nehemiah's great organizational skills, the work was hampered from the onset; this again reminds us that every true work of God will experience opposition of some sort.

The enemy first attempted to *sidetrack* the Jews from commencing the rebuilding project (2:19). Sanballat the Horonite, Tobiah the Ammonite, and Geshem the Arabian laughed at the Jews for even thinking about undertaking such an immense project and insinuated that if they did fortify Jerusalem, that the king would consider them rebels. Nehemiah's response was curt: *"The God of heaven Himself will prosper us; therefore we His servants will arise and build, but you have no heritage or right or memorial in Jerusalem"* (2:20). In the modern vernacular, Nehemiah was saying, "Butt out; this is none of your business; our God is with us, He has assigned us this task to do for Him, and that is all that matters." Consequently, the Jews were not diverted from the mission by the challenge, but rather became a more invigorated workforce.

As in Nehemiah's day, the devil never bothers with halfhearted believers, but once they become desperate for God and burdened for the work of God, he will intensify his opposition against them. Satan hates that which is precious to the Lord; namely, a testimony of His greatness through His people. Jerusalem was and will be the center of God's earthly purposes for His covenant people. Thus, Satan opposed the building of the wall in Nehemiah's time as he had stood against the building of the temple in Zerubbabel's day.

Likewise, in the Church Age, Satan opposes any true testimony of God's character and nature as established in gatherings of His people (i.e. assemblies of Christians). Today, it is not a temple or a wall that manifests the manifold wisdom of God, but the Church: *"To the intent that now the manifold wisdom of God might be made known by the church to the principalities and powers in the heavenly places, according to the eternal purpose which He accomplished in Christ Jesus our Lord"* (Eph. 3:10-11). It should therefore be no surprise that when a local assembly becomes burdened to remove the debris of religious pride, carnality, and spiritual slothfulness from their midst in order to erect a true testimony for Christ, the enemy will intensely seek to thwart the rebuilding program.

A notable example of this fact is contained in one of the oldest books of the Bible – the book of Job. One day when Satan had to present himself before God's throne in heaven, the Lord said to him, *"Have you considered My servant Job, that there is none like him on the earth, a blameless and upright man, one who fears God and shuns evil?"(Job 1:8).* God furnished a glowing character sketch of Job, whom He considered His righteous servant. The proclamation brought an immediate challenge from Satan who was allowed by God to initiate a series of horrendous circumstances to test Job's wherewithal. In the end, Job was greatly honored and blessed, and God was exalted before Satan.

Satan suffered his greatest defeat at Calvary; as a defeated foe, he hates everything about the Lord Jesus (John 12:31-33). The last thing he wants now is people on earth who remind him of Christ and who are doing the will of God. In the next several chapters of Nehemiah, we will notice that Satan's opposition will be from without and from within and will take on various forms. The severity of the opposition will increase proportionately with the resolve of God's people to labor for Him. Today, we must expect the same practice of hostility for those who are truly desperate for God and serve Him accordingly.

Being unable to *sidetrack* the Jews with idle words and fanciful questions, the enemy resorted to a more brazen tactic – *mocking and ridicule* (vv. 1-3). Sanballat and Tobiah belittled the Jews in front of the Samaritan soldiers, calling them "feeble." They further claimed that the task was too enormous to tackle and even if they did erect a wall around Jerusalem, it wouldn't be stable, saying that even a fox climbing on it would pull it down. The enemy wanted the work to fail in its infancy by insisting that the Jews did not know what they were doing and didn't have the means to accomplish the task anyway. The devil labors to plant doubt where God's people are grounded in faith.

Sanballat asked five questions in an attempt to cause the Jews to conclude their situation was hopeless: *"What are these feeble Jews doing? Will they fortify themselves? Will they offer sacrifices? Will they complete it in a day? Will they revive the stones from the heaps of rubbish – stones that are burned?"*(v. 2). The implication of these questions was the Jews had no idea of the immensity of the work, nor did they have the proper resources to do the work, and thus there would be no celebratory offerings. Nothing has changed today; there are still people who want God-honoring ministries to fail and if they cannot stop the work of God, then they will ridicule and mock the servants of God.

How did Nehemiah respond to the enemy's ridicule? He ignored what was said and resorted to prayer: *"Hear, O our God, for we are despised"* (v. 4). As we will see in following chapters, this was Nehemiah's first line of defense: his ministry plans and his response to attack were precipitated by prayer. Verses 4 and 5 record an imprecatory prayer similar to what David prayed in Psalms 35 and 71, and to what is uttered by the martyred dead in heaven during the Tribulation Period (Rev. 6:9-11). Was Nehemiah acting in the will of God to pray for divine judgment on the enemies? Gene Getz suggests four reasons why Nehemiah's prayer was permissible:

> First, in opposing the Jews, Sanballat "and company" were actually opposing God. Second, God had already pronounced judgment on Israel's enemies. Nehemiah was praying according to God's will – that God would deliver Jerusalem from her enemies (Josh. 1:5). Third, Nehemiah was praying that God would bring about what He had promised Abraham regarding those who curse His people (Gen. 12:3). Fourth, vengeance belongs to God, not to Nehemiah or other believers (Deut. 32:35; Rom. 12:19).[4]

While any of these reasons might justify Nehemiah's prayer for this particular situation, prayers asking for immediate wrath upon our enemies are not endorsed by Scripture for the Church Age. In the Age of Grace, Christians desire their adversaries to experience God's grace and to be saved. Though the Lord Jesus and Stephen suffered at the hands of their oppressors, both prayed that God would not judge at that time those who had ill-treated them (Luke 23:34; Acts 7:60). The Lord instructed His disciples, who would become His apostles during the Church Age, to pray for and show love to their enemies; perhaps some will repent and be saved (Luke 6:27-35). Such kindness demonstrates God's grace in action and can soften the hardest of rebel hearts. Thus,

Christians are not to pray for the destruction of their persecutors, as Nehemiah prayed, but are rather to pray for their salvation and strive to overcome their evil deeds by good works (Rom. 12:19-21).

So the Jews prayed for God's protection, but kept working. This is a great example for the Church to follow. If believers know the will of God in a particular matter and face opposition, they should pray for God's help but keep pressing on in faith. If the mind of the Lord is not known in a particular situation, believers should keep praying, while they continue to walk in faith so that open doors of opportunity can be recognized and closed avenues of service can be avoided. It is easier for the Lord to direct our path if we continue to pray and walk in faith, than if we stand still waiting for some spectacular sign from heaven (and there is a danger in this, since the enemy can counterfeit such things to mislead us).

Thankfully, the Jews had a mind to work and the wall was raised to half of its final height fairly quickly (v. 6). The enemy, fully aware of the Jews' persistence and their progress, countered them with more intense opposition (vv. 7-9). God's people are never more powerful than when they have a mind to work and a heart to pray! Seeing that the work was progressing quickly, the enemy gathered its forces and conspired together to fight against the Jews (v. 8). Nehemiah knew how to organize the people and to agonize in prayer; he asked for God's protection and set a watch against the enemy day and night. He had a heart for the people, which inspired them to move beyond what they thought they could ever do.

> People don't care how much you know until they know how much you care.
> — John Maxwell

Some Jews were taken from the rigors of building to the important task of watching and alerting others if the enemy attacked. Everyone was to be armed and in a state of readiness. If the alarm sounded, the Jews were to quickly depart from their designated work areas and engage their oppressors. This strategy would use the first line of defense to detain the enemy from penetrating into the ranks of God's people until reinforcements could arrive to drive off the attackers. The entire scene reminds us of Peter's exhortation to Christians who were under the constant threat of Roman persecution: *"Be sober, be vigilant; because your adversary the devil walks about like a roaring lion, seeking whom he may devour. Resist him, steadfast in the faith, knowing that the same sufferings are experienced by your brotherhood in the world"* (1 Pet. 5:8-9). Watchfulness is an important feature of the Christian life; a matter the Lord stressed several times to His disciples in the final days of His ministry on earth. Too often the enemy crouches in some unforeseen circumstance and then mercilessly pounces on unsuspecting believers who are caught completely off guard. The result can be personally devastating to the believer, but more importantly the name of the Lord Jesus is slandered by men. Believer, be blameless in your conduct and be alert for the enemy to strike at any time – when you least expect it, expect it. Rarely does the enemy attack where we anticipate. Consequently, we must be personally fortified with the whole armor of God at all times, otherwise Satan will eventually find out through observation where we are vulnerable and attack there.

Sanballat knew that the Jews were working with Artaxerxes' permission so a frontal assault by the Samaritan forces would not be a viable solution; however, guerilla warfare was. To engage in terrorist activities, especially if at night, would leave no credible evidence of the perpetrators, while it would incite fear and trepidation in the Jewish workforce.

Besides the constant threat of violence, the resolve of the Jewish labor force was waning (v. 10). As the enemy continued plotting without, the people grew faint within. There was a lot of debris from the previous wall that had to be cleared away before construction of the new wall could begin. Recall that Nehemiah was unable to navigate his horse through the debris field on the eastern side of the city during his nighttime inspection, but had to circumvent it and journey up the Kidron Valley (2:14-15). Many of the stones from the previous wall had been exposed to intense heat, causing them to be brittle and thus unusable. It would have been easier to build upon the existing rubble, but the walls would have been less stable and durable.

The unprofitable debris had to be cleared away to build on a solid foundation – this was necessary for a lasting testimony of God's eminence. The application for us is this: before we build up for God, we first need to look down on ourselves. Religious smugness, careless attitudes, coldness of heart, and pride in any form must be removed before we can see clearly to erect a testimony for God. His Word alone is the Rock that we can build on. Foundations laid on personal glory, false doctrine, and humanism will crumble away (Luke 6:46-49; 1 Cor. 3:11-15). It may seem like it would be easier to build on something that already exists, but ultimately only what is founded on Christ will stand the test of time and eternity.

If your local church has been struggling for years to raise up a testimony for Christ, it is time to investigate the foundation you are building upon; perhaps there is rubbish from the past which is hindering the building program. We should not feel sentimental about that which is hampering the work of the Lord; it must be dealt with. We must look down before we can build up! The Jews, despite the daunting task before them, were determined to clear away the debris first and build on a good foundation. They wanted a lasting testimony for Jehovah, not something that looked good at first and then crumbled away later.

However, discouragement, the persistent foe of the soul, was gaining ground in the hearts of the Jews. The enemy was threatening, the work was immense, and God's people were weary – this is when the devil's tool of discouragement is most effective in neutralizing the zeal of God's people. Discouragement is like a stout airborne virus that rapidly infects others. As this emotional epidemic progressed, a defeatist mentality began to sweep through the Jewish community.

Today as then, if discouragement is not quickly treated, those rising to build a testimony for God will become self-focused and cease to be profitable in the work. Nehemiah knew this and furnished the Jews with a battle cry to help them overcome discouragement: *"Remember the Lord ... Fight for Your Brethren!"* (v. 14). In the midst of overwhelming circumstances, if believers keep their eyes focused on the Lord, they will find less opportunity to be occupied with self; despair cannot thrive in a selfless environment.

Three centuries earlier King Jehoshaphat demonstrated his understanding of this reality when the Jews were being threatened by an innumerable host of Moabites, Ammonites, and Edomites. King Jehoshaphat cried out to the Lord for deliverance: *"O our God, will You not judge them? For we have no power against this great multitude that is coming against us; nor do we know what to do, but our eyes are upon You"* (2 Chron. 20:12). Then, he directed the Jews to march out to face their enemies with those singing and praising God leading the way. God responded to their demonstrated faith by completely wiping out the advancing armies without one Jew lifting his sword. Dear believer, God is able!

Battle cries have often been used to arouse people to action. In U.S. History, the slogan "Remember the Maine" was used to incite Americans to enter into the Spanish/American War. The Maine was a U.S. battleship which mysteriously blew up in Havana Harbor in 1898; she had been dispatched there to protect American interests in Cuba after the country rebelled against Spain. The battle cry "Remember the Lusitania" echoed as the United States entered into WWI: the Lusitania was a British passenger vessel sunk in the North Atlantic by a German submarine in 1915; 114 Americans perished in the attack. "Remember Pearl Harbor" was a battle cry that prompted the U.S. to enter WWII after the unprovoked attack on Pearl Harbor by the Japanese in 1941. In a similar vein, Nehemiah coined the battle cry "Remember the Lord – Fight for Your Brethren" to rally the Jewish brotherhood and inspire them to labor for the Lord.

As a safeguard, he organized families and clans into work groups which would be responsible for protecting each other as they labored together (v. 13). As a result, the enemy's counsel against them was defeated and the work continued (v. 15). This panorama reflects how the Church should respond to attempts to hinder God's work today. God was *among* His covenant people in the days of Nehemiah and working with them to establish a vivid testimony of His prominence over the nations. Today, God dwells *within* His people to accomplish the same purpose (Eph. 2:20-22). Through Zerubbabel's leadership a glorious temple was built as a testimony of Jehovah's character and nature. Nehemiah would accomplish the same feat through the construction of the wall. The way these physical structures were erected proved to the opposition that the God of the Hebrews was most powerful and dwelled among His people; this would serve as a warning to those who wanted to hurt them in the future.

Can believers today expect God to declare His glory through confounding of the opposition? Paul answers this question in his epistle to the Church at Ephesus. The apostolic ministry of Paul centered in declaring the gospel message of Jesus Christ to the lost and in revealing God's mysterious intentions for those who responded to it:

> *To make all see what is the fellowship of the mystery, which from the beginning of the ages has been hidden in God who created all things through Jesus Christ; to the intent that now the manifold wisdom of God might be made known by the church to the principalities and powers in the heavenly places, according to the eternal purpose which He accomplished in Christ Jesus our Lord* (Eph. 3:9-11).

Every Christian is part of God's vast spiritual house that He is assembling one soul at a time. Through the Church, the unregenerate witness the awesome nature of God and His capacity to do the unbelievable in His people. Paul also speaks of the local Church as the temple of God (1 Cor. 3:16). May each local church strive to establish a living declaration of God's grace within their communities. Whenever Christians come together in unity and in the name of Christ, Satan is certain to oppose their efforts to exalt the Savior. Remember the Lord and Fight for Your Brethren!

The work on the wall continued because Nehemiah assisted the Jews to look to the Lord alone for strength and to maintain close-knit working groups. While there was a national effort to build the wall, and certain individuals are mentioned for their personal achievements, it is these work-groups that formed the backbone of the effort. In the Church Age, there are individuals who do great things for Christ, but it is the "work-group" of the local church that displays the glory of God in a lasting way in a particular community. The local church provides accountability, responsibility, encouragement, edification, instruction, and correction when needed to ensure the spiritual growth of the individual living stones that compose it (1 Pet. 2:5). Consequently, there is a strong similarity between the Jewish family work-groups and the body-life to be enjoyed in the local assembly today.

Nehemiah further refined and optimized the strategy of the family/clan work-groups by instructing half of the people to have shields, bows, spears and coats of mail, while the other half worked (vv. 16-17). Even those working had swords girded at their sides or they carried a trowel in one hand and a sword in the other (v. 18). Both, in a spiritual sense, speak of the Word of God: the Trowel is to be used for the edification of the brethren and the Sword, which was once delivered to the saints, should be used to contend earnestly for the faith. Though in prison, Paul still used the Word of God *"for the defense and confirmation of the gospel"* (Phil. 1:7-8). He handled Scripture to both defend the gospel against nonbelievers and to build up understanding for those in the faith. We too should follow these examples – building and defending are important ministries for strengthening and preserving the vitality of the Church.

The appointed leaders of each group were to oversee their group's activities; this pictures the elders who form the oversight of each local church (Acts 14:23; Tit. 1:5). As the work-groups were spread out from each other, each team had a trumpet, which was to be blown if the enemy attacked in order to summon others to their assistance (vv. 18-19). Nehemiah reminded the people that this was Jehovah's work and, therefore, He would protect them from their enemies (v. 20). Nighttime security was bolstered to guard the workforce while they slept (v. 22). Other than to wash their clothes, the Jews remained fully dressed at all times in order to quickly respond to an attack (v. 23). The Jews were to be watchful and alert, but keep working as a united people for God despite the threatening situation.

As mentioned earlier, the need for Christian alertness and watchfulness is a repeated warning in the New Testament. Just a few days before the Lord Jesus would be crucified, He exhorted His disciples:

> *But watch out for yourselves, for they will deliver you up to councils, and you will be beaten in the synagogues. You will be brought before rulers and kings for My sake, for a testimony to them. And the gospel must first be preached to all the nations* (Mark 13:9-10).

Satan was defeated at Calvary by the Lord Jesus Christ. As a defeated foe, all that the devil can do today is to cast doubt on the person and work of the Lord Jesus Christ and try to hinder the Lord's people from proclaiming the truth. The Lord and the apostles knew that Satan would oppose anyone who would remind Satan of his Conqueror by living out that same life which he sought to destroy. Today, believers have the Holy Spirit, who equips them to live out the resurrected life of Christ: *"I have been crucified with Christ; it is no longer I who live, but Christ lives in me; and the life which I now live in the flesh I live by faith in the Son of God, who loved me and gave Himself for me"* (Gal. 2:20). This is why Satan will oppose any believer or group of believers who is determined to erect a testimony for God – it reminds the devil of his defeat and the One who accomplished it, the Lamb of God.

Charles Spurgeon began publishing a magazine in 1865 entitled, *"The Sword and the Trowel"* based on this section of text in Nehemiah. Spurgeon was highlighting the fact that God's people today can still exalt God when they unite for a divinely sanctioned cause and are determined to both labor for God and protect each other. The Jews understood that they were in a war; may the Church realize a spiritual battle rages on today and that the Lord is the believer's only means of victory.

Like the Jews who would not put off their clothes, believers have spiritual armor that is to be worn at all times (Eph. 6:12-16). Christians are to use the sword of truth and the weapon of prayer to confront the enemy (Eph. 6:17-18). Only by such spiritual help can we withstand the wiles of the devil and resist spiritual wickedness in high places (Eph. 6:11). Believer, if you seek to build for God, you will be a target of the adversary – expect it. May God's people today learn this important truth and follow the example of the Jews under Nehemiah's leadership who resolved in the Lord's strength to live the theme: Remember the Lord – Fight for Your Brethren!

A Revival Meditation

> Timidity is not humility. While *humility* is self-forgetfulness completely (forgetting both its weakness and strength) – *timidity* recalls all the weakness and hence is self-remembering. God does not delight in our cowardice and withdrawal.

> — Watchman Nee

Internal Problems
Nehemiah 5

In the previous chapters, the opposition to the work of God originated from external sources; in this chapter, Nehemiah will deal with a new threat – *internal strife* among God's people. Greed among the wealthy nearly bungled the entire effort, but again Nehemiah shows us how to rightly handle dissension among fellow laborers.

The problem of Nehemiah 5 is similar to the situation the apostles faced in Acts 6. The Church was caring for their widows, but there rose a division between the Hellenist and Hebrew widows; the former claimed that they were not receiving the same financial support as the latter. Up until that time the evangelistic fervor of a unified Church had successfully brought thousands of souls to Christ. Satan often employs a "divide and conquer" tactic against the Church by emphasizing the differences among believers in order to diminish our focus on what unifies us – Christ. Accordingly, there can be little doubt that he was behind the scene, planting thoughts and stirring up strife among the widows and their families. However, proactive leadership dealt with the strife in a way that pleased everyone and the entire congregation was quickly brought back into unity. Immediately after this, the work of evangelism became prosperous again (Acts 6:7).

Satan can use many things to divide the Lord's people today: political affiliations, schooling preferences, dress codes, diet choices, social classes, cultural orientations, etc. God's people must maintain the "big picture," understand what the enemy is attempting to accomplish, and seek unification under Christ and His cause, rather than divide over individual preferences and ideologies. To this end, Paul exhorted the believers at Philippi to keep focused on gospel ministry, to strive for unity, and to not fear the enemy:

> *Only let your conduct be worthy of the gospel of Christ, ... that you stand fast in one spirit, with one mind striving together for the faith of the gospel, and not in any way terrified by your adversaries, which is to them a proof of perdition, but to you of salvation, and that from God* (Phil. 1:27-28).

On the flipside, James warns believers that abandoning Christ-centered ministry will result in self-seeking misery: *"For where envy and self-seeking exist, confusion and every evil thing are there"* (Jas. 3:16). The Jews had been tenacious in the work and had remained strong against the opposition, but the problem that Nehemiah faced in this chapter was what James warned against – some self-seeking Jews were causing division among the brethren. The existing social structure promoted the comfort of wealthy Jews while oppressing their poorer brethren.

There was a food shortage in Jerusalem resulting from a famine coupled with an increase in population (v. 3). During the Babylonian captivity the land had received seventy years of agricultural rest (Jer. 25:11); this period ended with the Jews' renewed resolve to finish the temple in 520 BC (Hag. 2:18). Apparently, the Jews had been slow to till the land since that time, which contributed to the problem. In order to survive, the poorer Jews, many of whom were returnees from Babylon, were liquidating their assets in order to borrow money to buy food and to pay the king's tax (vv. 2-4). Donating their time to rebuild the wall only further hampered farmers from earning a livelihood and thus caring for their families. The situation was unresolvable, for even after they had mortgaged their land, houses, and vineyards, they were still lacking. Unfortunately, there will always be some people who will take advantage of others for their own profit in situations like this; apparently, the wealthy were charging high interest rates on the loans to their brethren – today we might refer to these people as "loan sharks."

It was a financial situation from which it was impossible to recover; as a last resort to survive, parents sold their children into slavery (v. 5). Consequently, there was an outcry of the oppressed against the wealthy (v. 1). Indeed, after learning of the situation, Nehemiah also was enraged by the ruthless behavior of his affluent countrymen (v. 6). Rather than showing compassion to their impoverished brethren, they were motivated by greed to serve themselves. After a brief time of introspection to bring his emotions in line with the will of God, Nehemiah pursued a course of action which would serve God and his people. Nehemiah knew that if the people had no reason to live, they certainly would not be motivated to construct a wall which would protect their oppressor's assets. As a divided people, it would be impossible to complete the wall.

I have never yet known the Spirit of God to work where the Lord's people were divided.
— D. L. Moody

Therefore, Nehemiah called for the Jews to assemble and a large congregation gathered, both to hear him and to stand with him on this matter of inequality (v. 7). He then proceeded to rebuke the nobles for their greed and cold-heartedness towards their brethren; it was unethical to profit from their hardship. The guilty could not answer the charge against them (v. 8). Nehemiah further admonished them:

What you are doing is not good. Should you not walk in the fear of our God because of the reproach of the nations, our enemies? I also, with my brethren and my servants, am lending them money and grain. Please, let us stop this usury! Restore now to them, even this day, their lands, their vineyards, their olive groves, and their houses, also a hundredth of the money and the grain, the new wine and the oil, that you have charged them (vv. 9-11).

Nehemiah exhorted the nobles to think about their testimony before the heathen, and, consequently, to regard their brethren highly as fellow servants of Jehovah. Otherwise, their greed would result in the Lord's name being disdained among the nations. In principle, the way in which we treat the lowliest believer in any situation shows our personal esteem for the Savior in all situations (Matt. 25:40). We need to learn to love people the way we have been loved by the Lord.

The nobles responded well to Nehemiah's rebuke and his request for them to restore previously seized property and to also provide compensation for the offense. They agreed to return the property that had been confiscated through unethical business practices and to also return a hundredth part of the value of this property as restitution for

145

their offense against their brethren (v. 11). Nehemiah called the priests to administer an oath to ensure the affluent would do what they had promised to do (v. 12). After witnessing the oath, Nehemiah shook out his lap, to symbolize what would happen to the nobles if they reneged on their vow – they would likewise be shaken out of their houses and professions by God. The proceedings pleased the whole congregation, who answered Nehemiah's final proclamation with an "Amen," and then they praised God together (v. 13). Nehemiah's leadership and quick justice unified the Jews again and the work on the wall continued. Nehemiah also notes that the nobles were truly repentant as demonstrated by the fact that they kept their pledge (v. 13).

> *Behold, how good and how pleasant it is for brethren to dwell together in unity!* (Ps. 133:1; KJV)

Nehemiah practiced what he preached; his leadership example is one to follow. He assisted the poor to overcome their financial hardship, and without extracting interest from them. He also operated a "soup kitchen" as a means of ministering to the needy; those who were hungry could enjoy a meal in his home. Instead of charging the people to sustain the governor's table, as his predecessors had done, Nehemiah provided for his own needs. He did not put any further burden on the people, though, as governor, he was entitled to do so (vv. 14-15).

Nehemiah feared the Lord more than he dreaded the possibility of being in lack. He was not a hypocrite; how could he ask the nobles to refrain from taking advantage of the working class, if he was sequestering their supplies for his private benefit? So instead of taking from the people, Nehemiah sought to serve them. Instead of taxing the people to enjoy fine dining, he provided from his own resources daily staples for 150 Jewish guests, plus those who were visiting from other nations, for the twelve years he was in Jerusalem (v. 17). Nehemiah notes the daily provision required to feed all of his guests: one ox, six sheep, and a number of fowls; one out of ten days they enjoyed wine (v. 18).

Furthermore, Nehemiah did not seek to buy up bargain-priced land from those in distress, but rather he sought to help them retain their property, as a heritage for future generations (v. 16). And, even though he was the king's governor, Nehemiah found time to labor alongside his brethren on the wall, as did his servants. Nehemiah was a team player who was not afraid of getting his hands dirty. He did not seek social status, but rather promoted a sense of collective oneness among the Jews. God was the ruler of His people and he was merely His servant. The Lord Jesus, speaking to His disciples, stated: *"But you, do not be called 'Rabbi'; for one is your Teacher, the Christ, and you are all brethren"* (Matt. 23:8). Christ is the head of the Church and all Christians are brethren: nothing more, nothing less.

Although no physical enemy is identified in this chapter, we have already acknowledged that Satan often strategizes to divide and conquer God's people to prevent them from laboring together for His glory. No doubt Satan manipulated the situation and stimulated lust among the wealthy Jews. He could have obsessed their minds with the desire of comfort and prestige. Perhaps Satan may have suggested to the poor that the situation was unfair and provoked them to despair: why keep working when they had nothing to live for?

We know from Scripture that Satan is able to directly inject evil thoughts into the human mind – this act is called *demonic obsession*. Paul acknowledges that there is a *"spirit that is now at work in the sons of disobedience"* (Eph. 2:2) and can affect the thinking of believers also (Acts 5:3). This is distinguished from *demonic possession* (Acts 16:16-19) and *external oppression* (2 Cor. 12:7-9). Obsession is a tool used by Satan to mentally torment believers. The enemy may plant thoughts to lure us into establishing a stronghold in the flesh (such as pornography), or he may observe a self-erected stronghold in the heart, such as bitterness, and seek to stir up unforgiving thoughts. Satan or his cohorts in crime then stimulate these strongholds with ungodly thoughts to inflict anxiety, distress, and depression. In the absence of these mental citadels (i.e. bitterness, anger, envy, etc.), Satan's efforts of obsessing the believer's mind would be ineffective, and he would soon terminate the mental attack (Jas. 4:7).

I liken obsessing the believer's mind to a spinning merry-go-round, where the circular energy represents a built-up stronghold (the energy of a bent that is unconfessed and unrepented of). Though Satan does not have the energy to start spinning the merry-go-round of the mind, he can keep the mental bastion whirling by suggestions much like a child on the playground continues to grab and pull the bars of the merry-go-round to maintain rotation. However, when the believer

147

resists by renewing his or her mind (or figuratively drags his or her feet in the illustration), the merry-go-round slowly stops until Satan realizes his efforts are futile and departs. The fortified idea has lost its hold. Matthew Henry refers to this subject as he comments on James 4:7:

> We are taught to submit ourselves entirely to God: "Submit yourselves therefore to God. Resist the devil, and he will flee from you" (verse 7). Christians should forsake the friendship of the world, and watch against that envy and pride which they see prevailing in natural men, and should by grace learn to glory in their submission to God. ... Now, as this subjection and submission to God are what the devil most industriously strives to hinder, so we ought with great care and steadiness to resist his suggestions. If he would represent a tame yielding to the will and providence of God as what will bring calamities, and expose to contempt and misery, we must **resist these suggestions** of fear. If he would represent submission to God as a hindrance to our outward ease, or worldly preferments, we must **resist these suggestions** of pride and sloth. If he would tempt us to lay any of our miseries, and crosses, and afflictions, to the charge of Providence, so that we might avoid them by following his directions instead of God's, we must **resist these provocations to anger**, not fretting ourselves in any wise to do evil. "Let not the devil, in these or the like attempts, prevail upon you; but resist him and he will flee from you." If we basely yield to temptations, the devil will continually follow us; but if we put on the whole armor of God, and stand it out against him, he will be gone from us. Resolution shuts and bolts the door against temptation.[1]

Ananias is an excellent New Testament example of satanic obsession that targets the mind. Apparently, a stronghold of greed or pride existed in the heart of this believer. He and his wife were quite willing to sell their property and give nearly all of the proceeds to the work of the Lord (Acts 5:1-2). The problem is that Ananias said that he gave the full sale price to the Lord. Perhaps he didn't want the diminished praise of others for not giving all, or he lusted after what he could buy for himself with part of the money (which had to be a small percentage in order for the lie to go undetected). But God knows all that is within the hearts of men and no lie goes unnoticed. Peter confronted Ananias with this sin.

*But Peter said, "Ananias, why has **Satan filled your heart to lie** to the Holy Spirit and keep back part of the price of the land for yourself?"(Acts 5:3).*

Again Matthew Henry remarks, "The origin of his sin: Satan filled his heart; he not only suggested it to him, and put it into his head, but hurried him on with resolution to do it."[2] Stanley D. Toussaint provides the following insight on the same passage of Scripture:

In response Peter accused Ananias by saying, Satan has ... filled your heart. The verb translated "filled" is *eplerosen*, from *pleroo*, which here has the idea of control or influence. The same verb is used in the command, *"Be filled with the Spirit"* (Eph. 5:18). Ananias, a believer, was influenced by Satan, not the Spirit! The fact that Peter asked, "How is it ...?" implies that Satan had gained control because Ananias had not dealt with some previous sin in his life.[3]

Warren Wiersbe also comments on Acts 5:

To begin with, the sin of Ananias and Sapphira was energized by Satan; and that is a serious matter. If Satan cannot defeat the church by attacks from the outside, he will get on the inside and go to work (Acts 20:28-31). He knows how to lie to the minds and the hearts of church members, even genuine Christians, and get them to follow his orders.[4]

Because Ananias had not previously repented and gained the victory over his bent, Satan was able to stimulate this established thought pattern through obsession. He injected musings into Ananias' mind that energized these controlling bents. If Ananias had renewed his mind and drawn near to God through obedience, there would not have been any stronghold for Satan to victimize. Consequently, the adversary would have fled from Ananias and scurried off to trouble someone else (Jas. 4:7).

It must be emphasized that Satan is not the direct source of all tempting thoughts. He may externally assault our minds with evil thoughts, or indirectly use an evil world system that opposes God: *"For all that is in the world, the lust of the flesh* [bodily appetites], *and the lust of the eyes* [coveting], *and the pride of life* [self glory], *is not of the Father, but is of the world"* (1 Jn. 2:16; KJV). The surrounding world system under the enemy's control stimulates our members, the flesh, to respond contrary to our spirit's order. Lustfulness, selfishness, and vain ambition do not proceed from the Father, but from the world.

Nehemiah is a great example of a godly leader. He did not seek status and fame, but rather the well-being of God's people and God's work. He was proactive when injustice occurred and would not rest until there was restoration among God's people and restitution had been made for the offenses. He was hospitable and used his own home to refresh others and provide for their basic needs. He was willing to labor with his hands alongside his brethren. Nehemiah closes the chapter with a short prayer: *"Remember me, my God, for good, according to all that I have done for this people"* (v. 19). We might be tempted to accuse Nehemiah of self-righteousness in this statement, but Harry Ironside warns against such a conclusion:

> This may seem to savor of self-complacency, but who of us would dare judge so devoted a servant? And again we need to remind ourselves that the dispensation of grace had not yet dawned. Law was still in the ascendant, and the spirit shown by Nehemiah is so beyond his age that we can only give thanks for what God had wrought in the soul of His dear servant, while we pray for wisdom and grace to serve His people in our own generation unselfishly, and in the Spirit of Christ, leaving all question of appreciation or reward to be settled at His judgment-seat.[5]

The Lord Jesus will reward all Christ-motivated and Holy Spirit-empowered service at His judgment seat. May God remember all God's shepherds who love Him and thus labor for His sheep in righteousness!

A Revival Meditation

> To a true child of God, the invisible bond that unites all believers to Christ is far more tender, and lasting, and precious; and, as we come to recognize and realize that we are all dwelling in one sphere of life in Him, we learn to look on every believer as our brother, in a sense that is infinitely higher than all human relationships. This is the one

and only way to bring disciples permanently together. All other plans for promoting the unity of the Church have failed.

— A. T. Pierson

Attack on Leadership
Nehemiah 6

Our attention is again directed to the ringleaders of the Jewish opposition: Sanballat, Tobiah, and Geshem (or Gashmu). No doubt every move within the city was being reported to them; accordingly, they must have enjoyed the news that *internal strife* among the Jews had delayed the construction project. The probable reason the narrative of Nehemiah 5 does not mention them is that if God's people get quarrelling among themselves, their enemies can afford to relax in their tents. However, as soon as unity is restored among God's people, the adversary is quickly aroused to engage in the conflict.

In the fourth chapter we learned that the wall had been raised to half of its final height (4:6). Nehemiah now confirms that the wall is nearly finished; all breaches have been repaired, but the gates have not yet been placed (v. 1). The chief enemy of the Jews was Sanballat the Horonite. He was deeply grieved after hearing that Nehemiah had come from Shushan to seek the welfare of the Jews (2:10). He despised the Jews and derided them in an attempt to *sidetrack* them from starting the building project after Nehemiah had rallied the people to do so (2:19). Later, he was enraged by the news that the Jews had actually begun to clear debris and repair the wall. However, all of his *ridicule and mocking* did not weaken Jewish resolve to rise and build (4:1). Sanballat then resorted to discouraging the Jews from building by terrorizing them (4:11-12). Yet, Jehovah was laboring among His people, and though the enemy incited fear, nothing came of his threats.

The insults, the ridicule, and the threatenings were merely flittering shadows which faded with the setting sun. Shadows may scare us, but they have no power to hurt anyone. It is only when we have a diminished opinion of God that the enemy's suggestions (or shadows) gain a foothold in our minds.

Having failed to slow their progress through these tactics, Sanballat, Tobiah, and Geshem would now concentrate their attack on the one who had inspired the Jews to do what they thought was an impossible enterprise. They were desperate; Nehemiah must be stopped at all costs – only then could this well-managed construction project become disorganized. The strategy, simply put, was "stop the leader to stop the work." The attack would focus on *God's leadership* and be the enemy's final attempt to stop the completion of the wall. Dear beloved, pray for your church leaders, for they will be prone to recurring attacks, including solicitations to do evil. Satan knows that if he can cause the undershepherds of the local assembly to fall, he can destroy the testimony that God has raised for Himself in a community.

The enemy mounted a four-pronged assault against Nehemiah. First, they solicited him to withdraw from the safety of his Jewish comrades to discuss the situation with them privately at a remote village in the plain of Ono (v. 2). The plain of Ono is situated some twenty-five miles northwest of Jerusalem. They requested his attendance four times in the same manner, but Nehemiah knew that they meant to do him mischief (v. 2). Nehemiah rejected each invitation with the same concise and trite response: *"I am doing a great work, so that I cannot come down. Why should the work cease while I leave it and go down to you?"*(v. 3). He knew what the Lord wanted him to do, and it did not include abandoning the work of God to dialogue with children of the devil.

Sometimes the devil breaks down the resolve of the believer to do what he or she knows is right through repeated solicitations; this is especially true when we are isolated from accountability. For example, Samson had supernatural strength, but succumbed to the temptation of one persuasive woman while he was away from his Jewish brethren. At first, Samson stood strong against Delilah's dramatic petitions to reveal to her the secret of his strength. She sought to betray him and profit from his capture. Even after three failed attempts, for some reason Samson continued to listen to her pathetic appeals (he had to know she had it in for him). He yielded to her fourth advance and revealed the secret of his power. He was shorn while he slept and was subsequently captured, blinded, and enslaved. Samson's weakness for women and separation from accountability made him susceptible to the enemy's repeated ploy.

It is one thing for a child of God to waste time entertaining goats instead of tending to God's sheep, and it is quite another to leave the safety of the sheepfold and to become the prey of ravenous wolves. Thankfully, Nehemiah did neither – he stayed focused on the important task before him, remained in the company of God's people, and ignored the solicitations of the enemy. How many Christians would not have shipwrecked their lives if they would have heeded Nehemiah's example! No doubt Nehemiah was criticized for not attempting to make peace with his adversaries, but what peace can a child of God and a child of the devil have with each other (2 Cor. 6:14-15)? None! Beware when the enemy says, *"come let us meet together."* The one behind the face of your aggressor is the father of lies, and the Lord Jesus said *"there is no truth in him"* (John 8:44). Dear believer, be discerning; not every religious movement and sympathetic appeal is of God; we must exercise care not to get involved with those who are actually opposing the Lord. Expect criticism for refusing to get involved, but this is much more desirable than to become a casualty of war.

The second strategy against Nehemiah was to slander him and then accuse him of wrongdoing through an open letter (v. 5). The enemy hoped that Nehemiah might want to avoid a scandal and thereby accept their cordial invitation to discuss the matter privately and then be immediately terminated. If this was not possible, the enemy hoped to at least cast doubt on Nehemiah's character by publicly criticizing and discrediting him.

> People who are constantly criticizing others are usually guilty of something worse in their own lives.
>
> — Warren Weirsbe

It was suggested in the "open letter" that Nehemiah wanted to be king of the Jews and was only building the wall to protect his kingship (v. 6). It was further suggested that he would appoint prophets to speak on his behalf in order to coerce the people into blindly following him (v. 7). These accusations cast Nehemiah as a self-seeking, power-hungry man who was secretly plotting treason against Artaxerxes. What was Nehemiah's response? He denied the accusation flatly and told his adversaries that they had quite an imagination; he then committed himself to God through prayer (vv. 8-9). Harry Ironside contrasts Nehemiah's response with the agenda of his adversaries:

> Nehemiah is not at all concerned about this. He knows he is personally right with God and he fears not suspicion and idle tales. "There are no such things done as you say," he retorts boldly, "but you feigned them out of your own heart." So was it also when evil workers sought to undermine the apostle Paul's influence, and so has it ever been when the truth was hated. To discredit, by fair means or foul, the messenger, is one of Satan's cunning devices in order to discredit the message, To do this, his tools often affect great humility themselves; and pretending to be zealous for the liberty of the people of God, they cry "Pope!" "Diotrephes!" "Heretic!" when any servant of Christ and the Church seeks to stand steadfastly against iniquity. They hope to thereby throw dust in the eyes of simple believers, in order to gain their own unrighteous ends. Trials like these are not easy to bear. To have one's good evil-spoken of, to be called a "lord over God's heritage" when trying to serve in lowliness, is painful indeed to any sensitive soul. But it is well not to retaliate, nor even to explain, but just to refuse the cowardly charge and leave results with God.[1]

Thankfully this despicable tactic did not work; Nehemiah did not heed the enemy's insinuations, but rather, he continued doing what God had assigned him. The third attempt on Nehemiah's life came through a Jew named Shemaiah, who we later learn had been paid by Sanballat and Tobiah to act against Nehemiah (vv. 10-12). Shemaiah prophesied that Nehemiah should go with him into the temple and shut the doors behind them. This action would protect Nehemiah against a supposed nighttime assassination attempt (v. 10). Nehemiah knew that the Law permitted only the priests to venture into the temple's sanctuary (Num. 3:10, 18:7). He was thus forbidden to hide there. Knowing that God would not contradict Himself, Nehemiah rightly discerned that Shemaiah was not speaking for God, but was in fact a defector, a paid puppet of the enemy (v. 12).

Nehemiah would rather let God defend him outside the temple than enter into it and sin against the Lord, which would provide the enemy with a legitimate grievance against him. Even if the Jews understood why Nehemiah had ventured into the temple, they would probably lose confidence in a man who was supposed to seek their welfare, but sought special treatment, which they were not privy to. Because Nehemiah both knew and obeyed the Law, the treachery of Shemaiah did not lead him astray. Nehemiah asks God to judge his enemies and to judge the prophets, including the prophetess Noadiah, who were speaking against him (v. 14).

Despite the enemy's attempts to snuff out the life of Nehemiah through solicitation, accusation, and treachery, Nehemiah was preserved and led his people to accomplish one of the greatest feats recorded in the Bible. Jerusalem's wall and its gates were built in just fifty-two days (v. 15). What effect did this achievement have on the enemy? Nehemiah tells us: *"And it happened, when all our enemies heard of it, and all the nations around us saw these things, that they were very disheartened in their own eyes; for they perceived that this work was done by our God"* (v. 16). Despite the wiles of the enemy, the wall was finished and thus supplied a testimony of God's greatness for all to witness. Even the opposition, seeing what a people so outwardly weak had accomplished in the presence of an enemy so strong, was forced to admit *"this work was done by the God of the Jews."*

The monumental feat was a bitter-sweet experience for Nehemiah, because the enemy continued to oppose him even after the city was secure. The fourth type of attack mentioned against Nehemiah in this chapter is treason. It is often after a great victory has been achieved that Satan does his worst damage. Believers, wearied after a laborious undertaking, feel that they deserve a break, some downtime to relax. Having let down their guard, the enemy's movements go undetected until it is too late.

God had miraculously brought His people out of Egypt by plaguing that nation and then opening the Red Sea as the means of their escape and their pursuing enemy's destruction. However, it was the secret attack after this which caused some of the Israelites to fall. After a few weeks in the wilderness, the Amalekites came against the Israelites stealthily. Their unprovoked assault focused on the tired and weary Jews who straggled behind the main group (Deut. 25:17-18). Though a phenomenal deliverance from Egypt had been achieved, the Jews learned that it was folly to relax in hostile territory. Yes, in the Lord, Nehemiah had accomplished a tremendous victory, but he had not earned a vacation. Likewise, the spiritual foes battling the believer never sleep. Believers must always stand ready and be vigilant against potential attack.

Tobiah corresponded with certain Jewish nobles in an attempt to intimidate Nehemiah as he was transitioning from construction to governing duties. Tobiah had gained some loyalists among the Jews through marriage alliances (vv. 17-18). His father-in-law was Shecaniah son of Arah (Ezra 2:5) and his son had married the daughter of Meshullam son of Berechiah, who worked to build two sections of the wall (Neh. 3:4, 30).

Jerusalem's wall could ward off an attacking army, but would not protect Nehemiah from treason from within the city. Would there be a coup attempt? Would a close advisor try to assassinate Nehemiah? Hence, the letters from Tobiah were meant to incite fear in Nehemiah (v. 19). Obviously, this situation was permitted by the Lord, so we must assume that God wanted Nehemiah to further learn to trust in Him alone for protection, and not to rely on human devices, such as a wall he had just finished. The nineteenth-century evangelist Charles Stanley claimed that Nehemiah's greatest trial came from these compromised Jews; he also suggested that false brethren, like those of Nehemiah's time, pose the greatest threat to the Church today:

> It seems to me the greatest trial and danger was from false brethren. The enemy knew that the wall was built: "They were much cast down in their own eyes: for they perceived that this work was wrought of our God." (Neh. 6:16). But the false brethren, even "nobles of Judah, sent many letters unto Tobiah, and the letters of Tobiah came unto them. For there were many in Judah sworn unto him." This is indeed sad, and a great trial, when those who outwardly take the place of being gathered to Christ, yet like these mixed marriages of Judah, we find some dear brethren in the Lord seeking to mingle the principles of the [Samaritan] camp with those of God. Nor should this surprise us, remembering the words of the apostle, "Also of your own selves shall men arise speaking perverse things." (Read Acts 20: 29-35.) No doubt these half-and-half brethren are the greatest stumbling-blocks in the way of inquiring souls. Let those gathered to Christ beware of evil associations — the greatest present danger.[2]

The enemy mounted a four-pronged assault against Nehemiah: First, they solicited him to withdraw from the safety of his Jewish comrades

(v. 2). The second strategy against Nehemiah was to slander him and accuse him of wrongdoing through an open letter (v. 5). The third tactic was the attempt on Nehemiah's life through the treachery of a Jew named Shemaiah (vv. 10-12). The fourth type of attack against Nehemiah was treason from within the Jewish community (vv. 17-18). Nehemiah's response to each tactic should prompt us to be spiritually alert for false brethren, to trust in God's Word for direction, to pray for deliverance when attacked, and to remember that Satan often assaults believers after their accomplishments.

Satan was defeated at Calvary (John 12:31) and further humiliated by the resurrection of Christ (Eph. 1:19-21). His only recourse since those events has been to cast doubt upon the work of Christ and to defame His person and character. Satan and his worldly domain hate the Lord Jesus and will go to any extreme to slander Him and to discourage and frustrate those who desire to live for Christ (John 15:18-19). The last thing Satan wants now is people on earth who remind him of Christ and who are doing the will of God – people who are, as Nehemiah put it, *"true servants of the Lord"* (1:11). Paul considered his spiritual son Timothy a servant of the Lord and exhorted him as such:

> *Flee also youthful lusts; but pursue righteousness, faith, love, peace with those who call on the Lord out of a pure heart. But avoid foolish and ignorant disputes, knowing that they generate strife. And a servant of the Lord must not quarrel but be gentle to all, able to teach, patient* (2 Tim. 2:22-24).

It was Nehemiah's unwavering faith in Jehovah and his irreproachable character that enabled him to undertake amazing feats for God. It is emphasized that the revealed character of the servant of God is as important as what that servant does. The servant of the Lord represents God in character and conduct; neither aspect can be missing from a true testimony of God. As a result of Nehemiah's resolve and leadership, the enemies of the Jews were forced to hang their heads and acknowledge Jehovah. The wall was a reminder to the Jews that God was with them. It would also serve as a testimony to the surrounding nations that the one true God resided in Jerusalem and dwelled among His people. Lastly, the wall would be constant reminder to the opposition of their defeat (v. 16). There is much to be gained when God's people revive, rise in unity, and build for the Lord!

A Revival Meditation

Oh! men and brethren, what would this heart feel if I could but believe that there were some among you who would go home and pray for a revival – men whose faith is large enough, and their love fiery enough to lead them from this moment to exercise unceasing intercessions that God would appear among us and do wondrous things here, as in the times of former generations.

— C. H. Spurgeon

Delegation and a Census
Nehemiah 7

At first glance the reader might consider skipping over Nehemiah 7; it is the longest chapter and most of the content is Jewish genealogies. To be sure, the Jews of bygone days were more excited about their genealogies than we are, but before concluding that Nehemiah 7 has no relevance, please ponder its placement in the book. The first six chapters pertain to the reconstruction of the wall and the last six chapters relate the reviving of the people under Ezra's ministry. Chapter 7 supplies the transition between these two major themes and suggests that God's people must first understand who they are before they can revive what they are.

Having completed the rebuilding of the wall, Nehemiah began the task of securing the city, delegating responsibilities, and strategizing how to repopulate Jerusalem. Hence, several valuable lessons in leadership can be gleaned from this chapter. It is noteworthy that Nehemiah, after completing the wall and consolidating Jerusalem, becomes a backdrop figure through the remainder of the book. He had accomplished what God required him to do; he had no desire to lord over the people or take on any position or role that would jeopardize the good of the people. Good church leaders are to serve God's people and to honor the Lord – they are nothing more than servants and nothing less than brethren.

With all the gates repaired and the wall about Jerusalem rebuilt, the final task to secure the city was to set the doors in the gates (v. 1). This done, Jewish citizens were appointed to act as gatekeepers (i.e. civil guardians) when the gates were opened during the day. The Jews were also to keep watch during nighttime hours from their own houses. To further reduce the opportunity for attack, Nehemiah ordered that the city gates only be opened a few hours each day (late morning to, presumably, dusk).

A mark of a good leader is to choose faithful individuals with sound character qualities who can be delegated to oversee important tasks; this Nehemiah did. There were many important duties to attend to and he could not possibly manage every task. The security of Jerusalem was of paramount concern and he could think of no one better for the job than his own brother Hanani, the one who had first informed him of the pathetic situation in Jerusalem. He was to coordinate with another man named Hananiah who had charge over the citadel. Nehemiah knew the integrity of his own brother, but how did he know to choose Hananiah for this important task? The answer lies in the following description of this man: *"He was a faithful man and feared God more than many"* (v. 2). That would be an honorable epitaph for any tombstone! Nehemiah picked experienced men of integrity, who feared God more than men, to be responsible for protecting God's people.

> A leader is one who sees more than others see, who sees farther than others see, and who sees before others do.
>
> — Leroy Eims

Nehemiah illustrates that it is necessary for those involved in leadership to prepare for the day when the responsibility must be passed on to others. Too often, church leaders become elderly and find themselves in the awkward situation of no longer being able to do the work and yet having no one available to assist them. Younger men who could have been potential elders were not identified, challenged, and mentored for the important task of shepherding the Lord's sheep. The overseers of each church must plan and pray towards the future handing over of the work to those the Holy Spirit calls in the next generation (Acts 20:28; 2 Tim. 2:2).

> Knowing how to do a job is the accomplishment of labor – showing others is the accomplishment of the teacher - making sure the work is done by others is the accomplishment of the manager – inspiring others to do better work is the accomplishment of the leader.
>
> — John Maxwell

With Jerusalem now secure, Nehemiah was faced with a logistical problem: not enough people lived in Jerusalem to support its economic infrastructure. Much of the city had not been rebuilt since it was decimated by the Babylonians about 140 years earlier. Nehemiah initiated a census of the people to clarify the population demographics. This information would help him understand where people lived, where residences were needed, and where personnel to support city operations could be obtained.

Nehemiah began the effort by examining the roster of those who returned with Zerubbabel about 90 years earlier. This was a list of the families who took advantage of Cyrus' offer to return to Jerusalem to rebuild the temple (this roster is also contained in Ezra 2). Nehemiah hoped to validate the Jewish heritage of the people by evaluating this list and available genealogies: thus removing imposters from their midst.

The roster began by identifying key civil and religious leaders (v. 7): Zerubbabel, the appointed governor of the province of Judah, and Jeshua (or Joshua), the High Priest. It is suggested that the twelve names that follow are either direct or symbolic representatives for each of the twelve Jewish tribes.

After the tribal leaders, eighteen specific families and clans are listed, then inhabitants from twenty-one towns and villages, the priests, the Levites, the singers, the gatekeepers, the descendants of temple servants or royal servants, and finally 642 returnees who could not prove their ancestry. Ezra provided a tally of the people associated with each of the above groups which totals 29,829; however, he then stated the aggregate number of Jews returning home as 49,897 (Ezra 2:64-65). The latter number is referred to as "the whole company," which probably included women and children, along with descendants from the ten northern tribes. Nehemiah records that 49,942 Jews returned to Israel at this time, which is slightly different than Ezra's total, the difference being that Nehemiah includes 45 additional singers (Neh. 7:66-67).

It is possible that Ezra and Nehemiah had good reasons, unknown to us, for compiling slightly different rosters. However, much of the discrepancy is probably best explained as a scribal error in copying the Hebrew numbers accurately. The original writings of Scripture were inspired, but the copyists were not inspired and they did make errors.

162

Through textual criticism, we can determine, with a high degree of confidence, that a Hebrew manuscript is very close to the original. In fact, ninety percent of the existing Old Testament manuscripts are without variants and nearly all of the remaining ten percent are stylistic, spelling, or word order differences. The Jews took great care in copying the manuscripts accurately, but no amount of carefulness is going to prevent mistakes from happening when a text is copied dozens of times.

Numbers often proved particularly difficult for scribes (copiers). The Hebrew numerical system was somewhat like the Roman in that they used letters for numbers. Some of the Hebrew letters were quite similar to one another, making the job of copying numbers even more difficult. However, these types of errors are often obvious when comparing parallel Bible passages or by using common sense. For example, when men from the small town of Beth-shemesh peered into the Ark of the Covenant and were judged, was it likely that 50,070 died (as recorded in 1 Sam. 6:19), or was the number perhaps 70 men? The answer is obvious. In a similar manner, the scribe copying the book of Nehemiah may have picked up the number of mules (245) traveling to Jerusalem in verse 68, and accidently placed that number in verse 67. Thus, 245 singers are noted in Nehemiah, rather than 200 singers, the number that Ezra provides. In all, we can say that about 50,000 Jews made the arduous 900-mile trip from Babylon to Israel and we need not lose any sleep over the trivial numerical difference in the text.

Besides establishing a legitimate Jewish population demographic, another reason for the census was that Nehemiah validate the purity of those who ministered in the temple, as Tirshatha commanded and Zerubbabel had enforced some 90 years earlier (Ezra 2:61-64). Only Levites and their servants could serve in the temple and only descendants of Aaron could function as priests. Those who were unable to demonstrate Aaronic lineage would be removed from temple service.

This examination of genealogies may have seemed somewhat harsh to some, for indeed faithful men who had labored on the wall and served in the temple may have been removed from the priesthood, depending on the outcome of the evaluation. For some, this may be considered a divisive action, but true unity among God's people can only be achieved when they are obedient to the will of God. In this case, the will of God was clearly stated in Scripture (Ex. 28:1).

Compromising truth for the sake of unity will always eventually divide God's people – it is better to follow Scripture and enjoy God's blessing than to create a temporary camaraderie without it. Most of the problems that local churches suffer from today are a direct result of ignoring biblical patterns and directives.

Nehemiah records not only the clan names of those Jews returning to Jerusalem from Babylon, but also the generosity of the people at that time to support the rebuilding of the temple (also recorded in Ezra 2). It was not necessary for Nehemiah to include this information (vv. 68-73) into his record, as it had no genealogical bearing, but evidently, he thought it worthy to note that God's work (building the temple) had been abundantly financed by God's people.

Christians are the Lord's representatives on earth (2 Cor. 5:20) and God provides for His own. God always pays for the work He orders. This support usually comes through the Lord's people; for example, we read the saints at Philippi had fellowship with Paul in the gospel several times (Phil. 4:15-19). Additionally, in the early days of the Church it is clear that itinerant workers were supported by their hosting families as they traveled to spread the gospel message; they took nothing from those they desired to see won to Christ (3 Jn. 5-8).

Historically speaking, on rare occasions the Lord moved Gentiles to give to His covenant people. The first example relates to the exodus. God judged the Egyptians because they harshly afflicted His people; the Israelites had served as an unpaid labor force and were entitled to monetary restitution. Thus, God instructed them to ask for it, and the Israelites left with the wealth of Egypt. Later, God moved the Persian kings to financially support the work of God in Jerusalem (i.e. the building of the temple and the wall), without being asked by God's people. In this case, God was merely returning to His people what the Persians had acquired from the Babylonians, who had despoiled the Jews.

In the dispensation of the Church Age there is no example or scriptural precedence to ask or plead for one's financial needs. Why? First, God is able to support His own work. Second, the unregenerate may think that they have earned a just standing before God by donating funds to His work without receiving His Son as Lord and Savior. Additionally, we have the example of Paul, who, while engaged in ministry at Corinth, did not request support from them to ensure that his motives would not be questioned and that the gospel message would remain clear to its hearers. However, during his eighteen-month stay in Corinth he did receive support from other churches who wanted to partner with him in the work (2 Cor. 11:7-9).

While God might prompt non-believers to support His work in unique situations (as in the days of Moses, Zerubbabel and Ezra), this is not His normative method of providing for His people and their ministries. Consequently, believers should follow the pattern contained in Scripture and not solicit the lost for financial assistance. The New Testament Church lived by this precedent: *"For His name's sake they went forth, taking nothing of the Gentiles"* (3 Jn. 7).

H. G. Mackay concisely summarizes the biblical pattern for supporting Christian ministries in his book *Biblical Financial Principles*:

> The book of Acts is the inspired missionary manual of the Church, recording the advance of Christianity, the spread of the gospel, and the establishing of local churches during the thirty years that followed Pentecost. It is doubtful if any other comparable period of time witnessed such progress in the dissemination of the truth (Col. 1:6, 23). One is startled, then, by the total absence in the record of two elements which occupy a prominent place in many missionary efforts today – appeals for workers and appeals for funds! Both are conspicuous by their absence from the account of apostolic enterprises.[1]

All Christian ministries should be sustained by the Lord as shown through the freewill giving of other saints. At times believers may make the needs of others known (Rom. 15:25-28; 1 Cor. 16:1-3; 2 Cor. 8). However, the benefactors should not be the ones who appeal for funding; rather, they themselves should be given to prayer and the ministry. Much time is wasted by the modern Church in trying to raise funds, instead of erecting a testimony for God – if God is in the work, the funds will be there. If the funds are not there, then the servant of the Lord knows that he or she is being redirected by the One who controls all such things.

If an emotional appeal for finances is issued, how will the Lord's servants know if their ministry has God's endorsement? It is possible that the devil might support a particular ministry in order to keep believers from doing what the Lord Jesus would really have them to do. Accordingly, fundraisers, marketing schemes, raffles, bingo, carnivals, pancake breakfasts, etc. are secular means of raising money and are poor substitutes for God's grace to His faithful servants. The One who owns the cattle on a thousand hills is certainly able to provide for His own children.

A Revival Meditation

A Godly leader ...
finds strength by realizing his weakness
finds authority by being under authority
finds direction by laying down his plans
finds vision by seeing the needs of others
finds credibility by being an example
finds loyalty by expressing compassion
finds honor by being faithful
finds greatness by being a servant

— Roy Lessin

The Water Gate Revival (Part 1)
Nehemiah 8:1-6

Three post-captivity revivals occurred among the Jews prior to their declension in the days of the prophet Malachi which prompted four centuries of divine silence. The first spiritual awakening occurred during the days of Zerubbabel at which time the temple was rebuilt. Two more revivals occurred during the ministry of Ezra the scribe; this chapter records the second of these. King Artaxerxes commissioned Ezra to teach the Jews their own Law and to maintain order in the region by enforcing it. He initially arrived in Jerusalem some thirteen years before Nehemiah did. Ezra was appalled at the spiritual condition of his people; besides being ignorant of God's law, some, including Jewish leaders and priests, had intermarried with pagans. His anguish over the nation's sin led him to publicly fall prostrate before the Lord in front of the temple – his prayer moved the people to repentance and to separation (Ezra 9 and 10).

Under Nehemiah's leadership, the Jews unified and rebuilt the wall with its gates to secure Jerusalem from its enemies. In previous chapters, we witnessed Nehemiah's unwavering resolve to erect this spectacular testimony of God's greatness. Although the opposition continually sought to distract and demoralize the much smaller workforce, the Jews, sustained by divine grace, built the wall nonetheless. Hopefully, every believer longs for such a working of God's grace within his or her life so that a lasting testimony of God's goodness will be recognized by others. We learn from Nehemiah that the key to triumphing over the enemy is to rely on the Lord for help and direction while at the same time refusing to be sidetracked from the objective, which is doing the will of God!

In the last chapter, Nehemiah instituted an elaborate security system to defend his people from a covert attempt by their enemies to infiltrate Jerusalem. He realized that the enemy had many ways to destroy a work of God. Though the threat of direct frontal assault had been virtually eliminated by the wall, they were still vulnerable to dangers from within.

Watchfulness is a Christian virtue often neglected, especially when one thinks he or she is secure. The elders of the Church at Ephesus were reminded by Paul that he had warned them day and night to be alert; the enemy may attack a local assembly at any time (Acts 20:31). Paul informed them that danger would come both from within and without the assembly and that they must be constantly alert for this double threat:

> *For I know this, that after my departure savage wolves will come in among you, not sparing the flock. Also from among yourselves men will rise up, speaking perverse things, to draw away the disciples after themselves. Therefore watch, and remember that for three years I did not cease to warn everyone night and day with tears* (Acts 20:29-31).

One of the greatest threats to the prosperity of the Jews was their poor spiritual condition – they were largely ignorant of the Law. Both Ezra and Nehemiah knew that they, as God's covenant people, were accountable to God to know the Law and obey it. God had already brought about the destruction of Jerusalem once because of willful sin, and certainly He could be provoked to do it again. Indeed, He did, in 70 AD after the Jews rejected His own Son as their Messiah.

The Jews had banded together to accomplish an incredible feat, but more than anything, they needed to draw near to God and experience ongoing spiritual revival. Without revival, their great accomplishments could easily be negated by moral decline; they must fully identify with Jehovah and live according to His Law. Thankfully, there was a second spiritual awakening among the people through the ministry of the scribe Ezra.

A careful study of Nehemiah 8 and 9 will reveal several key characteristics of spiritual revival. These same attributes are associated with other revivals recorded in Scripture and in Church history. We will examine each of these eight characteristics and hopefully encourage ourselves to yearn for spiritual revival in our lives also.

1. Deplorable Spiritual Conditions

As was the case when Ezra first arrived in Jerusalem thirteen years earlier, even after the rebuilding of the wall the Jews were a spiritually destitute people (Ezra 9). They knew that they were God's covenant people, but the teaching of God's Word had been generally neglected for a century and a half. Even two centuries prior to the Water Gate Revival, God's Word was not being publicly taught. The Book of the Law had been lost until priests instructed by King Josiah to repair the temple happened upon it (2 Kgs. 22). Because of neglect, the temple was in disrepair and the Word of God had been forgotten, though it resided right where it was supposed to be, in God's house.

In the Church Age, Christians are the temple of God (Eph. 2:19-22), and we too will fall into disrepair if we neglect the Word of God which is to be hidden within our hearts. The Psalmist declares: *"Your word I have hidden in my heart, that I might not sin against You"* (Ps. 119:11). If God's Word is merely in our Bibles and not hidden in the hearts, then we too, like the Jews before us, will experience spiritual decline. God's Word is the food of His people (Matt. 4:4) – spiritual starvation and moral decline stroll together. As demonstrated in Ezra's day, declension results when believers neglect to read, to understand, and to obey God's Word. On a positive note, however, it is observed that similar deplorable conditions existed just prior to all the great revivals in Judeo-Christian history.

2. Effectual and Fervent Prayer of the Righteous

James states that *"the effective, fervent prayer of a righteous man avails much"* (Jas. 5:16). Ezra's private and public prayers preceded the previous revival (Ezra 9:5-9). This pattern is also exhibited in Acts 1, where believers gathered for prayer and supplications while they waited for the coming of the Holy Spirit. When He did come, the Church was created and believers were empowered to preach the gospel message and 3,000 souls were saved that same day. These Christians obeyed the Lord's command to wait in Jerusalem until the Holy Spirit would come and take up residence within them (Acts 1:4-8). The blessings of God then spilled over from the believers to the lost – this is a true mark of spiritual revival. When God's people are revitalized by the Spirit of God, the lost are affected too.

Evangelism affects the other fellow; revival affects me.

— Leonard Ravenhill

Nehemiah was a man of prayer. His prayers and diligence brought about a tremendous work of God, which seems to have awakened the people to His abiding presence. Thus, they asked Ezra, the skilled scribe, to teach them about the Lord and what He expected of them: *"Now all the people gathered together as one man in the open square that was in front of the Water Gate; and they told Ezra the scribe to bring the Book of the Law of Moses, which the Lord had commanded Israel"* (Neh. 8:1). As noted earlier in the book, Nehemiah, Ezra, and other spiritually-minded Jews had been praying for their fellow countrymen. God indeed heard those prayers and was moving to draw His people to Himself; the Jews were awakened to their own spiritual need and they desired to hear from their God.

3. Renewed Reverence for God's Word

The Jews at this time were largely ignorant of the Law of Moses; they knew of generalities that had perhaps been passed down through the generations, but they did not know specifically what God expected of them. Their traditions and past idolatry had led them away from the Lord and had invoked His anger and parental discipline. Ninety years earlier, the Jews with Zerubbabel and Jeshua had been guided by the Law to build an altar at the site of the future temple and to offer burnt sacrifices upon it, thus bringing themselves under the efficacy of those sacrifices and Jehovah's protection (Ezra 3:1-4). After witnessing God's presence among them in the building of the wall, the Jews again were desirous to know more about Jehovah, their God.

A large congregation of Jews gathered at the Water Gate and asked Ezra and the Levites to teach them the Law, which they were obliged to do (vv. 1-2). Unbeknown to the Jews, their assembling coincided with the Feast of Trumpets, which was to be held on the first day of the seventh month (Lev. 23:24). During their sojourn in the wilderness, Moses used two silver trumpets to relay commands to the Israelites, including the call to assemble so God's will could be revealed to them (Num. 10:2-3). On this occasion also, God had a message for His people, so He assembled them on the first day of the seventh month, on the Feast of Trumpets.

On this day, Ezra and thirteen fellow priests took to a wood platform. Besides creating an environment in which the preachers could be more easily heard, the entire scene shows the prominence the Word of God is to have in public meetings of His people. While standing before the people, Ezra opened and read the Book of the Law. It is noteworthy that a great congregation of *"all who could hear with understanding"* gathered to listen to the preaching of God's Word (this fact is mentioned again in verse 3). In other words, men, women, and children were together while Ezra was speaking.

This was also the pattern of the early Church. Seven times in his first epistle to the Corinthians, Paul uses the expression "when you come together," or something similar, to speak of the entire assembly coming together for the meetings of the church (1 Cor. 5:4, 7:5, 11:17, 18, 20, 33, 34, 14:23, 26). For example, when he exhorts the believers about revamping their disorderly church meetings, he clearly states when his instructions apply, that is, when *"the whole church comes together in one place"* (1 Cor. 14:23). This is not to say that believers should not come together privately throughout the week in order to encourage each other, but rather when the church gathers, it is for a common purpose as a unified body under its Head – Christ.

The Old Testament provides many examples of God's people, both young and old, gathering for the public preaching of Scripture, for prayer, for confession of sin, and for worship; there are no examples in Scripture of separate meetings for children or for women. The references below provide examples of such congregational meetings and in some cases the proper usage of a congregational "Amen" by all in attendance to show their approval and agreement with what was said. This congregational affirmation was also a part of early church meetings and was a practice that Paul readily approved of (1 Cor. 14:16). The following are Old Testament examples of all God's people coming together for spiritual activities:

And the Levites shall speak with a loud voice and say to all the men of Israel: "Cursed is the one who makes a carved or molded image, an abomination to the Lord, the work of the hands of the craftsman, and sets it up in secret" (Deut. 27:14-15). (The pronouncement of God's

171

Word by the priests and the affirmation of it by all the people is repeated eleven more times through the remainder of Deuteronomy 27.)

The king went up to the house of the Lord with all the men of Judah, and with him all the inhabitants of Jerusalem -- the priests and the prophets and all the people, both small and great. And he read in their hearing all the words of the Book of the Covenant which had been found in the house of the Lord (2 Kings 23:2).

Oh, give thanks to the Lord! Call upon His name; make known His deeds among the peoples! ... Oh, give thanks to the Lord, for He is good! For His mercy endures forever. ... Blessed be the Lord God of Israel from everlasting to everlasting! And all the people said, "Amen!" and praised the Lord (selected portions of 1 Chron. 16:8-36).

Now while Ezra was praying, and while he was confessing, weeping, and bowing down before the house of God, a very large assembly of men, women, and children gathered to him from Israel; for the people wept very bitterly (Ezra 10:1).

Blessed be the Lord God of Israel from everlasting to everlasting! And let all the people say, "Amen!" Praise the Lord (Ps. 106:48).

Scripture shows a long-standing practice of God's people gathering together in one place for the hearing of God's Word, prayer, and worship. This Old Testament practice was continued by the early Church. If the unity of God's people is a manifestation of God's glory on earth, as the Lord Jesus states in John 17, why would local churches willingly splinter and hinder the body life of the local assembly? The sense of oneness and family life is critical for each gathering. Every believer needs to know and to appreciate the communal love and mutual respect that is enjoyed in family life.

The local church is a living body, a family of believers, and we should be careful of any activity that hinders its unified communion with Christ. Unfortunately, many local churches today are sick and feeble from self-inflicted ideologies and traditions which have hindered healthy body life. The local assembly ought to be a vibrant, joyful fellowship of God's people working together for the cause of Christ, not a sickly, poorly functioning entity on life-support.

The Jews had all come together to hear the Law of Moses. Their respect for Scripture and their desire to understand it was demonstrated in that they stood for six hours while God's Word was being taught. The Jews were attentive as Ezra stood on a wooden platform in order to be heard by the large congregation. History has yet to record a revival among God's people in which the Word of God did not first have a prominent place in their hearts. Other biblical examples include the revivals under King Hezekiah and then later King Josiah. Church history also records that the Reformation in the 16th century, the Great Awakenings in the 17th and the 18th centuries, and the General Awakening and the Brethren Movement in the 19th century all began with a renewed passion for God's Word and with intense prayers that it might be known.

4. The Worship of God

Prior to expounding Scripture, Ezra prayed. He praised the Lord, the one and only great God. This action had a profound effect on the people. It was essential for the people to be reminded of God's eminence and their own feebleness. The Jews were in full agreement and responded with *"Amen, Amen,"* or literally, *"this is true, this is true."* As the Jews declared this, they lifted their hands and arms up above their heads, their palms held heavenward, their faces downcast. Their posture silently proclaimed: "Lord, we are empty handed, we have nothing; all we need comes from You alone." Revival not only produces reverence for God's Word, but also deliberate recognition of the majesty of God – worship.

> When man loses sight of God's glory, he ultimately glories in his own depravity.
> — Mike Attwood

The Jewish revival of Nehemiah 8 began when the revealed Word of God was again appreciated and revered. Harry Ironside suggests this has been the beginning point of all the great revivals among God's people through human history:

In every genuine revival among God's people the revealed Word of the Lord has had a large place. It was so in Josiah's day, and in the awakening under Hezekiah. It has been so throughout the Church period. It was the recovery of the Word that brought about the Reformation of the 16th century, and every true awakening since has been based upon Bible study and Bible practice. Of no spiritual movement in history could this more truthfully be said than of that special work of God which began almost simultaneously in many parts of Great Britain and Ireland in the first half of the 19th century. Here and there little companies of devoted believers were found gathering together to search the Scriptures, seeking a right way for themselves and their children in the midst of the existing ecclesiastical confusion and dead formality. To them was revealed from the Word that Christ Jesus is the one Centre of gathering, that the Church is one body in which the Holy Spirit dwells and which He is to guide. Thus disowning everything for which they could find neither a plain "Thus says the Lord" nor a simple divine principle exemplified in Scripture, they turned away from all sects and systems to be known only as brethren in Christ, members of His body, seeking to walk in subjection to the Holy Spirit. For such, these remnant books are full of important and much-needed instruction. They have failed grievously and openly as did the restored Jews of old; but the same resource remains for these as for those the abiding, unerring word of God.[1]

Nehemiah 8 revealed four key characteristics of spiritual revival: First, a deplorable spiritual condition existed among God's people. Second, a righteous remnant effectually prayed for revival. Third, there was a renewed reverence for God's Word by His people. Fourth, the proper understanding of God's Word led the people to worship God. These and four more characteristics contained in Nehemiah 9 provide a recovery blueprint which can be repeatedly observed in other revivals recorded in Scripture and in Church history.

A Revival Meditation
During the Great Awakening in America in the late 18th century, George Whitefield joined Jonathan Edwards and revival swept America like a wildfire. Jonathan Edwards was not an eloquent preacher; in fact, he often read his messages, but when he preached his famous sermon, "Sinners in the Hands of an Angry God" many in the congregation fell

down as dead, crying out in agony and holding onto the pews and pillars in the church building as to avoid falling into the fires of hell. By the preaching of God's Word and the conviction of God's Spirit, the lost sensed the holiness of God in a profound way and agonized over their own sinful condition. After hearing God's Word, many lost sinners were overcome by the holiness of God and were thus profoundly compelled to be reconciled to Him. Hence, hundreds of thousands trusted the Lord Jesus Christ for salvation during this time frame.

The Water Gate Revival (Part 2)
Nehemiah 8:7-18

As previously mentioned, Nehemiah 8 and 9 reveal several key characteristics of spiritual revival, which seem to be consistent with other revivals recorded in Scripture and in Church history. We will continue to examine each of these eight features associated with the Water Gate Revival and hopefully encourage ourselves to yearn for personal revival also.

So far, we have seen that deplorable spiritual conditions existed among God's people just prior to revival. Next, a righteous remnant was engaged in fervent prayer for revival. This was followed by a renewed reverence for the Word of God. Lastly, a proper understanding of God's greatness and man's depravity was obtained; this realization culminated in the worship of God. We will observe in the remainder of the chapter that true revival must lead to reform.

5. Comprehension of Scripture

Ezra engaged in expository teaching of Scripture: *"So they read distinctly from the book, in the Law of God; and they gave the sense, and helped them to understand the reading"* (v. 8). After the Babylonian captivity, as a spoken language Hebrew had been largely displaced by Aramaic; therefore, the Hebrew words spoken to Ezra's audience required careful explanation. Thus, Scripture was read clearly, and then it was explained so all could both hear and understand it. It is quite doubtful that Ezra distracted the people with touching stories and funny jokes on this momentous occasion. Likewise, teachers today should be careful not to taint the teaching of divine truth with distracting human garnishments.

The Word of God well understood and religiously obeyed is the shortest route to spiritual perfection. And we must not select a few

176

favorite passages to the exclusion of others. Nothing less than a whole Bible can make a whole Christian.

— A.W. Tozer

In order to help the people to understand, thirteen teachers, plus other Levites, were dispersed among the congregation to answer specific questions about what Ezra was teaching (v. 7). Apparently, once the general populace understood what had been taught, Ezra continued by reading another portion of Scripture and explaining it. The Word of God had a wonderful effect on the people *"because they understood the words that were declared to them"* (v. 12). Ezra's teaching style was quite effective because he not only preached the Word, but also confirmed that his audience understood what he had taught before moving on.

Ezra was not interested in mesmerizing his hearers with fanciful words, funny stories, and dramatic emotional ploys – he realized that spiritual problems must be dealt with and with spiritual remedies, not humanistic substitutes. Once understood, God's Word through the conviction of the Holy Spirit would be sufficient to change sinful hearts. And that is exactly what happened; it is also what we need today. God's Word and His Spirit must reach through our inner man and take control of our minds. We do not need emotional appeals to prompt our flesh to superimpose itself on our decision-making. The former is spiritual, while the latter is carnal and usually results in devastating consequences.

6. Remorse and Repentance of Sin

Comprehension of Scripture brought brokenness: *"the people wept bitterly"* (v. 9). This same contriteness was observed during the revival some thirteen years earlier, after Ezra's public prayer (Ezra 10:1). Now again, the people were grieved over their personal conduct, knowing that it was not what God expected and demanded of them (v. 12). The people began confessing their sins, beginning with those in leadership, followed by the men, the women, and the children.

Although no public prayers are recorded in the narrative during Ezra's sermon, there can be no doubt that public prayers were uttered at this time. The earlier revival began when one brokenhearted man confessed the sins of the nation as his own (Ezra 9:10); this in turn prompted the people to be grieved over their own sins as well (Ezra 10:1-2). If Ezra were to visit our local churches today, he would have something to say to us about our spiritual adultery, cold hearts, materialism, and a lack of reverence for God and His Word. If we heard such a message, would it break our stony hearts? Might we too experience revival? The prophet Isaiah expounds this timeless principle:

> *For thus says the High and Lofty One Who inhabits eternity, whose name is Holy: "I dwell in the high and holy place, with him who has a contrite and humble spirit, to revive the spirit of the humble, and to revive the heart of the contrite ones"* (Isa. 57:15).

If we want to see revival in our lifetimes, we must step out of the darkness of sin and get real with God. Many who identify with Christ today are neither devoted to Him nor His Word, because of the blindness and despondency that sin causes. It is often these who covertly infiltrate Sunday mega-gatherings and then slip out again unscathed by personal accountability to God, His Word, and His people. Perhaps this is, historically speaking, why great revivals have always begun with small groups of believers desperate for God. A. B. Earl, who labored for fifty-eight years as an itinerant evangelist in the United States and Canada during the nineteenth century, noted this particular dynamic of those experiencing revival at that time:

> The multitudes flock to the house of God, when Christ's children enjoy the fullness of his love, and no more complaint is heard about small congregations .... For this reason, it is usually quite as well to commence a series of meetings with a small assembly, and in unpleasant weather; since, under such circumstances, the church – at least some portion of it – will be more likely to get fully into the work, and have power with God, than when the congregations are crowded, and the surroundings more promising.[1]

As the Scripture is understood, and we are compelled to compare our lives with the revealed will of God, we become more aware of our failed condition before God. While this realization should result in sorrow, regret alone does not change anything; we need a deep grieving that results in a change of heart. Paul puts the matter this way, *"For godly sorrow produces repentance leading to salvation, not to be regretted; but the sorrow of the world produces death"* (2 Cor. 7:10). Godly sorrow is more than mere regret for our failures; it is a desire to get things right with God through repentance. If one only experiences the conviction of God's Word apart from repentance, he or she will be most miserable.

However, true repentance and divine forgiveness release all the sequestered guilt in one's soul; then the joy of the Lord comes pouring in like a flood to fill every vacated memory. Accordingly, after the Word of God had accomplished its work, Ezra and the Levites told the people not to mourn any longer over past failures, for *"the joy of the Lord is your strength"* (v. 10). In fact, the Jews turned their day of reckoning with God into a day of feasting. Their mourning was displaced with joy (vv. 11-12).

7. Obedience to God's Word

The crowd dispersed, but the next day, the leaders of the various clans and families returned to learn more from God's Word (v. 13). These, the representatives of the nation, were taught about the Feasts of Jehovah, which they had neglected to keep for some time. They learned that the upcoming Feast of Tabernacles should be held on the fifteenth day of the seventh month (Lev. 23:34). Perhaps the Levites did not inform the people about the fast approaching Day of Atonement, designated for the tenth day of the seventh month, as there would have been only one week to both announce and prepare for it. The main participants of the Day of Atonement were the priests, especially the High Priest. However, the Feast of Tabernacles provided an opportunity for all Jews to participate and show devotion to God and His commands. A proclamation was sent; the Jews were going to commemorate the Feast of Tabernacles. Instructions were also delivered to the people as to how to construct the booths associated with the feast (v. 15).

The Jews obeyed God's Word and gathered olive, pine, myrtle, and palm branches, as well as branches from thick trees to construct makeshift booths (v. 15). These were fabricated on the housetops, in the courts of their homes, in the temple courtyard, and even in the streets (v. 16). For eight days, beginning with the fifteenth day of the month, the people obeyed the Law by dwelling in these booths. While the Feast of Tabernacles had been previously recognized in Israel through religious traditions, the Jews had not built and lived within booths for eight days since Joshua led them into Canaan (v. 17). In other words, their forefathers had not been compliant with the Law in this matter for over a millennium. As J. I. Packer notes, it is natural for us to drift with the current of human tradition, rather than to obtain our own bearings from Scripture and paddle against the flow of pious fiction.

> We approach Scripture with minds already formed by the mass of accepted opinions and viewpoints with which we have come into contact, in both the Church and the world.... It is easy to be unaware that it has happened; it is hard even to begin to realize how profoundly tradition in this sense has molded us.

— J. I. Packer

The Jews of Ezra's day delighted in knowing what God desired of them and they did it. Consequently, the Levites continued teaching the Word of God at the temple throughout the eight-day feast and the people eagerly listened. Likewise, it is a tremendous blessing to Christians today to gather for several days to hear the Word of God expounded. The Lord Jesus said, *"Blessed are those who hear the word of God and keep it!"* (Luke 11:28). The Lord also confirmed that only true disciples would obey His commands: *"If you abide in My word, you are My disciples indeed"* (John 8:31). May we, like the Jews, prove our devotion to the Lord by searching out the will of God as revealed in Scripture and then obey what we understand to be true. We can only experience the blessing of God by yielding to His will.

8. Rejoicing With God

Although the chapter began with sorrow over sin, it ends with joy, for *"there was very great gladness"* among God's people (v. 17). The Levites had reminded the people that the joy of the Lord was their strength (v. 10). Given the immensity of their failure, one might be tempted to think that the Jews should wallow in guilt and remorse for a while, but the instruction of the Levites to the Jews affirms that God wanted them to rejoice (v. 9); J. G. Bellett explains:

> The people, listening to the Law on such a day as this, are commanded by those who then sat in Moses' seat, to let their minds be formed by *the day,* and not by *the law.* That is, they were told not to mourn, but to be merry. Very right that they should mourn, if they heard the law alone, but hearing it on such a day as the first day of the seventh month, they heard it as in the presence of the grace and quickening and salvation of God, and their place and duty is to have their souls formed by grace. Right, again I say, it is, nay needful, that we should be brokenhearted in the sense of our sin and of our ruin, and under the hearing of the law; but when the healing of God visits us, we are to learn the joy that healing imparts, and have our minds framed accordingly.[2]

Through the preaching of and submitting to God's Law the Jews experienced renewed fellowship with God. They were sensing God's presence and an atmosphere of joy pervaded Jerusalem. This is the culmination of revival – the Spirit of God filling His people with power and joy. God renews and revitalizes His people to experience the wonder of His presence and to happily go on with Him in life – this is true spiritual fellowship. The result of this reality is that many souls are normally won to Christ by Christians who are experiencing revival. During such times entire communities have been transformed from bastions of sin to beacons for heaven.

For example, it is estimated that approximately 100,000 people turned from sin and confessed Christ as Savior during the Welch Revival of 1904-1905. Crime ceased. Taverns closed. People made their way home in the wee hours of the morning, holding hands and singing hymns beneath a starlit night. The mules pulling the coal wagons were nearly rendered useless, for they did not understand the commands of their drivers apart from swearing and yelling. The people sensed God's presence among them and the region was permeated with joy.

We too can experience vibrant fellowship with God, but we first must learn, as the Jews did in Ezra's day, the significance of hearing, understanding, and obeying God's Word. Continued revival depends upon our obedience to the truth and our devotedness to the Lord Jesus

Christ. A brief biography of Evan Roberts (1876-1951) shows us how prominent obedience to God's Word was to the Welsh revival. The author writes:

> Roberts worked in coal mines, but he walked in the heavenlies. Never without his Bible, he prayed and wept 11 years for revival in Wales. He entered the Preparatory School for the Ministry at Newcastle, Enlyn, when about 26, but he never finished. Compelled by the Holy Spirit, he returned in November, 1904, to his home village of Loughor, to tell of Christ. And fire fell! Evan did not preach (in the traditional sense) but he led the meetings, praying, "Bend us, O Lord!" and urging, "Obey the Holy Spirit. Obey!" The Calvinistic Methodist church was moved until all Loughor became a praying, praising multitude. They went from the pain of repentance to the joy of the Lord, resulting in empty taverns, closed brothels, and churches which were filled—daily. ... All Wales was brought in repentance to its knees at the cross.[3]

We should not be afraid of legitimate workings of the Holy Spirit. The early Church expected the supernatural to occur and consequently remained in a state of revival for many years as they carried the gospel message to the nations. They did not need to pray for revival, as they were living out the life of Christ in an ongoing manner. While Pentecost will not be repeated, believers today have the same God, the same Lord, the same Holy Spirit, the same dispensation of truth, and the same gospel – the problem lies with us. We have too low of an expectation of God and are satisfied with the status quo; thus, we have nearly no vision for what could be. As long as we are content with our mundane, self-centered existence, revival will elude the modern Church. It is time for God's people to awake from slumber and rise up and build!

A Revival Meditation

What happened to the Jews during the Water Gate Revival has occurred many times throughout the Church Age. The anguish of Ezra and Nehemiah over the poor spiritual condition of the Jews seems not too different than the apostles who travailed in prayer for the conversion of souls in the book of Acts or others who witnessed later revivals. Jonathan Edwards, for example, wrote much about the revivals that occurred in America during his lifetime. Below is Edwards' description of how the town of Northampton, MA was transformed for Christ through fervent prayer during the First Great Awakening (1733-35):

> On the evening of the day preceding the outbreak of the revival, some Christians met, and spent the whole night in prayer. There was scarcely a person in the town (Northampton), old or young, left unconcerned about the great things of the eternal world. The work of conversion was carried on in a most astonishing manner, and increased more and more; souls did as it were come by flocks to Jesus Christ. This work of God soon made a glorious alteration in the town; so that in the spring and summer following, the town seemed to be full of the presence of God; it was never so full of love, nor of joy, and yet so full of distress, as it was then. There were remarkable tokens of God's presence in almost every house. It was a time of joy in families on account of salvation being brought unto them; parents rejoicing over their children as new born, and husbands over their wives, and wives over their husbands.[4]

A Long Prayer
Nehemiah 9

Nehemiah 9 contains the longest recorded prayer in the Bible. Ezra leads the Jewish nation in a prayer that recounts their history as God's covenant people. In this prayer, he frequently transitions between the unfailing goodness of God to Israel and the recurring theme of their rebellion against God.

Revival had swept through the Jewish ranks. It began when men, women, and children gathered on the first day of the seventh month to hear the systematic teaching of God's Word. Family and clan leaders returned the next day to hear more from Scripture. In response to what they had learned, the nation gathered at Jerusalem to keep the Feast of Tabernacles, an eight-day feast beginning on the fifteenth day of the month. The Jews were under the preaching of God's Word daily during this eight-day period.

Apparently, the people dispersed at the conclusion of the feast, but, conscious of their spiritual need, they voluntarily regathered two days later (i.e. the twenty-fourth day of the month) to hear more. As the writer of Hebrews reminds us, the Word of God is powerful and will not return void, as demonstrated by the response of this people: *"For the word of God is living and powerful, and sharper than any two-edged sword, piercing even to the division of soul and spirit, and of joints and marrow, and is a discerner of the thoughts and intents of the heart"* (Heb. 4:12). The Jews continued to rejoice in their God even as His Word persistently exposed more defilement in them which needed to be dealt with. Accordingly, the impromptu gathering became a time of public repentance and confession of sin, not just their own, but also that of their forefathers (v. 2).

God's Word had cut deep into their hearts. The Jews fasted as an expression of self-mortification. They wore sackcloth, the humble attire of mourners, and threw dirt upon themselves to demonstrate their utter

184

distress and humility before their God (v. 1). This was a solemn convocation, for God's covenant people stood before Him untainted by strangers and foreigners (v. 2). God is holy and His people must be holy too. This act of consecration would remind the Jews that they must maintain separation from those who had and could again cause their spiritual and moral downfall. This solemn convocation before the Lord would certainly be a public indictment against those men who had taken foreign wives.

Scripture reveals the will of God for His people. The Jews were therefore eager to be directed by God in this matter. So they listened to the reading of Scripture for three hours and then engaged in prayer and worship for the next three hours. The study of God's Word and prayer should always go together. Believers are to read and contemplate the Word and then cultivate its meaning and application through meditation and prayer. Harry Ironside noted that Christians must first hear God speaking to them, before they can rightly speak back to Him:

One who gives himself preeminently to the Word, neglecting prayer, will become heady and doctrinal – likely to quarrel about "points," and be occupied with theoretical Christianity to the hurt of his soul and the irritation of his brethren. On the other hand, one who gives himself much to prayer while neglecting the Word is likely to become exceedingly introspective, mystical, and sometimes fanatical. But he who reads the word of God reverently and humbly, seeking to know the will of God, and then gives himself to prayer, confessing and judging what the Scriptures have condemned in his ways, and words, and thoughts, will have his soul drawn out in worship also, and thus grow both in grace and in knowledge, becoming a well-rounded follower of Christ. Apart from a knowledge of the Word, prayer will lack exceedingly in intelligence; for the objective must ever precede the subjective, but not be divorced therefrom.[1]

While in a spirit of reverence, the Jews prayed for the Lord to guide them. The fact that they spent as much time in prayer as they did studying Scripture speaks of their diligent desire for God's direction and blessing.

There is little doubt that Ezra was among this throng of people, but his name is not mentioned in Nehemiah 9 or 10. The Septuagint does insert the phrase "and Ezra said" at the beginning of verse 6 to indicate that he was the one speaking, but the Hebrew text does not refer to him. Ezra was the teacher who used Scripture to point God's erring people down the right way, but the matter of confessing sin, repenting of sin, and righting past wrongs now rested on the shoulders of the offenders. The guilty were now collectively before the Lord to know His mind and to honor Him. The High Priest Jeshua and other Levites led the congregation in a prayer of penitence, one that is similar to Ezra's prayer thirteen years earlier (Ezra 9).

In this prayer we have the history of the world as it relates to the nation of Israel:

The Creation of the World (v. 6)
The Call of Abraham (vv. 7-8)
The Exodus From Egypt (vv. 9-14)
The Wilderness Experience (vv. 15-23)
The Conquest of Canaan (vv. 24-25)
The Period of the Judges (vv. 26-29)
The Era of Pre-captivity Prophets (vv. 30-31)

In prayer the Jews repeatedly acknowledged God's goodness towards them and His holy character; God had been righteous in all His dealings with them. In fact, Jehovah had treated them much better than they deserved and they knew it. In an attitude of worship and praise, the Jews declared that Jehovah is the ...

God of Creation (v. 6)
God of Protection (v. 6)
God of Grace (vv. 7-8)
God who Answers Prayer (v. 9)
God of Deliverance (vv. 10-12)
God of Revelation (vv. 13-14)
God who Provides (v. 15)
God of Mercy (vv. 17-19, 27-28, 31)

What God did to create the nation of Israel and bring it into the Promised Land is summarized in verses 6-15. How Israel failed to keep God's Law and His righteous response as tempered with mercy is the focus of verses 16-32. The Jews had suffered much for their own disobedience, but they did unequivocally know that they worshipped the one true God, the Creator of all. Jehovah had uniquely revealed Himself to the Jews through the prophets and through Scripture and desired to be known and appreciated by them. He did the miraculous and answered their prayers to demonstrate His awesome presence among them, and in love, He had chastened them for their rebellion.

As the writer of Hebrews confirms, God's chastening of His children is a proof of His love for them (Heb. 12:6). God loves us too much to leave us the way we are. The Jews realized that as God's covenant people, they had repeatedly failed Him, but still He had not deserted them. Paul reminds Timothy of this wonderful truth: *"If we are faithless, He remains faithful; He cannot deny Himself"* (2 Tim. 2:13). We have the Lord's promise to bring us safely through to the conclusion of our salvation – glorification with Christ: *"Being confident of this very thing, that He who has begun a good work in you will complete it until the day of Jesus Christ"* (Phil. 1:6). *"For our citizenship is in heaven, from which we also eagerly wait for the Savior, the Lord Jesus Christ, who will transform our lowly body that it may be conformed to His glorious body, according to the working by which He is able even to subdue all things to Himself"* (Phil. 3:20-21). The Lord is faithful and has been shown faithful to His Word throughout Scripture and throughout history.

During the Water Gate Revival, the people came to appreciate the character of God, and they therefore knew that they had been the benefactors of His long-suffering nature. They discerned God's justness in all of His dealings with them (v. 33). Consequently, the prayer transitions from Israel's past to their present situation in verses 32-38. Understanding both the character of God and His past faithfulness, the Jews plead for His mercy to be shown to them. As David acknowledged, the only means of receiving forgiveness and being restored to God is by departing from sin and obtaining His mercy:

He is ever merciful, and lends; and his descendants are blessed. Depart from evil, and do good; and dwell forevermore. For the Lord loves justice, and does not forsake His saints; they are preserved forever, but the descendants of the wicked shall be cut off (Ps. 37:26-28).

187

This is also our incentive to turn back to the Lord, to confess our past failures, and to request forgiveness and restoration. History has shown that He longs to be in good fellowship with His children and, thus, always extends His loving arms to the wayward who are determined to come home again (Luke 15:20).

In pleading for mercy, the Jews confessed their failures and acknowledged that their punishment had been just. They were still suffering because of the sins of their forefathers and they knew it. They lamented over their present situation: they were servants of Persia (v. 36), heavily taxed, and subjected to forced labor and military service (v. 36). Past sin had caused them to be a distressed people, but they had experienced a change of heart through divine chastening and were eager to change their ways. They now wanted to obey God's Law and were willing to enter into a covenant with God promising their future allegiance and obedience (v. 38).

This should be the desire of every true child of God! Unfortunately, this high water mark in Jewish history did not last long, for when Nehemiah returned from Babylon a few years later, the Jews has regressed back into old sinful patterns; they broke their covenant. It was at about this time that God prompted the prophet Malachi to issue a final rebuke to His people. Divine silence then followed for four centuries until God's final message to the lost sheep of Israel would be delivered by His own Son, the promised Messiah (Heb. 1:1-3).

A Revival Meditation

Missionary and evangelist Roy Hession describes what must happen within our souls for the power of God to be outwardly demonstrated in our lives:

> Our wills must be broken to His will. To be broken is the beginning of revival. It is painful, it is humiliating, it is the only way. It is being 'Not I, but Christ,' and a 'C' is a bent 'I.' The Lord Jesus cannot live in us fully and reveal Himself through us until the proud self within us is broken. This simply means that the hard unyielding self, which justifies itself, wants its own way, stands up for its rights, and seeks its own glory, at last bows its head to God's will, admits it's wrong, gives up its own way to Jesus, surrenders its rights and discards its own glory – that the Lord Jesus might have all and be all. In other words, it is dying to self and self-attitudes.[2]

Consecration and Service
Nehemiah 10

In the last chapter, we witnessed that true confession of past sins and genuine repentance leads to a change in behavior. This is the type of repentance that is not to be repented of (2 Cor. 7:10). Sincere repentance is not just being sorry for the consequences of sin, but being sorry enough to forsake sin and obey God. As the Jews reviewed their history, they realized that their past failures were controlling their present conditions. There is an insanity to sin, but gripping truth restores a sound mind.

The Jews desired to go on with the Lord and to have His blessing and fellowship, rather than His chastening hand. Paul reiterates this same principle to new believers in Galatia: *"Do not be deceived, God is not mocked; for whatever a man sows, that he will also reap. For he who sows to his flesh will of the flesh reap corruption, but he who sows to the Spirit will of the Spirit reap everlasting life"* (Gal. 6:7-8). The Jews understood there could not be a genuine blessing unless they were obedient to the Word of God; therefore, the people entered into a signed covenant with the Lord in this chapter. The family and clan leaders willing to put their seal to the covenant are listed in verses 1-27.

The leaders of the people effectively put those they were accountable for under the obligation of the covenant. Nehemiah thus acknowledged that *"the rest of the people,"* having understood the Law, separated themselves from foreigners and consented to the terms of the covenant (v. 28). The first name on the list, as one might expect, was Nehemiah, the governor (v. 1). Next the religious leaders signed the covenant, including twenty-one priests (vv. 1-8) and seventeen Levites (vv. 9-13). The final group of signers consisted of forty-four family heads from the tribes of Benjamin and Judah (vv. 14-27). In all, eighty-three leaders of the people signed the covenant with God.

It is noteworthy that the Jewish leaders did set a good example to follow and that the Jews consented to follow their leaders, as unto the Lord. Peter affirms this is a good pattern to follow: *"Shepherd the flock of God which is among you, serving as overseers, not by compulsion but willingly, not for dishonest gain but eagerly; nor as being lords over those entrusted to you, but being examples to the flock"* (1 Pet. 5:2-3). Elders are to lead and be paradigms to those entrusted into their care. Recognizing that their leaders must give account to Christ, the Lord's people are commanded to obey them as unto the Lord, thus making the overseers' jobs easier (1 Thess. 5:12-13; Heb. 13:17).

The Jews did not consent to follow the Law of Ezra, nor of Nehemiah, but rather they were compelled to obey the Lord. Their forefathers had followed self-manufactured traditions which had resulted in the nation's divine chastening and their own exile. The preaching of God's Word produced sincere repentance within them, and they were now determined not to repeat previous offenses. With one accord, God's covenant people had progressed towards consecration by acknowledging their desire to obey God's Word.

In all, there were four areas of conduct that the Jews committed to be faithful in: they would not intermarry with foreigners (v. 30), they would keep the Sabbath day holy (v. 31), they would honor the Sabbath year agricultural prohibition (v. 31), and they would fund the upkeep of the temple and its workers through a yearly donation (v. 32). While the Law directed the Jews in these matters, Christians in the Church Age may glean application from these also.

The first offense to be corrected pertained to intermarriages with people of the land (v. 30). God's people throughout all dispensations of His working are to be holy, because He is holy (1 Pet. 1:16). Holiness has at its core the idea of separation – God is unique and separate from all of creation. Thus, His people are also to be unique in behavior (i.e. to morally act as He would) and to be separate from the world's enticing influences. The world has different forms: political, artistic, musical, religious, economic, etc. Biblically speaking, the "world" may refer to the world we live on (Earth), the world of things, the world of people, or the world system controlled by Satan. In the latter instance, the world represents a human society built up apart from God; it is human civilization with base motives and desires, the outworking of mankind's depraved state.

Worldliness, then, is any sphere from which the Lord Jesus is excluded. The world stands in opposition to Jesus Christ and His message because Satan is behind the scene, controlling the various systems of the world, and he despises Christ and those who identify with Him. Paul identifies Satan as *"the god of this age"* (2 Cor. 4:4) and *"the prince of the power of the air"* (Eph. 2:2). On three occasions the Lord Jesus said that Satan is *"the prince of this world"* (John 12:31, 14:30, 16:11). The world is Satan's delegated domain, but he must function within divine boundaries. God is holy, and He cannot tempt anyone to sin (Jas. 1:13), but Satan is allowed to test man's resolve to obey God.

Thus, Paul instructed the believers at Rome to present their bodies as a living sacrifice by not being conformed to the world (Rom. 12:1-2); he also exhorted the Christians at Corinth not to be unequally yoked with non-believers in associations, such as marriage and business partnerships (2 Cor. 6:12).

Israel had failed in both aspects; they had been conformed to corrupt Babylonian ideologies and they were intermarrying with the heathen of the land. Marrying and socially mingling with the people of the land had been a snare to this nation since the exodus from Egypt. Balaam successfully corrupted the Israelites, who were poised to enter the Promised Land, by leading them into idolatry through seductive Midianite women (Num. 25:1). The pagan prophet Balaam understood that no human army could defeat the approaching Israelites because God had blessed them. However, he also knew that Jehovah was a holy and jealous God and would be moved to punish His people if they provoked Him to do so. If we want God's blessing in our homes and in our local churches, we had better learn to practice separation from all that would defile ourselves and grieve the heart of God.

The second topic on the agenda of the covenant was failure to keep the Sabbath day holy (v. 31). Although the pattern of sanctifying the seventh day for the Lord was set up at the time of creation by God Himself (Gen. 2:1-3), it was not commanded until the Israelites were alone with God at Sinai. The fourth of the Ten Commandments issued by Moses at Sinai relates to the Sabbath day:

Remember the Sabbath day, to keep it holy. Six days you shall labor and do all your work, but the seventh day is the Sabbath of the Lord

191

your God. In it you shall do no work: you, nor your son, nor your daughter, nor your male servant, nor your female servant, nor your cattle, nor your stranger who is within your gates. For in six days the Lord made the heavens and the earth, the sea, and all that is in them, and rested the seventh day. Therefore the Lord blessed the Sabbath day and hallowed it (Ex. 20:8-11).

The first four of the Ten Commandments were decreed to enable the Jews to remain loyal and devoted to Jehovah by preventing misplaced affections. The prophet Isaiah explains why honoring the Sabbath day was important to the Lord and why the Jews would be blessed if they did so:

If you turn away your foot from the Sabbath, from doing your pleasure on My holy day, and call the Sabbath a delight, the holy day of the Lord honorable, and shall honor Him, not doing your own ways, nor finding your own pleasure, nor speaking your own words, then you shall delight yourself in the Lord; and I will cause you to ride on the high hills of the earth, and feed you with the heritage of Jacob your father. The mouth of the Lord has spoken (Isa. 58:13-14).

The Sabbath day, Saturday, was set aside to rest and to honor God. The Jews, their slaves, and their beasts of burden were all to rest on the Sabbath. Albert Barnes notes that the Jews were rewarded in three ways for keeping the Sabbath day holy: "(1) in great national prosperity, (2) in the lasting welfare of Jerusalem, and (3) in the wealth and piety of the people generally, indicated by their numerous sacrifices."[1] God always commands us to do what is morally right to do, but sometimes, what we are to do is right only because He commands it. Keeping the Sabbath day falls into the latter group, but regardless of why the commandment was issued, man is always blessed by doing what God says.

Why did God consider the Sabbath day observance to be an important part of Jewish life? Irving L. Jensen explains that it provided a challenging test of practical obedience for the Jews:

The real test of the heart's relation to God is obedience to His Word. One of the laws of Israel was the hallowing of the Sabbath by not working on that day (Jer. 17:21-22). The constant pressure of materialism upon the lives of all, including the people of God, made the keeping of such a commandment difficult, and for this reason this one commandment of the ten was a real test of the priority of the temporal or the eternal in the heart.[2]

God honors those who obey His commandments. Thus, the Sabbath day ordinance provided a simple test as to what God's people really valued – their own private affairs or what the Lord deemed important. The Lord is honored when His people remember and honor Him as requested, instead of doing what they are inclined to do for themselves on the day set aside for God. Today, the Church is not under the Law (Gal. 4:19-5:1); in fact, the Jews are no longer under the Law either (2 Cor. 3:6-18; Heb. 13:12-13), but the Ten Commandments still reflect God's moral standard to be lived out in His people (Rom. 3:20). The Law is not dead, but we are dead to it; that is, it has no judicial hold on Christians (Rom. 7:4-6). Christians are not commanded to keep the Sabbath, but there is a principle throughout Scripture of setting aside one day in seven to honor God, and the early Church set a precedent for gathering for this purpose on Sunday.

To draw a distinction between Christianity and the Law (and, more importantly, the humanized system of Judaism derived from it), the early Church met on Sunday, rather than Saturday. Christians continued to gather corporately on one day in seven to worship the Lord, but they did so on the first day of the week, the day of Christ's resurrection (Acts 20:7; 1 Cor. 16:2). This day is also referred to as "the Lord's Day" by the apostle John (Rev. 1:10). Let us seek to make the Lord's Day a special day for the Lord. Saints should put aside their own personal ambitions and gather to hear the preaching of the Word, to break bread, to pray, to encourage each other, and to engage in ministry which would draw people to Christ. The Lord's Day should be a special day for all spiritually-minded Christians – a day set aside to remember and honor the Lord with other believers.

For Nehemiah and his people, a third area of renewed commitment pertained to honoring the regulation of the Sabbatical year (v. 31). The Sabbatical year was to remind the Jews that God owned the land they dwelled in and that they were merely stewards of it (Lev. 25:23). Every seventh year the fields, the olive groves, and the vineyards were to receive a full year's rest. Whatever grew naturally during the Sabbath year was to be freely gleaned by the poor, and anything that remained was considered God's provision for the beasts of the field.

This was God's law of the land; unfortunately, the Jews had ignored this commandment. God kept track of this offense, and, in one lump sum of years, He gave the land its due – seventy years of rest (i.e. one-seventh of the four hundred ninety years the Jews did not honor the Sabbath year, per 2 Chron. 36:21). This judgment was realized during the Jews' exile to Babylon, proving once again that there are no loopholes in God's judicial system (Ex. 23:10-13).

The fourth grievance to correct related to maintaining and supporting the temple, or "the House of God," a term employed nine times by Nehemiah in verses 32-39. The Jews apparently realized they had neglected the temple built by Zerubbabel, even as the proper maintenance of Solomon's temple had been neglected at various times in their history. God's House should have been a high priority in the Jewish social economy; in fact, it should have been at the center of it. The temple was the location in which God desired the Jewish nation to gather for worship, sacrifice, and prayer.

What the people now realized was that their neglect of God's house was a direct reflection of their devotion to Jehovah. They were willing to take responsibility for the house of God, including its necessary financial support and upkeep. Each Jewish man was to contribute a third part of a shekel for the service of the temple (v. 32). Lots would be cast to see who would provide wood for the burnt offerings (v. 34). The Jews were to bring the firstfruit offerings to the temple and to pay their tithe to the Lord in order to support the priests, Levites, gate-keepers, and singers serving at the temple (vv. 35-39). In this section of Scripture (pertaining to the fourth commitment), the term "firstfruits" occurs three times, and terms "firstborn" and "firstling" are also mentioned. Clearly the Jews realized that God demanded and deserved their very best. If we withhold our best from the Lord, we commit a selfish form of idolatry (i.e. we value earthly relationships and things above heavenly things and the Lord Himself).

In the Church Age, the House of God is the Church, a living spiritual temple (1 Tim. 3:15). This is where we find the opportunity to engage in Christian service for the benefit of other believers. Every believer has their work of ministry to perform for the good of the entire body (Eph. 4:12, 16). Just as the Jews were not to forsake the House of

God, Christians should not forsake gathering together to worship, to learn, to pray and to enjoy fellowship with the Lord (Heb. 10:25).

Although Christians are not under the Law, they can, in effect, commit the same offenses against the Lord that the Jews did long ago. Just as the Jews entered into some commitments to right wrong behaviors, it is time for Christians to do the same. Mike Attwood suggests that believers contemplate these four areas of growth as they aspire to please the Lord:

1. To live a separated life, abstaining from that which is evil and clinging to that which is good! Not to marry an unbeliever, or to compromise with an unbelieving world when it comes to divine things.

2. To be subject to the Word of God, not just hearers but doers also.

3. To honor the Lord's Day and determine to be with the Lord's people unless our name is in the obituary column.

4. To work, serve, and support the activities of the House of God and make it central in my life.

The goal: To be done once and for all with me-first religion and acknowledge the crown rights of Jesus Christ to rule over my life.

A Revival Meditation

Does it grieve you, my friends, that the name of God is being taken in vain and desecrated? Does it grieve you that we are living in a godless age?... But, we are living in such an age and the main reason we should be praying about revival is that we are anxious to see God's name vindicated and His glory manifested. We should be anxious to see something happening that will arrest the nations, all the peoples, and cause them to stop and to think again.

— D. Martyn Lloyd Jones

Decision Time
Nehemiah 11

In the previous chapter, the Jews entered into a covenant with Jehovah. They pledged to refrain from marrying Gentiles, to honor the Sabbath day and the Sabbath year, and to financially support the temple's upkeep and ministers. Jewish leaders signed the contract under oath and acknowledged divine judgment would be warranted if they broke their agreement (10:29). Hopefully, the covenant would preclude a regression into old sinful patterns. The moral issues now dealt with, Nehemiah turned his attention to the practical matters of sustaining and securing the city of Jerusalem.

The Water Gate Revival recorded in chapters 8-10 rightly interrupted Nehemiah's logistical efforts to secure the city, which began in chapter 7. Chapter 11 picks up by addressing two main questions: Where should the Jews live? How should they serve the Lord? Jerusalem, as secured by the newly rebuilt wall, was voluminous but contained relatively few inhabitants; thus, the city was vulnerable to attack. In the event of an attack, the Jews who lived elsewhere could disappear into the rocky terrain, numerous caves, and deep caverns prevalent in the surrounding foothills, but the city-dwellers must depend on the defense of the city to elude trouble. The problem was that Jerusalem did not have enough citizens to defend it, nor to function properly, nor to adequately support temple operations. How would Nehemiah be able to encourage Jews to relocate to Jerusalem?

No doubt this would have been an arduous task if revival had not occurred. However, having experienced a spiritual awakening to the things of God, a notable group of Jews willingly volunteered to move to Jerusalem (v. 2). The Jewish rulers already resided in the city, thus setting a good example for others to follow (v. 1). Those who did not volunteer to relocate did willingly participate in the casting of lots. This was an acceptable method of determining the will of God in the Old

Testament era. *"The lot is cast into the lap, but its every decision is from the Lord"* (Prov. 16:33). The apostles also used this method to choose an apostle, Matthias, to replace Judas (Acts 1:26). There is no scriptural example of using lots to determine the will of God by Christians in the Church Age; instead of this, Scripture, the Holy Spirit, and the providential care of God are to guide the decisions of believers.

It was decided that one tenth of the remnant, as determined by the casting of lots, would take up residence in Jerusalem, while the remainder would abide in other cities. Thus, the chief concern of the people was not where they should reside, but rather, where was it that God wanted them to be. Some Jews seemed to sense God was beckoning them to live in Jerusalem, while others, not so sure, wanted an indication from the Lord where best to serve Him. Both attitudes are honoring to the Lord: answering the call of the Lord and being willing to go if called.

Missionaries are often asked to explain their call into a foreign land, but how many believers today have any spiritual justification for living where we do? Often we dwell where we do because of family influences, to pursue financial prosperity, or to enjoy a comfortable lifestyle or a pleasing view. Would not every Christian be better able to serve the Lord if he or she adopted the attitude of the Jews in Nehemiah 11 and said, "Lord, I want to reside at whatever location I can best serve You?" If we are not aspiring to this type of thinking, then what we are living for becomes quite evident – ourselves! The Lord Jesus put the matter this way: *"But seek first the kingdom of God and His righteousness, and all these things shall be added to you"* (Matt. 6:33-34).

The lots were cast and the matter was decided. Two lists of names finish out Nehemiah 11: those who did or would reside in Jerusalem (vv. 4-19), and those who would live elsewhere (vv. 20-36). After the casting of lots, Nehemiah was careful to assign and delegate municipal responsibilities in a way that everyone was involved and that promoted the orderly operation of the city. For example, the priests, as directed by their leadership, were to manage all the affairs associated with the temple sacrifices (vv. 10-14), the Levites and their leaders were to repair and maintain the temple and supervise its daily operation (v. 15-18), while others were chosen to guard the gates (v. 19). Pethahiah was appointed to be the official representative of Jewish interests at the Persian court (v. 24).

In the local assembly as well, good leadership recognizes the callings and gifts of individuals and then directs each person to the work of ministry for which they are best suited within the community of God's people. Every believer in the body of Christ has a work of ministry to perform for the good of the Church and for the glory of God (Eph. 4:12, 16). Thank the Lord for godly leaders who set a good example to follow and who can direct and equip others in such a way to reach their full potential for Christ. All members of the body are needed and all must be willing to serve the Lord wherever they are and in accordance with their divine appointment. Jim Elliot concisely put the matter this way: "Wherever you are – be all there!"

A Revival Meditation

MORAVIAN REVIVAL

This revival began in 1727. Prior to this, the settlers at Herrnhut could not live together in peace. Finally Count Zinzendorf gave all his time to work for a settlement of their differences. On the 12th of May, 1727, they all, with great joy, gave themselves afresh to God, and promised to bury their disputes forever. The following account of the revival is taken from the *History of the Moravians* by A. Bost:

> From that time there was a wonderful effusion of the Spirit on this happy church, until August the 13th when the measure of Divine grace seemed absolutely overflowing. Every day brought some new blessing.

> On the 22nd of July some brethren agreed to gather at stated times to a hill near Herrnhut, in order to pour out their souls to God in prayer and singing: On the Lord's day, the 10th of August, the minister Rothe was seized, in the midst of the assembly, with an unusual impulse. He threw himself upon his knees before God, and the whole assembly prostrated themselves with him under the same emotions. An uninterrupted course of singing and prayer, weeping and supplication, continued till midnight. All hearts were united in love.

The brethren held a Communion service on Friday, 13th. It was full of deep spiritual power and emotion. The whole assembly united in prayer to God, and then sang, 'My soul before Thee prostrate lies,' amidst tears and sobs, so that it could hardly be distinguished whether they were weeping or singing. The scene was so moving that the pastor could hardly tell what he saw or heard. A few days after the 13th of August, a remarkable revival took place among the children at Herrnhut and Bertholdsdorf.

On the 18th of August, all the children at the boarding school were seized with an extraordinary impulse of the Spirit, and passed the whole night in prayer. From this time, a constant work of God was going on in the minds of the children, in both places. No words can express the powerful operation of the Holy Spirit upon these children.

On the 25th of August the brethren began the ministry of continual prayer which continued for over a hundred years. They considered that, as in the ancient Temple the fire on the altar never ceased to burn, so in the Church, which is now the Temple of God, the prayers of the saints ought always to ascend to the Lord.

In January, 1728, the brethren held their first missionary meeting. This meeting was celebrated by meditations on different portions of Holy Scripture, and fervent prayers; in the midst of which the church experienced a remarkable enjoyment of the presence of the Spirit.

The Moravian Missions began in 1731. Work was commenced in the West Indies and Greenland. In the years that followed missionaries were sent to Labrador, North America, South America, South Africa, Asia, Australia, and many islands of the sea. The Moravians Missions have been a mighty force in the evangelization of the heathen, but we must remember that it all began in the revival in 1727.[1]

The Dedication of the Wall
Nehemiah 12

Chapter 12 is the climax in the book of Nehemiah: the wall has been marvelously finished, the Jews have experienced revival, and they have renewed their commitment to follow the Lord; now it is time to dedicate the wall. Nehemiah had publically praised God for each victory along the way, but it was appropriate at this time for the Jewish nation to publicly acknowledge God's greatness in this accomplishment. It would be a ceremony involving everyone and, hopefully, one not soon forgotten.

Before noting the details of this festive occasion, Nehemiah first records four distinct lists of names. The first list is of the priests and Levites who had returned from Babylon with Zerubbabel a century earlier (vv. 1-9). The second list comprises the names of Israel's high priests during the Babylonian captivity (vv. 10-11). Nehemiah realized that the lists of high priests, priests, and Levites in 1 Chronicles 6 concluded with the fall of Jerusalem: Jehozadak became the High Priest after his father Seraiah was killed during the Babylonian invasion of Jerusalem (1 Chron. 6:15). Nehemiah now supplies the names of the post-exilic high priests beginning with Joshua (Jeshua), who returned with Zerubbabel (Ezra 2:2) and concluding with Jaddua, a contemporary of Nehemiah. The third list contains the names of post-exilic priests (vv. 12-21), and the fourth, the names of post-exilic Levites (vv. 22-26). Nehemiah compiled the most up-to-date genealogies in his book, which he finished writing early in the reign of Darius the Persian (i.e. Darius II who began to reign in 423 BC).

Nehemiah had previously recorded the clan names of the priests and Levites who returned with Zerubbabel (Neh. 7), but apparently he thought it necessary to specifically identify those who had exercised faith and returned to Israel. These priests and Levites would have no lands to reclaim for a legacy, for Jehovah alone was to be their inheritance and they would dwell in cities. Why did Nehemiah prominently list the names of this former generation in his record? Matthew Henry provides an insightful answer to this question, saying it was "to keep in remembrance those good men, that posterity might know to whom they are beholden, under God for the happy revival and reestablishment of their religion among them."[1] In a sense, the Jews of Nehemiah's day owed a debt to these men, for they were building upon the heritage left behind by them – these names would remind the Jews of this fact.

Believers in the Church Age should also remember those who have left us with a godly heritage from which we still benefit. Many godly men and women have hazarded their lives to carry the precious gospel message to remote areas. Others have labored in doctrine to ensure we have a secure foundation of truth to build upon. Some have inspired us to think beyond where we are today to what could be. The writer of Hebrews thought it good for Jewish Christians to remember those from the Old Testament who had finished well, and to recall God's past faithfulness to them until their own sojourn on earth was complete (Heb. 11).

The same writer also reminds Christians to remember their leaders who finish their course honorably for the Lord: *"Remember those who rule over you, who have spoken the word of God to you, whose faith follow, considering the outcome of their conduct"* (Heb. 13:7). We too owe a debt to those who have gone before us that we might continue the work they willingly received and faithfully committed to us. May believers today endeavor to acquaint themselves with the stories of faithful saints from yesteryear. These men and women inspire us to move forward with optimism for the cause of Christ. May their zeal for God be a rebuke to our creature comforts and halfhearted Christianity. As Nehemiah and Ezra have shown us, it only takes a few sincere believers to rise up in unflinching faith and rebuild what has fallen into disgrace. These are saints of vision, of prayer, and of the Word of God; they have paved the way for others to experience revival also.

As previously alluded, Darius the Persian mentioned in verse 22 refers to Darius II, the successor of Artaxerxes I Longimanus. Darius II ruled from 423-404 BC. Since there are no references to Nehemiah's age in the text, it is hard to estimate how long he may have lived. When the book opens, he is second-in-command under King Artaxerxes. If he were 40 years old then, and 41 when he reached Jerusalem in 444 BC, he would have been 62 years old in 423 BC. when Darius II replaced Artaxerxes. Consequently, he probably wrote the book not long after 423 BC, and almost certainly before 400 BC.[2]

The dedication ceremony is discussed in verses 27-47. The ceremony needed to be announced and then sufficient time was required to gather the people, including the Levites, to Jerusalem. Next, the priests, the people, the gates, and the wall itself had to be purified by blood (vv. 27-30). The people were defiled and accordingly what they had built with their hands was also tainted in God's evaluation. This precedent was established by Moses before and after the tabernacle had been constructed and erected. The blood of a bullock and of a ram was used to purify the priests and the altar of sacrifice (Ex. 24:6-8, 29:12-21). Likewise, before reinstituting temple sacrifices and worship, King Hezekiah had the priests, the temple, and all of its articles ceremonially cleansed by blood. The priests also offered at that time sacrifices of reconciliation for the nation to make restitution to God for their past paganism (2 Chron. 29:20-24). Apparently, Nehemiah's wall dedication ceremony was patterned after Hezekiah's temple cleansing efforts.

Before the Jews ventured to the base of Mt. Sinai to meet Jehovah, Moses required the people to bathe and wash their clothes. Nehemiah and the rest of the Jews likely did the same thing before the dedication of the wall. By washing with water and purifying with blood, the Jews were acknowledging that they had defiled by sin what God had declared holy. God had accomplished a great feat in His people, but "dedication" means devotedness to God and consecration to serve Him, thus, that which has been devoted to God must first be cleansed and made acceptable (holy). The Jews were to dedicate their best to God, not just any unclean thing (Mal. 1:6-14). The same is true today; God desires believers to be daily consecrated to Him in holiness – to be living sacrifices.

> *I beseech you therefore, brethren, by the mercies of God, that you present your bodies a living sacrifice, holy, acceptable to God, which is your reasonable service. And do not be conformed to this world, but be transformed by the renewing of your mind, that you may prove*

what is that good and acceptable and perfect will of God (Rom. 12:1-2).

These verses summarize the New Testament equivalent to a dedication ceremony, which is to recur day after day – it is not a onetime event. We must keep ourselves clean from worldliness (Jas. 4:4), humanism (Col. 2:8), from unlawful lusting (Gal. 5:16-17), and the deeds of the flesh (Col. 3:5). A holy life is essential for dedicated service: this is a valuable lesson shown to us in Nehemiah 12.

The ceremony itself was to be an exhilarating event for the Jews who had gathered outside the western wall of the city (apparently at the Valley Gate). The fact that the Jews were not carrying swords and spears at this time indicates that the enemy had withdrawn from Jerusalem in defeat. Accordingly, with glad and merry hearts the people, as guided by their leaders, engaged in singing, music, and prayers of thanksgiving (v. 27). In elaborate fanfare, the Jewish procession divided into two groups and marched round the top of the wall; one group, led by Nehemiah, traveled counter-clockwise (v. 31), and the other group, following Ezra, journeyed clockwise about the city (v. 36). Both groups would meet again at the court of the Temple, where the dedication service would take place.

Nehemiah had the people walk on the wall they had labored to build as a testimony of their triumph. Tobiah had mocked them by asserting that even if a fox walked on the wall the Jews were building it would collapse (4:3). The journey of the entire Jewish remnant about the wall would remind them of all that God had accomplished, despite their adversaries! Their past investment of tears and perspiration now resulted in abundant joy and spectacular achievement. On this point, Mike Attwood shares a practical application for Christians to consider today:

> If there is no investment, there is no interest! The more we have invested in the work of God, the more precious it will be to us! We have a real concern for it, if our blood, sweat, and tears have been put into it. What is your interest in your local assembly? The more you put into it, the more precious it will become to you.

— Mike Attwood

As the Jews recalled Jehovah's faithfulness, they were prompted to praise, thank, and extol Him. The following key words define the tenor of the festive occasion: "joy" and "rejoicing" are mentioned six times (vv. 43-44), "singing," "singers," and "songs" occur eight times (vv. 27-29, 42-47), and "thankfulness" is referred to six times (vv. 24, 27, 31, 38, 40, 46). The entire scene is fostered in joy and thanksgiving. So resounding were their voices and instruments, *that the joy of Jerusalem was heard afar off"* (v. 43). When hearts are clean and dedicated to God, joy and thankfulness walk hand and hand. Likewise, it is good for us to call to mind what past feats the Lord has accomplished for us, that we too might be prompted to rejoice in Him.

> If true dedication marks us, God will receive His portion in praise and thanksgiving; we shall have joy in heart; and there will be no lack of gifts for the support of the work of God and of His servants.

> — F. B. Hole

In recent years the Jews had not experienced much to be happy about; their homeland had been brutally conquered and many of their countrymen slaughtered, while others were taken to Babylon as captives. In Babylon, the Jews at large did not feel like rejoicing; in fact, they did not want to sing the songs of Zion even when requested to do so by their captors:

> *By the rivers of Babylon, there we sat down, yea, we wept when we remembered Zion. We hung our harps upon the willows in the midst of it. For there those who carried us away captive asked of us a song, and those who plundered us requested mirth, saying, "Sing us one of the songs of Zion!" How shall we sing the Lord's song in a foreign land?* (Ps. 137:1-4).

The solution to their dismal outlook was a national revival. After returning to Israel by faith, they experienced a spiritual awakening; now their singing could not be restrained. Spiritual revival prompts praise, worship, thanksgiving, and a desire to return to the Lord a portion of what He has graciously bestowed. The Jews willingly gave tithes and firstfruit offerings to the Lord, which was God's provision to sustain the priests and Levites (vv. 44-47). As Harry Ironside notes, rejoicing in the Lord and giving to Him are always to be found together, no matter the dispensation in which one resides:

> One is reminded of the twofold offering of Heb. 13:15-16: *"By Him therefore let us offer the sacrifice of praise to God continually, that is, the fruit of our lips, giving thanks to His name. But to do good and to communicate, forget not: for with such sacrifices God is well pleased."* These two offerings should never be divorced – thanksgiving going up to God from grateful hearts, and benevolence flowing forth toward men, the practical expression of that gratitude. There is no surer indication of a low state in God's people than to find the poor among them left to suffer want, and the Lord's servants permitted to endure privation.[3]

The singing of God's covenant people was so robust, it could be heard from a great distance. Likewise, the joy of the Lord should inspire vigorous singing among Christians today! Might the redeemed, wherever they gather to the Lord Jesus Christ, lift their voices so that God's goodness might be known afar off. You might be a part of a small church gathering, but what we have to sing about is marvelous and spectacular – so let us lift the shingles off the roof for the glory of God!

A Revival Meditation

REVIVAL IN ROCHESTER IN 1830

After receiving many pressing calls to preach, Finney felt that as Rochester was the most needy – there were three Presbyterian Churches in a very low and divided state – it was the Lord's will that he should go there. Soon after he began to preach, the ministers came together, and a great improvement in the spiritual state of the churches was manifested. Finney said, "The three churches, and indeed Christians of every denomination, seemed to make common cause, and went to work with a will, to pull sinners out of the fire. The spirit of prayer was poured out powerfully, so much so, that some persons stayed away from the public services to pray, being unable to restrain their feelings under preaching. Mr. Abel Clary continued in Rochester as long as I did. The burden of his soul would frequently be so great that he would writhe and groan in agony. He never appeared in public, but gave himself wholly to prayer."

Soon there were some very marked conversions, one of the first being the wife of a prominent lawyer. The meetings became thronged with lawyers, physicians, and merchants. Many of the lawyers became very anxious, and freely attended the enquiry meetings. The revival took a tremendous hold of the High School. Nearly every teacher and student was converted. As a result, forty of those students became ministers, and a large number became foreign missionaries. The majority of the leading men and women in the city were converted. Some years later Dr. Beecher talking to Finney of this revival in Rochester, said, "That was the greatest revival of religion that the world has ever seen in so short a time. One hundred thousand were reported as having connected themselves with the churches as the result of that great revival." The mighty working of the Spirit of God, as in this revival, continued throughout Finney's long ministry.[4]

Spiritual Declension
Nehemiah 13

After governing Jerusalem for twelve years, Nehemiah returned to Babylon to resume his duties in the Persian court (5:14, 13:6). This interval of time had been requested by Nehemiah, and approved by Artaxerxes, prior to the cupbearer's departure from Babylon (2:6). Not long after his return to Babylon, Nehemiah became aware that the situation in Jerusalem had deteriorated. He again sought and obtained leave of the king in order to return to Jerusalem.

It is uncertain how long Nehemiah had been in Babylon, but an interval of six to ten years seems likely. Certainly Nehemiah would not have tolerated mixed marriages while present in Jerusalem and some of these unions (at his return) had produced children old enough to intelligently speak other languages (v. 24). Nehemiah's own age limits an interval much longer than ten years. It is also unknown how long he remained in Jerusalem to correct the problems identified in this chapter, but the trip was likely of a short duration. A stay longer than a few months may have been an affront to Artaxerxes' generosity in the matter.

Previously, the Jews had signed a covenant with Jehovah to refrain from the marriage of foreigners, to honor the Sabbath day and Sabbath year, and to support the temple and its Levite ministers (Neh. 10). Revival had occurred after Ezra had confronted the wayward nation with the Word of God. Yet, in a relatively short time, spiritual decline had again beset the Jewish nation. Ironically, the Jews were doing what they had promised not to do and were neglecting what they said they would do.

This blatant regression into apostasy likely prompted the ministry of Malachi, whose prophetic rebuke would initiate more than four centuries of divine silence. After that time, God would speak to His covenant people again by sending His own Son, the Lord Jesus Christ, to them. This would be God's greatest declaration of love for His people, for the message of peace that His Son would offer would ultimately require His own life to secure (Luke 2:8-14).

Nehemiah specifically acknowledged how the Jews had departed from the truth. First, they had failed to separate themselves from paganism; both Ammonites and Moabites were being accepted within their congregation. Even the temple had become home to foreigners, thus defiling it (vv. 4-7). Furthermore, some of the Jews had defiled themselves by marrying women of the land (vv. 23-30). Both of these offenses had been previously dealt with in recent history. Ezra and Nehemiah had each confronted the matter of forbidden associations some fifteen years earlier (9:2, 10:28), and Ezra had dealt with the intermarriage problem about thirty years earlier (Ezra 9 and 10).

Why were the Ammonites and Moabites restricted from worshipping Jehovah with the Jews? This was because they did not assist, but rather opposed, the pilgrimage of the Israelites from Egypt to Canaan (v. 2). Consequently, God forbade their acceptance into the congregation of God's people (v. 1). God desired a holy people that would be consecrated to Him alone, but throughout their entire history the Jewish nation displayed a propensity towards being a *"mixed multitude"* (v. 3). They had again proven that their spiritual resolve to live for God was weakened by unchecked lust.

Seeing that spiritual compromise was again rampant among God's people, Nehemiah was prompted to take stern measures. As in the days of the Water Gate Revival, correction began with the reading of the Law of Moses. After hearing God's Word, the Jews fell under prompt conviction and *"they separated from Israel all the mixed multitude"* (v. 3). Regrettably, the problem of associations ran deep and would require Nehemiah to directly confront the leaders of the people. Even Eliashib, the High Priest, had developed an alliance with the enemies of God.

Specifically, Eliashib had partnered with Tobiah (v. 4), the Ammonite who earlier had opposed Nehemiah's efforts to rebuild the wall so vehemently (4:3). Eliashib transformed a temple chamber in the court of the house of God into a stately residence for Tobiah (v. 5). This chamber had been originally used to store offerings and temple supplies (12:44, 13:7). Nehemiah entered this chamber and threw out all of Tobiah's belongings. He then had it cleansed, and the temple vessels and the meal offering supplies (including frankincense) restored to the room (vv. 8-9).

Nehemiah's courage and zeal for the house of God resembles that of the Lord Jesus Christ, who centuries later would also cleanse the temple. Having fashioned a whip out of several cords, He drove the animals, the merchants, and the money-changers from the temple and overturned the money-changers' tables (John 2:14-17). Sinful men had converted His Father's house, a place designated for prayer and worship, into a den of thieves and the Lord keenly felt the offense. Paul informs us that the body of the believer is the temple of the Lord (1 Cor. 6:19-20). Do we allow the enemy of God to enter into our inner chamber and dwell in the sanctuary of God? If the Lord held a whip over us, what behaviors would He adamantly want to drive out from our bodily temples?

Righteous indignation further motivated Nehemiah to also confront the matter of mixed marriages; some Jewish men had married foreign women, in direct violation of their covenant signed just a few years earlier (v. 23). As our first parents learned, forbidden fruit has an enticing appeal, but disastrous consequences. The Law of Moses clearly prohibited the Jews from marrying foreigners (Deut. 7:1-4), but nonetheless, some Jewish men were attracted to what was different and unfamiliar to them. Perhaps these foreign women looked more sensual and their lawless ways were more appealing to the Israelites. In Proverbs 7, Solomon warned his son of the destructive charm that a strange woman can have on a young man destitute of knowledge. Her seductive assault battered all five of his senses and, his lust aroused, he cast reason aside and yielded to her urging: *"He goes after her straightway, as an ox goes to the slaughter"* (Prov. 7:22). The sexual sin of the woman is to lure and the sin of the man is to follow after what he knows is morally wrong. Some Jewish men had cast reason aside and ignored the prohibition of the Law – now they would reap what they had sown.

However, there was more at play in this situation than the blatant disregard for the Law; the children of these mixed marriages could not speak Hebrew (v. 24). Their pagan mothers did not teach them the language of Zion, which meant the children would not receive biblical instruction, but would rather learn to worship the false gods of their mothers. Accordingly, these marriages angered the Lord; in fact, the prophet Malachi calls these mixed marriages an act of treachery and promised divine retribution on any Jewish man who married a foreigner (Mal. 2:10-12).

Nehemiah was so distraught over this widespread sin that he verbally and physically confronted the guilty:

> *So I contended with them and cursed them, struck some of them and pulled out their hair, and made them swear by God, saying, "You shall not give your daughters as wives to their sons, nor take their daughters for your sons or yourselves"* (Neh. 13:25).

Likely in his sixties, Nehemiah demonstrated all the tenacity and strength of a young man zealous for the Lord. The joy of the Lord was his strength (8:10). After literally knocking some sense into these rebel Jews, Nehemiah reminded them of how God had profoundly loved and blessed King Solomon; in fact, there was no king like him in all the earth (v. 26). Yet, even he, after marrying foreign women, engaged in idolatry and trespassed against God. If the wisest man upon the earth entered into sin by the marriage of foreign women, why then would any Jew now think this would be a wise thing to do (v. 27)?

Regrettably, even some of the priests, who were only to marry within the tribe of Levi, had also married foreigners (v. 28; Deut. 23:8-11). Eliashib, the high priest, had a grandson (the son of Joiada) who had wed Sanballat's daughter. Sanballat was the governor of Samaria and had strongly opposed Nehemiah's wall-building efforts (2:10, 19, 4:1-7, 6:1-14). This left Israel's high priest in league with God's enemy, thus Nehemiah showed no mercy to the son of Joiada, but chased him away, presumably out of the city. Josephus, in his *Antiquities*, states that this young man, Mathias, fled to Mount Gerizim with a copy of the Torah and created the rival religion of the Samaritans (John 4:20).

Nehemiah was a man sensitive to sin and mindful of the devastating consequences of unrepented transgressions. He called on God to judge all the violators, for they had defiled the priesthood. He personally ensured that all the priests and Levites purged themselves of their foreign wives and that they fulfilled their duties at the temple (v. 30).

Besides their failure to separate themselves from the heathen, a second area Nehemiah had to correct was the neglect of the house of God (v. 11); apparently, the temple and its servants were not being supported. The Jews had promised just a few years earlier to financially maintain the temple and its workers as part of their covenant with God (10:32-39). They had failed miserably in this commitment.

It seems that the Levites and singers were still performing their duties, but as soon as their obligations were complete, they rushed to labor in their fields. In other words, they needed secular employment in order to provide for their families; the Jews were not financially supporting their ministry through tithes and donations. Nehemiah reinstituted the tithing of grain, wine, and oil so that the Levites could serve with joy without being anxious about supporting their families. Nehemiah also appointed four men: a priest, a scribe, a Levite, and an assistant, who were all trustworthy, to oversee the distribution of the collections. These faithful men were to collect, store, and distribute fairly among their brethren what had been dedicated to the Lord by the people.

A third area of offense was the Jews' failure to honor the Sabbath day (vv. 15-22). They had pledged to honor God by keeping the Sabbath holy, as the Law demanded (10:31). Yet, Nehemiah observed people treading winepresses and loading and transporting of all kinds of agricultural goods on this day (v. 15). Merchants from Tyre even came to Jerusalem on the Sabbath day to sell fish and all kinds of other wares to God's people (v. 16). The Jews had again blatantly violated their agreement with the Lord – they had profaned this commandment (v. 17) and, accordingly, brought God's wrath upon Israel (v. 18).

Nehemiah's solution was to shut the city's gates as darkness fell on the eve of each Sabbath day and keep them closed until after the Sabbath (v. 19). This would prevent merchants from pulling carts loaded down with their wares into the city. Nehemiah also positioned men at the gates to ensure no one entered or left the city carrying a burden on the Sabbath. The merchants thought that they could out-smart Nehemiah's reforms by camping outside the gates of Jerusalem. Perhaps they were hoping to gain entrance after dark, or that some of the Jews would sneak out at night to buy some of their merchandise. Nehemiah warned the merchants to disperse or be removed by force; rather than having their goods confiscated or damaged, they chose to leave. Commenting on this scene, Charles Stanley encourages believers to also maintain a closed gate of separation from worldliness:

Then beware of the men of Tyre, who will offer their tempting wares before the wall. Keep the gates shut – oh, keep the gates closed. Let nothing come in to break your rest in Christ – your joy in God. We need much the lesson of the last chapter to keep the gates shut; it will be most offensive to men of Tyre, but most pleasing to our God. He alone could have given us such a picture of the day in which we live, and He alone could give us such a light for our feet. May He sanctify us by His word – His word is truth![1]

The Samaritan merchants learned Nehemiah was quite serious about enforcing the Sabbath day regulation of the Law – as long as he held a position of authority in the Persian Court, it would be a day completely set aside to honor the Lord. The wall of worldly exclusion would stand!

Summary

There are many lessons to learn from the book of Nehemiah, but perhaps this chapter presents one of the most important. With the Lord's help, it is possible to rebuild a ruined testimony, but such an effort must continue in the same truth it was established on. The nature of the depraved human heart is to withdraw from God. Sincere statements of dedication can effortlessly flow from our lips, but maintaining spiritual vigilance requires more than an emotional high.

The book of Nehemiah also shows us that the enemy is observant and will quickly move to confront a true work of God. Whether a personal ministry or the work of a local assembly within a community, Satan will vigorously oppose any true testimony of Christ. Various devices were employed by the adversary in an attempt to impede or stop the work on the wall: sidetracking God's people with questions and arguments, frustrating them by constant ridicule, threatening them with harm and death, stimulating greed to cause internal strife, and attacking God's leadership. Believers should not be ignorant of Satan's devices and expect such evil tactics as they labor for the Lord also. Nehemiah was able to keep focused on the objective because he committed his enemies to the Lord for judgment and continually prayed for and relied on God's grace to accomplish the work. This is a good example for us to follow!

Another important aspect of the book of Nehemiah is that God outlines His future plan for the nation of Israel through their experiences. Both Nehemiah and Ezra witnessed brief revivals which restored and consecrated the Jews to Jehovah and, thus, they received His blessing. Hamilton Smith explains that in a future day (i.e. the millennial reign of Christ), Jerusalem will be the scene in which God's covenant people will be restored to Him once and for all:

> In regard to Israel it was God's purpose to have His house in the city of Jerusalem, in the midst of a people dwelling in His Land. Connected with this purpose are three important principles. With the house there is the thought of God *dwelling;* with the city God *ruling;* and with the Nation and the Land God *blessing.* Where God dwells, there God must rule; and when God rules, God blesses. It is thus God's purpose to dwell in the midst of a redeemed people, ruling over them for their blessing. This purpose will be realized in a day to come.[2]

Lastly, Nehemiah teaches us that we are not only to respond to God's Word and come to Him in faith, but that we are to walk with Him in faith also. The Jews frequently responded with brokenness to calls of repentance, but then failed to continue in God's Word, thus regressing back into the same pitiful condition that had previously ensnared them. Today, those who respond to the gospel message must not only come to the cross to receive forgiveness, but must also be willing to follow Christ while bearing their own cross (Luke 9:23-24). This is Nehemiah's example; his devotion to the Lord never wavered. Whether confronted by intense opposition or the disappointing regression of his own people, Nehemiah learned to trust and rejoice in His God. In such times of distress, may we too recall to mind Nehemiah's charge to his fellow countrymen: *"The joy of the Lord is your strength"* (Neh. 8:10). Rejoicing is a choice (Phil. 1:18), and it is a command (1 Thess. 5:16). Rejoicing in truth revives the heart of the redeemed and opens the way for God to perform the spectacular – O God, revive us again!

A Revival Meditation

Evangelism, fine as it is, is not revival. After a singularly successful meeting, Billy Graham was asked, "Is this revival?" Graham replied, "No. When revival comes, I expect to see two things which we have not seen yet. First, a new sense of the holiness of God on the part of Christians; and second, a new sense of the sinfulness of sin on the part of Christians." We might add a third and closely-related indication of revival: a new working of the Holy Spirit in the local church. Why? For two big reasons, among others; first, because the Word of God calls for it; and second, because the world challenge calls for it.[3]

Closing Charge

I hope some of you will agree with me that it is of far greater importance that we have better Christians than that we have more of them! If we have any spiritual concerns, our most pressing obligation is to do all in our power to obtain a revival that will result in a reformed, revitalized, purified church. Each generation of Christians is the seed of the next, and degenerate seed is sure to produce a degenerate harvest – not a little better than but worse than the seed from which it sprang. Thus the direction will be down until vigorous, effective means are taken to improve the seed. Why is it easier to talk about revival than to experience it? Because followers of Christ must become personally and vitally involved in the death and resurrection of Christ. And this requires repentance, prayer, watchfulness, self-denial, detachment from the world, humility, obedience and cross carrying!

— A. W. Tozer

Esther

Overview of Esther

The Author
Though the writer supplies an eye-witness account of events occurring in Shushan during the reign of King Ahasuerus (Xerxes), no hint to the author's identity is provided. Some have speculated that Ezra or Nehemiah wrote this account, as both men had prominent positions during the reign of King Artaxerxes, Xerxes' son. Jewish tradition ascribes authorship to Mordecai. However, nothing in the text or its literary style can validate these conclusions. The New Testament does not refer to the book of Esther, so no help in identifying its author is found there. Given the pro-Hebrew theme and its exceptional outcome, the book was likely written by a Jew, not necessarily a prominent individual of that era.

The Date
The book supplies a firsthand account of the toppling of Haman and the thwarting of his evil plot in the early months of 473 B.C. The author also refers to the conclusion of King Ahasuerus' rule and the prominence of Mordecai in the kingdom at that time (10:2). Hence, the book was likely penned shortly after the king's death in 465 B.C, that is, in the early years of Artaxerxes' reign (464-424 B.C.). Artaxerxes would have certainly remembered the bizarre Jewish drama which unfolded during his father's reign, which may partly explain his generosity to both Ezra and Nehemiah a few years later.

Outline
1:1-2:18 – Esther's Rise to Prominence
2:19-4:3 – Haman's Plot to Exterminate the Jews
4:4-7:10 – Esther's Deliverance of Her People
8:1-9:19 – The Jews Overcome their Enemies
9:20-32 – The Feast of Purim

10:1-3 – Mordecai's Greatness

The Setting

Although Ezekiel, Daniel, and Jeremiah vividly describe the destruction of Jerusalem and the taking of Jewish captives, little is known of their actual captivity in Babylon. Only the books of Esther and Daniel supply a brief view of Jewish life while in that foreign land. The events chronicled in this book occur in the fifty-seven-year gap between Ezra chapters 1-6 (the rebuilding of the temple under Zerubbabel's leadership) and Ezra chapters 7-10 (the spiritual rebuilding of the people by the scribe Ezra).

The narrative commences in the third year of King Xerxes, 483 B.C. (1:3). Many Jews failed to return to Jerusalem under Cyrus' edict some fifty-five years earlier. The prophet Jeremiah had foretold that God would hand over His wayward people to Babylon for the purpose of purging their idols, then He would restore them to Israel and Himself after seventy years of exile (Jer. 25:11, 29:10). When this opportunity availed itself, the Jews were to leave Babylon and return to Palestine; there God would begin afresh with them (Jer. 50:8, 51:6). Unfortunately, the majority of the estranged Jewish nation had become acclimated to pagan and affluent Babylon and refused to return with Zerubbabel to rebuild Jehovah's temple. The events recorded within the book of Esther may have excited some Jews to return to Israel a few years later with Ezra and then Nehemiah.

Unique Tenor

Whenever God's people are settled in the world, they will lack reverence for Him and devalue the things important to Him. Accordingly, a cold spiritual tone permeates the entire story: God's name does not appear in the text, nor is He referred to by title or even a pronoun; neither is there any reference to His laws, His priesthood, His feasts or sacrifices. Other post-exile books, such as Ezra and Nehemiah, are marked by prayer, but no prayers are recorded in Esther, though fasting is mentioned. Obviously, prayers without God would be meaningless and at this juncture God is hidden from His disobedient people still residing in Babylon.

Though the Lord is not specifically referenced in the text, J. Sidlow Baxter notes that His personal name *Jehovah* is secretly revealed four times in the Hebrew text as an acrostic at crucial points in the story (1:20, 5:4, 5:13, 7:7). Also, the name *Ehyeh* (meaning "I am who I am"; Ex. 3:14) is found once in acrostic form (7:5).[1] These occurrences cannot be by chance because of the difficulty of constructing such form within the original language. These concealed occurrences of God's name in the text indicate that although God's people were estranged from Him, He was ever present with them. As John N. Darby elaborates, it is important to understand the spiritual tenor of the book in its dispensational context:

> The Book of Esther shows us the position of Israel, or, to speak more accurately, the position of the Jews, out of their own land, and looked at as under the hand of God, and as the object of His care. That He still cared for them (which this book proves to us), when they no longer held any position owned by God, and had, on their part, lost all title to His protection, is an extremely touching and important fact in the dealings of God. If, when His people are in such a state as this, God cannot reveal Himself to them – which is manifest – He yet continues to think of them. God reveals to us here, not an open interposition on His part in favor of His people, which could no longer take place, but that providential care which secured their existence and their preservation in the midst of their enemies.[2]

God was with His people, but He was standing in the shadows as He watched over them. Despite Jewish despondency, the narrative affirms God's faithfulness and devotion to His covenant people and His ability to safeguard them through the most unlikely means, including an orphaned Jewish captive named Esther.

Esther Devotions

Too Much Feasting
Esther 1

Ahasuerus (Xerxes) came to power in 486 B.C; he ruled over 127 provinces from Northern Africa to India (v. 1). His court was located in Shushan, one of three principal capital cities of the Persian Empire, the others being Achmetha and Babylon (v. 2). Located about two hundred miles east of Babylon on the Ulai Canal, Shushan had been the winter headquarters of the Babylonian Empire. This ancient city is within modern-day Iran and is sometimes referred to as Susa. Daniel resided there approximately sixty-six years earlier (Dan. 8:2) and in about forty years Nehemiah would serve as King Artaxerxes' cupbearer at this same location (Neh. 1:1).

This intriguing story begins in 483 B.C., the third year of Xerxes' reign (v. 3). The narrative mentions a 180-day feast hosted by Xerxes for his nobles from all districts in the empire (v. 4). It is likely that various officials arrived and departed at different times during this 180-day period. F. C. Cook notes that "feasts of extensive scale were not unusual in the East. ...Even ordinarily, the later Persian monarchs entertained at their table 15,000 persons."[1] Xerxes' purpose for this festive event was to impress his subjects with his wealth and dominion in order to solidify support for his planned invasion of Greece. He needed to convince his subordinates that he had sufficient resources to launch the incursion. His father Darius was killed at Marathon during Persia's first invasion into Greece in 490 B.C. Xerxes, desiring to avenge his father's death, had already spent two years planning to mount a second invasion (which he did launch in 481 B.C. after four years of preparation).

At the conclusion of the former feast for his nobles, an all-out seven-day bash was hosted by Xerxes; this party was held in his

221

elegantly decorated garden court and was open to the public (vv. 5-8). The royal colors of Persia, white and blue (or violet) were displayed in a canopy of high hanging awnings above the guests who were reclining on comfortable couches below. Besides plenty of food, the banquet furnished as much wine as each individual desired to drink. A vast number and variety of gold goblets were available to further enhance the imbibing experience. While the men were getting smashed with Xerxes, Queen Vashti also hosted a banquet for the women in the royal palace (v. 9). These women were mostly the wives of those men attending Xerxes' party.

Vashti may have been Amestris, who Xerxes married before ascending to the throne. If this is correct and she was deposed, as the text states, she may have recovered her former dignity in the latter years of Xerxes' reign. The Greek historian Herodotus writes: "I am informed that Amestris, the wife of Xerxes, when she had grown old, made return for her own life to the god who is said to be beneath the earth by burying twice seven children of Persians who were men of renown."[2] Amestris was remembered as a cold and cruel woman.

An inebriated Xerxes ordered seven of his eunuch-chamberlains to escort Queen Vashti to the men's party; the king desired to show his guests her stunning beauty (vv. 10-11). Although there is nothing in the text to suggest that the king was asking his wife to behave lewdly, Persian modesty required women to be veiled in public, meaning that the king's drunken whim was a breach of social etiquette. For Vashti to be displayed in front of a group of intoxicated men was beneath the dignity of a queen. Vashti chose not to degrade herself; she refused the king's inappropriate command which infuriated Xerxes (v. 12).

Clearly the relationship between the king and his queen was not an intimate one, nor one of common respect, but of form. It would be unconscionable for a Christian husband to parade his wife in front of other men for the purpose of inciting their lust or for her to desire such an exhibition. Paul exhorts women to dress modestly and to adorn themselves in non-enticing ways to better express godliness in good works (1 Tim. 2:9-11). A sister in the Lord should have no desire to cause another man to lust after her (excluding her husband, of course). Solomon explains to us that the sexual sin of the woman is to lure (Prov. 7:21) and the sexual sin of the man is to follow (Prov. 7:22). It seems that after one thousand wives and concubines, Solomon finally understood that unchecked gazing leads to more lusting and more lusting promotes immoral behavior. He said, *"The eye is not satisfied with seeing, nor the ear filled with hearing"* (Eccl. 1:8). Our flesh nature is never gratified – it always wants more than what is reasonable and what God permits.

Practically speaking, a wife needs to work at appealing to her husband's senses to arouse him, while her husband should appeal to his wife's emotions to affirm security and his singular devotion. The goal is mutual satisfaction, so there will be no need or yearning for sexual gratification elsewhere. Sadly, Xerxes' request told Vashti that she was not significant to him, nor was she secure in his love, a fact that he would soon prove. Vashti was wrong to disobey her husband's authority, but the eagerness of Xerxes to publicly degrade his wife was the greater offense – an insult to decency.

Persian Law endorsed the death penalty for anyone rebelling against the king's command (vv. 13-15). The king consulted with his wise men on the matter. Memucan, speaking on behalf of the group, informed the king that Vashti's behavior not only set a bad precedent of rebellion, but also would inspired women throughout the empire to despise their husband's authority (vv. 16-18). Their counsel was to dispose of the queen (perhaps by death, but more likely through banishment) and to transfer *"her royal position to another who is better than she"* (v. 19), the idea being, that Vashti's harsh punishment for disobeying her husband would send a solemn warning to all women throughout the kingdom not to dishonor their husbands (v. 20).

Xerxes is manipulated to render rash and imprudent decisions by conniving men more than once in this story. Memucan's advice pleases the king and he signs it into law (v. 21). Vashti is deposed and letters detailing her crime and punishment along with a decree stating that a *"man should be master in his own house"* were dispatched in various languages to every province in the kingdom (v. 22). Clearly all Xerxes' luxurious pleasure seeking and intoxicating revelries created the opportunity for foolishness to reign over Shushan and the queen, who had shown better commonsense than the king, paid the price.

Meditation

Comfort and prosperity have never enriched the world as much as adversity has.

— Billy Graham

Esther Becomes Queen
Esther 2

The king later realized that he had overreacted and regretted his decision to banish Vashti (v. 1). There is approximately a four-year interim between Vashti's dismissal in chapter 1 and Esther's wedding recorded in this chapter in late 479 B.C (v. 16). History records that Xerxes had withdrawn from the palace for about two years while warring with Greece. Although he had enjoyed initial successes in Greece, Xerxes returned to Babylon shortly after the Greek fleet decimated his navy forces in the ill-planned Battle of Salamis in September, 480 B.C. Since the women potentially selected to replace Vashti went through a one year preparation period, it seems likely that Xerxes' remorse over Vashti aligned with his disappointing retreat from Greece.

The king's counselors perceived that Xerxes was having second thoughts about what he had done to Vashti, so they proposed that a thorough search be made for young beautiful virgins in order to find a suitable woman that could replace Queen Vashti (v. 2). These young women would then be sequestered within the women's quarters of the Shushan citadel (v. 3). The young virgins would be in the care of Hegai, the king's eunuch, while they underwent excessive preparation (beautification and purification treatments) before spending a night with the king. The one he fancied the most would become queen. This idea appealed to the carnal appetite of the king and he agreed to the proposition (v. 4).

The counselors, who had persuaded the king to dispose of Vashti previously, probably felt that they needed to devise an irresistible plan to prevent themselves from becoming recipients of the king's wrath. After all, they were the ones who had coaxed him into doing something that he really did not want to do. There was also the possibility that Vashti (i.e., if she was banished and not executed) might avenge herself

225

against the king's counselors if she regained her royal position. This was a pagan culture ruled by licentious cravings, so it should be no surprise that their proposed plan defamed women.

The Bible exhorts men not to judge a woman by her outward features, but to value her for her inner beauty (i.e., purity, virtuous character, diligence, and devotion to the Lord). The psalmist likens a virtuous wife to a fruitful vine adorning the home with beauty: *"Your wife shall be like a fruitful vine in the very heart of your house"* (Ps. 128:3). Peter informs us that God considers the wholesome character and a gentle and submissive spirit in a woman very precious – this is true beauty that is to be appreciated (1 Pet. 3:2-4). A woman's outward beauty can be completely negated by acts of indiscretion (Prov. 11:22). The believer realizes that *"though our outward man is perishing, yet the inward man is being renewed day by day"* (2 Cor. 4:16). May we learn to appreciate what God values as precious in others and not be conned into glamorizing what appeals to the flesh and is but a fading glory.

In chapter 1, we met King Xerxes and Queen Vashti (who then abruptly disappears from the narrative forever). In chapter 2 we are introduced to two more protagonists in the story, Mordecai (v. 5) and Hadassah (v. 7). Mordecai was a descendant of Kish, a Benjamite (v. 5). Kish had been among the Jewish captives exiled to Babylon with King Jeconiah by Nebuchadnezzar in 597 B.C (v. 6). The prophet Ezekiel was also among these enslaved Jews; Daniel had been exiled to Babylon eight years earlier in 605 B.C. Kish was probably Mordecai's grandfather. We learn that Hadassah was a young and beautiful Jewish woman who had been orphaned at an early age. She was adopted by her older cousin Mordecai, who cared for her as his own daughter (v. 7). Hadassah's Persian name was Esther (v. 7).

In regards to the king's command, many young virgins were forcibly removed from their homes and brought to the citadel and placed in Hegai's care (v. 8). Some commentators pose the notion that Esther entered a beauty contest to earn the privilege of being a woman in the king's harem, but this is a mistaken idea. The passive Hebrew voice indicates that these women were not invited, or given a choice in the matter; they "were gathered." To resist the king's command would certainly have resulted in death.

Why did the Lord permit this indecent practice to occur? Why would He allow these young women to be degraded to mere objects of sexual pleasure? All of man's misery in the world is the result of human sin. God's Law to the Jews identified what sin was and put restraints on some wrong behaviors in an attempt to curb unchecked selfishness which would harm their society (e.g. adultery and slavery). Humanity cannot blame God for the terrible consequences of our sin. For reasons beyond our understanding, He often chooses not to directly intervene, but mysteriously operates within deplorable situations to accomplish a greater good which is usually so improbable, that we must conclude that God is great! Although Esther's circumstances are most distasteful, God would use Esther to achieve good out of them. Thankfully, God works to glorify Himself and preserve His people even when His name is not being made known among them.

Joseph endured thirteen years of slavery and imprisonment because of his brother's jealousy, but God used that experience to exalt Joseph to a position in Egypt where he could effectively preserve the nation of Israel during a seven-year famine. He explained to his brethren: *"But as for you, you meant evil against me; but God meant it for good, in order to bring it about as it is this day, to save many people alive"* (Gen. 50:20). Decency cannot endorse Esther's circumstances, but God would use this repulsive situation to elevate her to a position in which she could be an advocate for her people. The fact that Hegai immediately favored Esther and provided her with the best accommodations and an ample allowance indicates that divine providence was at work (v. 9). James Vernon McGee defines for us the meaning of "providence":

> Providence is the way that God is directing the universe. He is moving it into tomorrow − He is moving it into the future by His providence. Providence means "to provide." ... Providence means that the hand of God is in the glove of human events. ... The Book of Esther provides us with the greatest illustrations of the providence of God. Although His name is never mentioned, we see His providence in each page of this wonderful little book.[1]

Esther obeyed Mordecai's instruction and did not reveal her Jewish ethnicity (vv. 10, 20). Mordecai was trying to protect Esther from the

227

anti-Semitic mood prevalent in the empire. Esther's name was Persian and evidently she looked enough like the locals to pass for one of them. Mordecai took Esther's care seriously; he ventured to the women's quarters every day until she was married to receive word as to how Esther was faring (v. 11). He was not permitted to see her as these women were in isolation to protect their moral purity and to undergo beautification treatments. Each maiden would undergo a year's preparation for a single purpose – to have sex with the king when it became her turn (v. 12). Josephus summarizes the scene before us:

> So she was handed over to one of the eunuchs to take care of her; and she was given every attention, and was anointed freely with spices and with costly ointments, such as women's bodies required. This treatment was enjoyed for six months by the virgins, who were in number four hundred. When the eunuch thought the virgins had been sufficiently purified in the forementioned time and were now fit to go to the king's bed, he sent one every day to have sex with the king. After the king had intercourse with her he sent her straight back to the eunuch. But when Esther came to him, he was pleased with her and fell in love with the maiden, and made her his lawful wife. He held a wedding for her on the twelfth month, which was called Adar, of the seventh year of his reign.[2]

When the time came to spend a night with the king, each woman was given whatever apparel, jewelry, cosmetics, adornments, etc. she requested in an attempt to impress the king (v. 13). After having sexual interaction with the king, the women were kept at a different location as part of the king's harem. As the king's concubines, they would only be sent for again if summoned by name (v. 14). According to F. C. Cook, Persian monarchs maintained, besides their legitimate wives, as many as 300 or 400 concubines.[3] Obviously, many women never saw the king's face again after losing their virginity. They would be cared for and protected in the palace, but would never know the joys of true family life, including bearing and nurturing children.

When Esther's turn came, she adhered to Hegai's counsel and received nothing more than what he thought was best for her to have. Because *"Esther obtained favor in the sight of all who saw her"* (v. 15), it is likely that Hegai instructed Esther to rely on her natural beauty instead of outward garnishments to sway the king. Her turn came in the tenth month of the seventh year of Xerxes' reign (i.e., 479 B.C.; v. 16). Xerxes' harem was large, so the fact that Xerxes favored Esther above all other women again indicated that the Lord was controlling the selection process (v. 17). Some have suggested that Esther's behavior was one of a harlot. This is an ignorant conclusion, as Esther was not paid for her services, nor did she voluntarily agree to be one of the women in the selection process. Matthew Henry reminds us of the sordid royal practices of Persian kings at this time:

> Esther was preferred as queen. Those who suggest that Esther committed sin to come at this dignity do not consider the custom of those times and countries. Everyone that the king took was married to him, and was his wife, though of a lower rank.[4]

When the king slept with a woman, it was understood that she was now married to him, she was set aside for him only, and she would receive his protection and care. But Esther was more than a concubine; she became Xerxes' wife of highest standing and the Queen of Persia. A royal holiday was proclaimed throughout the kingdom (this may have included the release of taxation for one year) and all of Xerxes' officials and servants were invited to attend an elaborate wedding feast, where the king bestowed gifts to the attendees in accordance with his great wealth (v. 18).

Although enthralled with his new queen, verse 19 notes the king's erotic disposition. More *"virgins were gathered together a second time."* Xerxes was still intent upon building his harem to ensure his sexual pleasure despite his marriage to Esther. We also learn from the same verse that Mordecai was a man of some political stature, for he sat within the king's gate. In the Jewish economy, that would indicate some sort of judicial role, but in the Persian culture he may have only been a doorkeeper tasked with protecting the king.

In the execution of his duty, Mordecai overheard a plot by two of the king's eunuch-doorkeepers, Bigthan and Teresh, to assassinate Xerxes (v. 21). Such plots were not uncommon in Persian history; in fact, Xerxes would be later murdered by Artabanus, the captain of the guard, and Aspamitras, his chamberlain.[5] Mordecai informed Esther, who told the king in Mordecai's name (v. 22). The plot was foiled, the accused were tried and hanged; the matter was recorded in the court chronicles in the presence of the king (v. 23). The final three verses of chapter 2 have an immense bearing on events later in the book, which is why the information is recorded.

As previously mentioned, some commentators attack Esther's character, for she did not have the same moral convictions of young Daniel who would not eat the king's food because it violated Jewish Law and his conscience. However, Daniel was a young man who was taught the Law from his youth and had a unique prophetic calling in the affairs of Israel. Esther was a Jewish orphan whose family had lived in pagan Babylon for nearly 120 years without the Law of God being publicly taught. Certainly the Mosaic Law prohibited fornication and marrying a Gentile, but what Esther knew of the Law is uncertain and she had no choice in being accosted and sequestered in the palace. This author wonders what the moral condition of Christians would be today if all their Bibles, commentaries, recorded messages, and Christian literature and music had been suddenly confiscated 120 years ago. Let us be careful in condemning the conduct of others who may be yet ignorant of God's ways; rather, let us concentrate on obeying what we do understand of God's will so that others will have a good example to follow.

Meditation

None are more unjust in their judgments of others than those who have a high opinion of themselves.

— Charles Spurgeon

Haman's Conspiracy
Esther 3

The initial phrase "After these things" refers to a five-year pause in the narrative from Esther's coronation in the seventh year of Xerxes (2:16) to the instigation of Haman's plot against the Jewish people in the twelfth year of Xerxes (v. 7). Chapter 3 introduces us to the final key character of this story, Haman. He was an Agagite, a royal descendant of Hammedatha of the Amalekites (Agag was a royal title; 1 Sam. 15:8). Xerxes promoted Haman to a position over the princes of his kingdom and apparently was second in command after Xerxes (v. 1).

The King ordered his subjects to honor Haman when in his presence; most chose to bow; however, Mordecai would not show respect to Haman in this manner. Whether this was a matter of personal pride or religious conviction is difficult to assert, but there is nothing in the text to indicate that Mordecai was rebelling against Haman's authority (v. 2). Those with Mordecai at the king's gate noticed his behavior and challenged his actions, insinuating that he was disobeying the king's command (v. 3). Mordecai likely showed respect in another manner, but he did refuse to bow down before Haman as others did. After Haman's plot was made public, Mordecai did not even stand up in Haman's presence (5:9).

Mordecai explained to his colleagues that he was a Jew (v. 4). The Law prohibited Jews from revering anyone but their God, Jehovah (Ex. 20:5, 23:24), a conviction that three Jewish captives in Babylon named Shadrach, Meshach, and Abed-nego were willing to die for (Dan. 3:16-18). The fact that Haman had not noticed Mordecai's behavior until others desiring to earn Haman's favor informed him about it, suggests that Mordecai's public actions were not disrespectful; rather, he did not render the type of homage Haman coveted (v. 5).

Haman was infuriated by the news and after learning that Mordecai was a Jew, he sought vengeance not only on Mordecai, but all Jewish people everywhere (v. 6). A superstitious Haman sought direction from his heathen gods to determine the proper date for annihilating the Jews. The Pur (a lot) was cast on the first day of the New Year (perhaps by a pagan priest or magician) to determine the proper month for the genocide; the twelfth month was indicated. Ironically, *Pur* later became the basis for choosing the name of *Purim* to commemorate the foiling of Haman's plot.

Although the lot here was cast by a corrupt man, Proverbs 16:33 states that God controls the lot to confirm His purposes: *"The lot is cast into the lap, but its every decision is from the Lord."* In Joshua's day, through the casting of two lots, each tribe received the very portion that had been promised to them by prophetic utterance centuries earlier. This confirmed that a sovereign God was in full control of the distribution process. When God governs His creation, nothing is left to chance. This can be seen in that the twelfth month was chosen, providing the maximum time, nearly a full year, for the situation to be remedied.

Having the date for his sinister plot decided, the next step was to convince King Xerxes of its essential good for the Persian Empire. Haman propositioned the king:

> *There is a certain people scattered and dispersed among the people in all the provinces of your kingdom; their laws are different from all other people's, and they do not keep the king's laws. Therefore it is not fitting for the king to let them remain. If it pleases the king, let a decree be written that they be destroyed, and I will pay ten thousand talents of silver into the hands of those who do the work, to bring it into the king's treasuries* (vv. 8-9).

It is interesting that Haman did not identify the specific people group he wanted to exterminate, as perhaps Xerxes knew some of them and would balk at his plan. Haman briefly noted how different these people were from the normal populace and that their laws were contrary to the king's laws. Haman probably knew nothing of Jewish laws, but was merely thinking of the one instance where Mordecai refused to bow down before him as the king commanded. Sadly,

Xerxes did not ask who these people were, indicating that either he explicitly trusted Haman or that he was an apathetic monarch who cared more about his finances than the welfare of his subjects.

The war with Greece had gone poorly and Xerxes had debts to pay, so the idea of an additional ten thousand talents (about 375 tons) of silver in his coffer was appealing. This was an incredible sum of money (about 240 million dollars in today's economy; 2016). According to Herodotus, the regular revenue of the Persian king consisted of 14,560 talents of silver.[1] If the same talent is meant, Haman was offering Xerxes about two-thirds of a year's total revenue in order to enact his law. The king did not hesitate; he took the signet ring from his hand and passed it to Haman, which gave him the authority to draft a law of his liking: to eliminate his enemies and plunder their possessions (vv. 10-11). The king's scribes were called and Haman's law, written in the king's name, was signed on the thirteenth day of the first month (v. 12). This meant that in exactly eleven months the law was to be executed.

When used metaphorically in Scripture, each of the numbers from one to forty holds a particular meaning; the following are a few examples of how the number thirteen is used in Scripture to show rebellion. The number thirteen is first mentioned in the Bible when five Jordanian kings rebelled against Chedorlaomer (Gen. 14:4). There were thirteen years of silence after Abraham doubted God's promise and fathered Ishmael, after which God reminded Abraham of His covenant thirteen times (Gen. 17). There were thirteen judges who ministered to Israel during the time when *"every man did what was right in their own eyes"* (Judg. 17:6). Satan, or the Dragon, is spoken of thirteen times in Revelation. Throughout Scripture, the number thirteen is associated with rebellion, and this is likely the determining factor as to why Haman's plot to destroy the Jews was set for the thirteenth day of the month (Est. 3:13). The choice of day and month indicates that God was controlling this situation, despite all Haman's conniving.

Letters announcing this ruthless statute were swiftly delivered by couriers throughout all 127 provinces of the empire (vv. 14-15). Subjects of the kingdom were *"to destroy, to kill, and to annihilate all the Jews, both young and old, little children and women, in one day, on the thirteenth day of the twelfth month, which is the month of Adar, and to plunder their possessions"* (v. 13). After the law was signed and sent out by couriers, the king and Haman toasted their accomplishment.

However, the law was not well-received by those in the capital city of Shushan; in fact, many were bewildered by it (v. 16).

Even for a society marked by brutality, this senseless and cold-blooded atrocity was shocking. The Jews were not traitors; they had committed no crimes against the empire to justify this massacre. Perhaps other minorities within the kingdom were wondering whether they might be next to be eradicated by Xerxes. In the minds of the common people, the king and his high minister had greatly erred. In time, Xerxes would realize just how wrong he was to nonchalantly affirm Haman's law.

Beyond the narrative, there is a broader truth revealed in Scripture concerning the ongoing confrontation between the Jews and the Amalekites, which commenced during the Israelites' exodus from Egypt a millennium earlier. Amalek was the grandson of profane Esau, *"who for one morsel of food sold his birthright"* (Heb. 12:16). Consequently, both Esau and Amalek are used in Scripture to picture lusting flesh which continues to war against God's people. The children of Israel had hardly quenched their thirst from the water flowing out from the rock at Horeb when they were threatened by the Amalekites (Ex. 17). Amalek means "war-like" and Amalekites have always lived up to their patriarch's name. The attack of the Amalekites occurred about two months after the Exodus when God's people were tired and weary (Duet. 25:17-18) – this is often when the flesh is most successful in swaying believers from doing what is honoring to the Lord.

Under Joshua's leadership and Moses' intercession, Amalek was beaten that day, but not destroyed; indeed, the war against the Amalekites would rage on from generation to generation (Ex. 17:16). The new nature of the believer received at regeneration cannot sin (1 Jn. 3:9) and therefore also continually wars against the flesh nature: *"For the flesh lusts against the Spirit, and the Spirit against the flesh; and these are contrary to one another, so that you do not do the things that you wish"* (Gal. 5:17). There is nothing in the old nature that can please God (Rom. 8:8) – only when our vessels are under God's control do we have the capacity to please Him.

Like the Amalekites, the believer's flesh lives on and must be defeated again and again for the Christian to be a witness for Christ in the world, for the deeds of the flesh oppose God. Paul understood what would happen if he did not keep his flesh under control – he would suffer a shipwrecked testimony for Christ.

> *And everyone who competes for the prize is temperate in all things. Now they do it to obtain a perishable crown, but we for an imperishable crown. Therefore I run thus: not with uncertainty. Thus I fight: not as one who beats the air. But I discipline my body and bring it into subjection, lest, when I have preached to others, I myself should become disqualified* (1 Cor. 9:25-27).

Victory over one's flesh requires the removal of that which entices the flesh to dissatisfaction and, as Paul says, a willingness to land blows against one's own carnal appetites. To keep the flesh in subjection requires constant discipline, no matter how mature one is in Christ. Such is the believer's conflict until glorification; then, every soldier of the cross will have the final victory. At the Judgment Seat of Christ, those who took this challenge seriously will be rewarded with an imperishable crown.

Though there will be no literal Amalekites in the Millennial Kingdom of Christ, sinful flesh will still exist on earth during that era, but in submission to Christ's rule. This means that it will not be until the Eternal State that Exodus 17:14 will ultimately be realized: *"I will utterly blot out the remembrance of Amalek from under heaven."* At the Great White Throne Judgment, God will completely do away with any wicked thing throughout all His new creation; no sin of any kind will exist in God's kingdom and all believers will be eternally thankful for its eradication!

Meditation

> Till that day [Christ's rule on earth] come, whatever may be the vivid picture of coming blessing, there is always a dark shadow. There is an enemy; there is one that tries to frustrate all the plans of God: and, of all the races of the earth, there was one that was particularly hostile to God's people of old – the Amalekites; so much so that Jehovah swore and called upon His people to carry on perpetual war against that race. For He promised to blot them out from under heaven.[2]

— William Kelly

Fasting and Courage
Esther 4

The Jews, as an enslaved people in the Persian Empire, had no rights per se, thus they perceived the king's edict as a serious threat to their existence. Many, including Mordecai, tore their clothes, wore sackcloth, fasted, and mourned bitterly (vv. 1-3). Such was the Jewish custom to publicly signify deep sorrow and anguish of soul (Jer. 49:3; Dan. 9:3). Mordecai probably felt the travesty of Haman's plot more keenly than anyone, for it was his impertinence that spawned the lethal decree against his people. Mordecai's example of publicly identifying with God's people and their unjust plight is one to follow, suggests Matthew Henry:

> Mordecai cried bitterly, rent his clothes, and put on sackcloth (vv. 1-2). He not only thus vented his grief, but proclaimed it, that all might take notice of it that he was not ashamed to own himself a friend to the Jews, and a fellow-sufferer with them, their brother and companion in tribulation. ... It was nobly done thus publicly to espouse what he knew to be a righteous cause, and the cause of God, even when it seemed a desperate and a sinking cause.[1]

Civil affairs and edicts that disdain the name of Christ and oppress His Church should cause us to do more than to sorrow privately. Believers should be willing to expose the unfruitful works of darkness and beseech the Lord openly to act against what is known to be corrupt (Eph. 5:11). A few years later, Ezra (a Jewish priest with political rank in the Persian Empire) tore his clothes and cast himself down in the dirt in front of the new temple in Jerusalem to publicly pray and bewail the pitiful spiritual condition of God's people. A great revival immediately broke out among God's people (Ezra 8). Here Mordecai identifies with his people and traverses the streets of Shushan weeping bitterly in response to the injustice of Haman's law.

236

Because he was wearing sackcloth, he could not assume his normal occupation within the king's gate, but rather remained in the city square in front of the king's gate. After hearing of Mordecai's civic exhibition from her attendants, Esther sent him proper attire. Mordecai refused her provision – he would not discard his sackcloth, but would continue mourning publicly (v. 4). Esther then sent Hathach, one of the king's eunuchs assigned to her, to inquire of Mordecai about the matter (vv. 5-6). Mordecai informed Hathach of the deal Haman had struck with the king to destroy the Jewish people and provided him a copy of the law to show Esther (v. 7). Mordecai further requested that Esther would petition the king on behalf of her people; Hathach then returned to Esther and told him all that he had learned (vv. 8-9).

After hearing this information, Esther relayed the following answer to Mordecai through Hathach (v. 10):

All the king's servants and the people of the king's provinces know that any man or woman who goes into the inner court to the king, who has not been called, he has but one law: put all to death, except the one to whom the king holds out the golden scepter, that he may live. Yet I myself have not been called to go in to the king these thirty days (v. 11).

We might wonder why Esther had to converse through a third person with Mordecai, her cousin and father by adoption. Esther was the Queen of Persian; she lived an isolated life within the palace walls, which better ensured her protection and purity. She was unaware of Haman's edict because of her secluded environment; she was cut off from public information and normal lines of communication. In order to speak with Mordecai, she would have needed the king's permission, which would have then aroused suspicion about her ethnicity, a matter that she had kept secret.

From Esther's reply, we may suppose that Xerxes may not have been quite as enthralled with Esther as he initially was five years earlier, for she had not even seen the king for thirty days. Perhaps a rub had developed between the king and the queen and he was satisfying his sensual pleasure by other women in his harem. Regardless, Esther understood the law of the royal court – no one was permitted into the king's presence unless summoned. Anyone who dared encroach was executed unless the king extended his golden scepter to that individual, symbolizing that mercy was being offered to the intruder. Esther informed Mordecai that since a month had passed without her interacting with the king, a favorable response by the king towards her intrusion into his court was at best questionable. Certainly the king's rash dealings with Vashti weighed heavily on Esther's mind.

Esther's message was delivered to Mordecai, who immediately answered Esther (v. 12):

Do not think in your heart that you will escape in the king's palace any more than all the other Jews. For if you remain completely silent at this time, relief and deliverance will arise for the Jews from another place, but you and your father's house will perish. Yet who knows whether you have come to the kingdom for such a time as this? (vv. 13-14).

Mordecai warned Esther that this decree was against her and her family also. The law of the Persians could not be rescinded or ignored, meaning that even though she was the Queen of Persia, she would still be executed for being a Jew. If Esther did nothing, she would perish anyway and God would deliver His people through another means. Given the circumstances, would it not be better to risk petitioning the king?

Esther's reply to Mordecai conveyed her resolve to honor Mordecai's wishes and to seek the king's assistance no matter the personal cost to her (v. 15):

Go, gather all the Jews who are present in Shushan, and fast for me; neither eat nor drink for three days, night or day. My maids and I will fast likewise. And so I will go to the king, which is against the law; and if I perish, I perish! (v. 16).

Her infamous response to Mordecai, *"If I perish, I perish"* conveys her selfless courage, an underlying hope in divine intervention, and her desire to please Mordecai. After hearing her reply, Mordecai departed from the city square and fasted for three days as Esther had requested; Esther and her maids did the same. There is nothing in the narrative to suggest that Mordecai and Esther were deeply religious, but their actions do show an overall confidence in Jehovah concerning the welfare of His covenant people. Prayer is not mentioned in the text, yet Mordecai's reference to inevitable "deliverance" in verse 14 indicates his faith in divine assistance to resolve their distressing situation. In summary, their fasting could have had no other objective but to gain God's favor in the course of events Esther was determined to pursue.

The writer of Hebrews explains to us what true faith is: *"Now faith is the substance of things hoped for, the evidence of things not seen"* (Heb. 11:1-2). Why could the Lord's disciples face death with confidence? Because they knew who Jesus Christ was and trusted Him explicitly. Mordecai realized that he could not just pull himself up by his bootstraps and smile and say today is a happy day and everything is going to be great. True faith is not displayed with fake smiles or by acting happy when all is disturbing, but rather in knowing God and trusting Him to not act contrary to His character or His promises. In mourning and fasting, Mordecai and Esther are displaying that kind of resolve in their God, though as a third generation of exiled Jews, they knew little of His ways. It is encouraging to know that no matter what measure of spiritual growth we have attained, the Lord is always ready to act on the genuine prayers of His people when offered with confidence and in humility.

Meditation

Faith is a deliberate confidence in the character of God whose ways you cannot understand at the time.

— Oswald Chambers

Esther's Banquet
Esther 5

Esther was true to her word, and after three days of fasting with her attendants, she put on her royal attire and stood at the entrance to the king's inner courtroom (v. 1). Xerxes was sitting on his throne, which faced this entrance. At this moment Esther is completely helpless – she now has two death sentences against her, although Haman's law condemning her to death is still unknown at this time. The king looks up and notices his queen; no doubt there was an intense silence as everyone was wondering what Xerxes would do in response to this imposition. Given his favorable response, perhaps Xerxes even smiled at his queen as he held out his golden scepter to her (v. 2). The only way for Esther to avoid execution was to acknowledge acceptance of the king's mercy. This she does by stepping forward and touching his scepter.

What a wonderful picture of God's mercy we have before us. Each of us was born into this world bearing two death sentences: an appointment with physical death, because we were born spiritually dead (i.e., separated from God; John 3:18; Rom. 5:12). Thankfully, the Lord Jesus nailed our death sentences to His cross (Col. 2:14) and bore the judgment for our sin two thousand years ago. This one time act satisfied God's judicial anger concerning our offenses against Him. Hence, the solution to both calamities is found in the One who sits on God's throne in heaven and Who is quite willing to extend mercy to those who request it by faith. The Lord Jesus said that He was the only means for lost sinners to be restored to God: *"I am the way, the truth, and the life. No one comes to the Father except through Me"* (John 14:6). And Peter reminds us that God *"is longsuffering toward us, not willing that any should perish but that all should come to repentance"* (2 Pet. 3:9). Through Christ, God can extend the divine scepter of mercy to all those who will acknowledge their sinful condition and trust in Christ alone for salvation. Through Him we avoid hell and receive eternal life and spiritual restoration with God; we also have the hope of overcoming physical death through resurrection and the receipt of a glorified body (1 Thess. 4:13-18).

Understanding that the Queen would not risk death to venture into his presence unrequested unless the matter was urgent, Xerxes addresses Esther kindly: *"What do you wish, Queen Esther? What is your request? It shall be given to you – up to half the kingdom!"* (v. 3). "Up to half the kingdom" was a common figure of speech which meant the king would grant any request of his queen, if reasonable. Here we are reminded that the Lord does not merely grant mercy to the undeserving, but also abundant grace to satisfy all legitimate need. Hence Paul could encourage the believers at Philippi with this promise: *"And my God shall supply all your need according to His riches in glory by Christ Jesus"* (Phil. 4:19). How is this possible? Grace is always available to those in need or distress *"because He* [Christ] *continues forever, has an unchangeable priesthood"* (Heb. 7:24). Presently, Christ sits on His Father's throne in heaven and is the believer's High Priest (Heb. 6:20). Xerxes did not invite Esther to come to the throne, but the writer of Hebrews reminds Christians that they have an open invitation: *"Let us therefore come boldly to the throne of grace, that we may obtain mercy and find grace to help in time of need"* (Heb. 4:16). In Christ, we find mercy to escape judgment and grace to overcome every trial and to satisfy all our needs.

What a relief to Esther's heart – the king favored her and encouraged her! In regards to the just cause that she was willing to die for, she had said, *"If I perish, I perish"* but it was not to be. Esther exhibits the same kind of dedication the Lord Jesus exhorts believers to have in their service to Him: *"If anyone desires to come after Me, let him deny himself, and take up his cross daily, and follow Me. For whoever desires to save his life will lose it, but whoever loses his life for My sake will save it"* (Luke 9:23-24). Esther was willing to lose her life to gain a better one for her countrymen. She put herself in the hands of a pagan Gentile king, but as Matthew Henry points out, believers today have a much better throne to seek and Advocate to petition:

Esther came to a proud, imperious man; but we come to the God of love and grace. She was not called, but we are; the Spirit says, Come, and the Bride says, Come. She had a law against her, we have a promise, many a promise, in favor of us; Ask, and it shall be given you. She had no friend to go with her, or to plead for her; on the contrary, he that was then the king's favorite, was her enemy; but we have an Advocate with the Father, in whom he is well pleased. Let us therefore come boldly to the throne of grace.[1]

Esther did not reveal the particular burden of her soul at this time, but merely requested the king and Haman attend a banquet that she had prepared for them (v. 4). Evidently, the Lord put it in her heart not to reveal the matter at this juncture. The king agreed and Haman was immediately summoned to attend. That very day, the two most powerful people in the Persian Empire privately dined with Esther as she had requested (v. 5).

After the main meal was eaten, it was customary in Persia to continue the banquet with fruits and wine. It was at this time that Xerxes, sensing that Esther had much more on her mind than feasting with her king, again inquired of her request. Before she answered, he again affirmed his desire to grant her request if it was reasonable (v. 6). Given Xerxes' readiness to oblige Esther, we might wonder why she only bid the king and Haman to return tomorrow for another banquet before informing the king of her dire appeal (vv. 7-8). William MacDonald suggests several reasons why Esther reacted this way:

1. She wanted time to ingratiate herself with the king, having apparently been out of favor with him (4:9-12).
2. Her courage failed her both times (i.e., in the throne room and at the first banquet).
3. She wanted to build up an element of suspense and impress upon the king that her business was vitally important and no mere whim.
4. She wanted to inflate Haman's pride and take him off guard before she exposed him as a vicious murderer.[2]

Perhaps elements of some or all the above entered into Esther's patient strategy, one that she had carefully thought through during the previous three days of fasting. She epitomizes the words of Isaiah: *"Whoever believes will not act hastily"* (Isa. 28:16). True faith is not easily rattled or fostered in rash behavior; it serenely rests in the providential care of an omnipotent and omniscient God. For this reason, *The Christian's Friend* magazine extols Esther's patient resolve to overcome the adversary of her people:

> Esther may be observed to stand in very near fellowship with the mind of God. She seems as though she had observed the divine method with these proud adversaries; for she takes God's own way exactly with wicked Haman. She is not in haste. She lays her plans to let the heart of that Amalekite fill itself to the brim with pride that he might fall, according to the divine way, in the moment of its most towering presumption. She has "the golden scepter" on her side and with it the king's promise to give her whatever she might ask, even to the half of his kingdom. But she is patient. She bids the king and Haman to her banquet of wine. They come; and again the half of the kingdom is put within her grasp. But she is still patient, and bids them a second time. Is this, I ask, mere patience? Is this mere calmness and self-possession, or nothing more (however excellent that would be) than the contradiction of the heat and impatience of the wicked?[3]

Regardless of what her reasoning may have been, it becomes clear in chapter 6 that certain elements of God's sovereign plan had yet to be realized in order to achieve the greatest deliverance of His people – Esther's patience was therefore rewarded.

A joyful Haman was puffed up more than ever after departing from Esther's banquet for home, that is, until he saw Mordecai in the king's gate (v. 9). Mordecai did not even stand up, per Persian protocol, to acknowledge Haman's presence. Haman suppressed his indignation towards Mordecai and once home, called together his wife Zeresh and his friends to boast of his wealth, prosperity, and political achievements (vv. 10-11). He also informed them of the banquet he had enjoyed with the king and the queen that day and that Queen Esther had again invited both of them to attend a second feast the following day (v. 12). Since Haman was boasting of the second banquet, we can assume that the king did accept Esther's second invitation, although this point is not mentioned in the text.

From Haman's perspective, all was going well except for the irritation of the Jew Mordecai at the king's gate (v. 13). Self-admiring and self-flattering people are self-deceived, and the higher they exalt themselves, the more impatient their contempt is for those who defile them or rather, reject their exaggerated self-assessment. Haman was a proud, self-centered man – he was high on himself.

Those in his audience suggested that Haman should have gallows seventy-five feet high quickly constructed and that in the morning he should suggest to the king that Mordecai should be hung on the gallows that he had prepared (v. 14). If the request was granted he would be able to happily attend Esther's banquet because the man who vexed his soul would be dead. Perhaps Haman viewed Mordecai as the only Jew with enough clout to mount opposition to his extermination plans. Regardless of his egotistical reasoning, one fact is inescapable; Haman wanted a noose around Mordecai's neck.

Meditation

> The natural life in each of us is something self-centered, something that wants to be petted and admired, to take advantage of other lives, to exploit the whole universe.
>
> — C. S. Lewis

> Self-righteousness is the devil's masterpiece to make us think well of ourselves.
>
> — Thomas Adams

The King's Insomnia
Esther 6

In this chapter we learn of the benefit obtained because Esther did wait an extra day to reveal her petition to the king. Xerxes had asked his queen twice as to the nature of her request, but she chose to delay answering him. The queen had risked her life to approach him, then twice denied his inquiries to know what the urgency was – that did not make sense to the king. Whether there were other pressing matters of state we do not know, but certainly this domestic quandary was on the king's mind and sleep evaded him (v. 1). Haman had every reason to sleep well that night: he had enjoyed a lovely banquet with the king and queen and looked forward to another; he also was comforted by his plans to end Mordecia's life and to wipe out the Jews altogether. But Haman did not know that the God of the Jews inscribes his sovereign subplots within the plots of evil men to accomplish His purposes.

What better way to try to fall asleep than to read something quite boring, so the king commanded one of his attendants to read aloud the court chronicles. It was during this recitation that Xerxes was reminded that his servant Mordecai had foiled a plot against his life by two disgruntled doorkeepers at the king's gate (2:21-23), but nothing had been done to honor him (vv. 2-3). Note the improbability of all the following events occurring together: the king's insomnia, the decision to read the chronicles (now containing twelve years of history), the reading of the exact portion about Mordecai's heroics, the king's inquiry as to how Mordecai was rewarded, the king's desire to immediately honor Mordecai, and Haman's planned visit the next morning to ask for Mordecai's life.

Clearly, God was exercising His sovereign control over the king's heart to ensure he would have a favorable opinion of Mordecai at the time of Esther's banquet the next day in order to react unfavorably against Haman. Jehovah had already worked in the hearts of the two previous Persian kings: Cyrus had fulfilled Isaiah's prophecy of returning the exiled Jews to Jerusalem to rebuild the temple (Ezra 1) and Darius had promoted the prophet Daniel to be second in command under him (Dan. 6).

When Haman came to see the king the next morning, he had every intention of asking Xerxes for permission to hang Mordecai, but immediately after being admitted to the inner courtroom, the king interrupted Haman's intended request with a question (vv. 3-4): *"What shall be done for the man whom the king delights to honor?"* (v. 6). Egotistical Haman had no thought of anyone but himself and hence he was caught in his own snare (v. 7): "I am prime minister; I was given the king's signet ring; I alone attended Esther's banquet with the king – who else could the king possibly be thinking of but ME?" Having ensured himself that the king could only be thinking of him, Haman suggested that an honor higher than any ever conferred to one of the king's subjects be granted to the individual who the king highly esteems. Then Haman went on to describe exactly what should be done to accomplish this goal:

> *Let a royal robe be brought which the king has worn, and a horse on which the king has ridden, which has a royal crest placed on its head. Then let this robe and horse be delivered to the hand of one of the king's most noble princes, that he may array the man whom the king delights to honor. Then parade him on horseback through the city square, and proclaim before him: "Thus shall it be done to the man whom the king delights to honor!"* (vv. 8-9).

This all sounded good to the king, so he responded favorably to Haman's suggestion: *"Hurry, take the robe and the horse, as you have suggested, and do so for Mordecai the Jew who sits within the king's gate! Leave nothing undone of all that you have spoken"* (v. 10). Haman must have been speechless; the king delighted in the same individual he wanted to execute that very day and worse, Haman was commanded to parade his chief antagonist through the streets of Shushan and proclaim to everyone the king's esteem for him. Haman was to honor Mordecai, the Jew, in the exact manner he had ascribed to the king and this he did (v. 11). This is the first of five times Mordecai is called "the Jew" apparently to highlight the fact that one from the people group Haman sought to extinguish had received high repute in the Persian Empire.

It is relatively easy for us to rejoice in Haman's shame and snobbishly conclude, "He got what he deserved," until we realize that we are fashioned from the same corrupt moral fabric that Haman was cut from. Each of us has the same propensity to be selfish and proud. May we not merely cheer Haman's deserved downfall, but consider Matthew Henry's warning against the destructive nature of deceitful pride:

> See how men's pride deceives them. The deceitfulness of our own hearts appears in nothing more than in the conceit we have of ourselves and our own performances: against which we should constantly watch and pray. Haman thought the king loved and valued no one but himself, but he was deceived. We should suspect that the esteem which others profess for us is not so great as it seems to be, that we may not think too well of ourselves, nor trust too much in others. How Haman is struck, when the king bids him do honor to Mordecai the Jew, the very man whom he hated above all men, whose ruin he was now designing![1]

Solomon informs us that pride is the primary fountainhead from which strife springs: *"By pride comes nothing but strife, but with the well-advised is wisdom"* (Prov. 13:10). Nothing good can come from pride! This is why Paul admonished the believers at Philippi to follow Christ's example of selfless humility: *"Let nothing be done through strife or vainglory; but in lowliness of mind let each esteem others better than themselves"* (Phil. 2:3; KJV). As R. C. Chapman attests, this is the best defense against the pride that naturally consumes us:

> In 1 Corinthians 15:28 we read: *"Then shall the Son also Himself be subject,"* and in Revelation, *"The throne of God and of the Lamb."* Christ is forever the Shepherd and forever the Lamb, and it is the lowly or little Lamb, the diminutive being used. There is an infiniteness in the lowliness of the blessed Lamb, and He is now at the utmost of His lowliness. Satan took upon himself the form of a master, being created a servant; instead of serving in obedience he would be lord, and "the condemnation of the devil" is in his self-will; he chose to take to himself what belonged only to God. What a

rebuke to the devil the exaltation of the Son of God will be to all eternity – a mirror in which to see his own folly! Acquaintance with the Cross of Christ brings me to nothing! Let any thought of self-exaltation be to me as a serpent; I have nothing to do but to kill it![2]

Strife is the devil's way to get one's way, but lowliness permits God to judge legitimate wrongs His way, which is always the best outcome. How do we know this is true? Vengeance (justified wrath for sin) is the Lord's alone (Rom. 12:19); only He can rightly dispense wrath to humble the proud heart (Job 40:11-12); the wrath of man does not work the righteousness of God (Jas. 1:20). Harry A. Ironside suggests genuine humility is evidence that one possesses God-fearing wisdom:

> Nothing is more detestable in God's sight than pride on the part of creatures who have absolutely nothing to be proud of. This was the condemnation of the devil – self-exaltation. ... Humility is an indication of true wisdom. It characterizes the man who has learned to judge himself correctly in the presence of God.[3]

Although our determination and natural abilities, as in Haman's case, may secure for us fame and wealth, such status will be short-lived if accompanied by pride, an attitude void of proper reverence for God: *"The righteousness of the blameless will direct his way aright, but the wicked will fall by his own wickedness"* (Prov. 11:5). Let us therefore not trust in the uncertainty of riches, but rather let us put our confidence in the Lord, who freely bestows to us all good things to enjoy (1 Tim. 6:17-19; Jas. 1:17).

Through God's providential care of His people, Haman, the enemy of the Jews, was brought low, and Mordecai, the weeping humble Jew, was exalted. Haman could not bear his shame; he covered his head and quickly made his way home. In contrast, Mordecai was not puffed up by the king's honor; he returned to his normal duties at the king's gate (v. 12). Indeed, honor is well bestowed on those who do not think themselves above their calling and place of service.

Haman's wife and friends saw the king's honoring of Mordecai at Haman's expense as a bad omen that the Jews would have victory over Haman, and they were correct (v. 13). But at least Haman was consoled by the fact that he was in good favor with the king and that he had been summoned alone to Esther's private banquets (v. 14).

Meditation

The fear of the Lord prolongs days,
But the years of the wicked will be shortened.
The hope of the righteous will be gladness,
But the expectation of the wicked will perish.
The way of the Lord is strength for the upright,
But destruction will come to the workers of iniquity.
The righteous will never be removed,
But the wicked will not inhabit the earth (Prov. 10:27-30).

Esther's Urgent Plea
Esther 7

King Xerxes had suffered a sleepless night and Haman had a busy morning parading Mordecai before the people, but both arrived at Esther's banquet at the appointed time (v. 1). Xerxes asked his wife for a third time what her request was and his utmost intention of granting it, if reasonable (v. 2). Neither the king nor Haman had any idea of what was coming.

The long suspense was over; Queen Esther revealed her petition to Xerxes: *"If I have found favor in your sight, O king, and if it pleases the king, let my life be given me at my petition, and my people at my request"* (v. 3). The king was stunned by this request, flabbergasted that his beloved wife, the Queen of Persia, had become a beggar in his presence. Esther continued, *"For we have been sold, my people and I, to be destroyed, to be killed, and to be annihilated. Had we been sold as male and female slaves, I would have held my tongue, although the enemy could never compensate for the king's loss"* (v. 4). If the decree had pertained to the hardship of slavery only and not the annihilation of her people, she would have remained silent. Esther had no desire to meddle in political affairs, but being a woman of sincere conviction she could not sit idly by in the safe confines of the palace and watch the slaughter of her people. On their behalf she was compelled to plead for mercy. Having identified her ethnicity, Esther bravely takes her place with her condemned people. William Kelly suggests that Esther's emotional appeal struck the right chord with her husband:

> Not only all the affections of the king burst out at this insult that was done to the one that he loved above all in the kingdom; but more: there was the audacious presumption that should attempt the

destruction of the queen and all the queen's people — of all her people without even the king's knowledge. Who could be the traitor?[1]

The intensity of the story has been building since her initial intrusion into the king's courtroom two chapters earlier, but now the passionate and articulate appeal of Esther had reached deeply into the king's heart. He immediately demands, *"Who is he, and where is he, who would dare presume in his heart to do such a thing?"* (v. 5). In other words, "Tell me, my beloved, who wants to kill you?" Having brought the discussion to its desired crescendo, a likely sobbing Esther blurts out: *"The adversary and enemy is this wicked Haman!"* (v. 6). Haman was a selfish man who only thought of himself. He thought he was the man the king wanted to honor in chapter 6, but was not, and it is doubtful that he thought he was the awful scoundrel that Esther was describing until the moment she indicted him. Strike one against Haman.

This is one of the greatest moments of surprise recorded in Scripture; neither Xerxes nor Haman had a clue that Esther was a condemned Jew. Haman is instantly filled with terror – he knows his life is in jeopardy. The king never thought that Haman's plot would have such far-reaching implication to him personally. Enraged Xerxes leaves the room in order to clear his head and think through his options: *"Then the king arose in his wrath from the banquet of wine and went into the palace garden"* (v. 8). Those who act in self-will sooner or later will suffer self-reproach.

Haman, however, felt no remorse or regret for his actions; rather, to preserve his life, he pleads with the only person who could sway the king's anger against him, the queen, *"for he saw that evil was determined against him by the king"* (v. 8). Apparently, the king lingered in the garden long enough for Haman to cast himself on the couch that Esther was sitting upon to grovel for his life. This behavior was a breach of proper etiquette and after returning to the room and finding Haman in such a position next to Esther, the king accused Haman of wanting to assault the queen and in his very presence (v. 9). Strike two.

Immediately upon hearing this charge, the king's servants quickly arrested Haman and covered his head. Then, strike three: Harbonah, one of the eunuchs said to the king, *"Look! The gallows, fifty cubits high, which Haman made for Mordecai, who spoke good on the king's behalf, is standing at the house of Haman."* The king was further shocked by this news; Haman wanted to hang the very man he had just publicly honored, a man who had foiled a plot against his life. The king's reply was curt, *"Hang him on it!"* And that is what happened; afterwards we read the king's wrath subsided (v. 10).

Solomon's warning rings true: *"He who earnestly seeks good finds favor, but trouble will come to him who seeks evil. He who trusts in his riches will fall, but the righteous will flourish like foliage"* (Prov. 11:27-28). Paul also reminds us: *"Do not be deceived, God is not mocked; for whatever a man sows, that he will also reap. For he who sows to his flesh will of the flesh reap corruption"* (Gal 6:7-8a). The enemy of God's people had social status, political clout, vast wealth, and even the king's ear, but God brought it all to nothing in a moment of time through the courage and patience of Esther.

What began as a bad day for Haman turned out to be his last day to trouble God's people – the Lord knows how to humble our adversaries, silence our critics, and remove those who would cause us harm. At this juncture we might well consider God's question to Abraham after being told that he and his elderly wife were going to have a baby boy: *"Is anything too hard for the Lord?"* (Gen. 18:14). It is a rhetorical question that God continues to answer in miraculous ways!

Meditation

In consideration of Esther's petition to Xerxes, Matthew Henry provides this lovely devotional thought:

> If the love of life causes earnest pleadings with those that can only kill the body, how fervent should our prayers be to Him who is able to destroy both body and soul in hell! How should we pray for the salvation of our relatives, friends, and all around us! When we petition great men, we must be cautious not to give them offence; even just complaints must often be kept back. But when we approach the King of kings with reverence, we cannot ask or expect too much. Though nothing but wrath be our due, God is able and willing to do exceeding abundantly, even beyond all we can ask or think.[2]

252

A Royal Decree
Esther 8

God had ensnared the Jew's cruel adversary in his own evil plot against them. But though Haman was dead, his devilish work against God's people had not been undone; they were still in peril. Jews throughout the entire empire remained under a death sentence according to Persian law.

For the first time Esther informs Xerxes that the man who saved his life, Mordecai, was her cousin, and also her adoptive father (v. 1). The trust which the king had erroneously extended Haman by the giving of his signet ring was now conferred to Mordecai to do what was right – the king trusted Mordecai (v. 2). Even after his death, we see how God had reversed the roles of Haman and Mordecai; the latter now had the honor and political power of the former.

There is another facet of this story which is quite remarkable. About six centuries earlier King Saul was to totally obliterate the Amalekites as one of his first duties in office. Because of his failure to obey God's command in the matter, Saul lost the kingdom and the Amalekites lived on to war against God's people for centuries. It is ironic then that Mordecai, like Saul, was also a Benjamite and that Haman was an Agagite, a royal descendant of Hammedatha of the Amalekites (1 Sam. 15:8). If King Saul would have obeyed the Lord's command, there would have been no Haman to threaten the Jews in this story. For instructive purposes, God's people are often permitted to drink from their own cup, that is, the consequence of our obstinacy is used to teach us submission to God's will.

Although Haman was dead, the edict he put in place to slaughter Esther's people was still law – something had to be done. Esther, for a second time, intruded into the king's inner court without an invitation; Mordecai was still conversing with the king. She fell at the king's feet and tearfully requested that he counter the evil law that Haman had put in place in the king's name (v. 3). For a second time Xerxes extended his golden scepter to Esther to spare her life. After receiving this mercy, she rose to her feet and stood before the king (v. 4). Having already informed the king why she was there, she more specifically requests the king to revoke Haman's law to annihilate her people, for she cannot *"endure to see the destruction of my countrymen"* (vv. 5-6).

The king's response is twofold (v. 7): First, he reminds Esther what he had already done for her. He had hanged Haman for conspiring against the Jewish people and he had transferred the assets of Haman's estate to her. Given this royal judgment, John A. Martin suggests that Haman was considered to be a criminal and not just offensive to the king.[1] Second, he permitted Esther and Mordecai to write another royal decree to supersede the one Haman had drafted. (Haman's law could not be revoked because it had been sealed by the king's signet ring; v. 8.) The royal scribes were summoned and a new law was drafted in Xerxes' name and sealed by his signet ring on the twenty-third day of the third month (slightly more than two months after Haman's law was affirmed; v. 9).

Couriers were quickly dispatched and the new law allowing the Jews to defend themselves against their enemies (those who sought to hurt them or to plunder their possessions) was disseminated throughout the kingdom (v. 10). The Jews were permitted to use whatever force was necessary, including the destruction of their enemies (v. 11). Mordecai's statute was delivered to all 127 provinces and in the language of all people groups to ensure everyone understood that the Jews could lawfully avenge themselves (v. 12). What amounted to a twenty-four-hour civil war would occur on the thirteenth day of the twelfth month – the same day that Haman had ordered the extermination of Mordecai's people (vv. 13-14).

Mordecai was arrayed in royal apparel including a purple linen robe; this attire was appropriate for his high rank and authority. He also wore a crown, but it was not like the king's royal crown, rather a golden band or coronet (v. 15). Earlier he had publicly mourned clothed in sackcloth, but now Mordecai departed the palace wearing robes of splendor and a heart bursting with gladness.

Those who sow in tears shall reap in joy. He who continually goes forth weeping, bearing seed for sowing, shall doubtless come again with rejoicing, bringing his sheaves with him (Ps. 126:5-6).

You have turned for me my mourning into dancing; You have put off my sackcloth and clothed me with gladness (Ps. 30:11).

The people of Shushan also rejoiced that a good man, a champion of his people, had been promoted by Xerxes. The anti-Semitism which Haman had fostered in the kingdom was squelched; in fact, many Gentiles became Jewish proselytes *"because fear of the Jews fell upon them"* (v. 17). The Jews were now esteemed throughout the Persian kingdom and they all rejoiced in their phenomenal deliverance through Mordecai's decree in the king's name (v. 16).

Meditation

The essence of optimism is that it takes no account of the present, but it is a source of inspiration, of vitality and hope where others have resigned; it enables a man to hold his head high, to claim the future for himself and not to abandon it to his enemy.

— Dietrich Bonhoeffer

Vengeance and Purim
Esther 9

The permitted civil war occurred on the prearranged day. Although the enemies of the Jews had hoped to overcome them, it was the Jews, who had assembled in fighting regiments, that were crushingly victorious (v. 1). The account provides two reasons for their triumph: *"No one could withstand them, because fear of them fell upon all the people"* (v. 2) and the political officials under Xerxes *"helped the Jews, because the fear of Mordecai fell upon them."* Mordecai had become famous and well-favored throughout Persia and no one wanted to suffer his disfavor (vv. 3-4). How is the sudden change in demeanor of the general populace towards the Jewish people best explained? God put fearful compulsion into the hearts of men to serve His purposes, a stratagem repeatedly witnessed in Scripture (e.g., Gen. 20:6-7, 31:24; Ex. 11:3, 12:33; Judg. 7:22).

Whether motivated by hatred of the Jewish people or by greed of what could be gained by plundering them, those opposing the Jews had no public support. Consequently, when the fighting broke out, they were slaughtered by a well-organized opposition: Five hundred fell at Shushan in the citadel; this number included key leaders plus Haman's ten sons (vv. 6-9). The narrative specifically notes that the Jews did not plunder their enemies, lest some might conclude that they were merely a greedy, blood-thirsty people that took undue advantage of Mordecai's position (v. 10).

Xerxes was likely astounded by the casualty report in the citadel and thought things must be going as equally well for Esther's people in the other provinces. He informed her of this news and asked if there was anything else she would like to request of him. She immediately responded to the king's generous offer: *"If it pleases the king, let it be granted to the Jews who are in Shushan to do again tomorrow according to today's decree, and let Haman's ten sons be hanged on the gallows"* (v. 13). These ten men were already dead, but the public display of their dangling bodies would further confirm the king's support for the Jewish people. Xerxes grants Esther's request and an additional day was permitted for Jewish vindication in Shushan (v. 14). The next day 300 additional enemies of the Jews were slain near the citadel (v. 15).

The Jews could not venture into the palace to avenge themselves, but rather the reference to Shushan in verse 6 was to the upper city, a residential district of some 100 acres. It is likely that the lower town (roughly the same size) lying to the east of the upper district is what was referred to in verse 13 on the second day of slaughter.[1] There are many who cannot understand Esther's vicious request because they somehow typify Esther with the Lord's dealings with the Church, but as William Kelly explains, that is an erroneous association:

> One sees at once what profound confusion is made by that [assumption]. Not so. It is the Gentile discarded, and it is the Jew called in; but righteousness will be the character of the reign of the kingdom by and by. Grace is what suits the church now. It would be perfectly unintelligible therefore to have Esther representing the church now. The execution of righteous vengeance would be altogether incompatible with the calling of the Christian – with the church's place. But with the Jew called in to share the kingdom by and by – called into the honors of the kingdom – it is exactly in season. Then – when Messiah shall reign, and Jerusalem shall be His queen – will be found that word verified, "The nation and kingdom that will not serve thee shall perish."

> Our proper place now is to act suitably to Him who is at the right hand of God. But when the Lord Jesus leaves heaven for the earth – when He comes to reign, then righteousness will be the character of His kingdom, and terrible things will be done in righteousness, according to the 45th Psalm. Thus the execution of the ten sons of Haman is not the smallest difficulty when this is understood, for the Lord will not only smite at the beginning, but there will be a repetition of the blow: there will be a thorough clearance of the adversary, and of all that render but feigned obedience. The Lord will deal with them in that day that is coming.[2]

Any enemy of the Jewish people is also God's enemy. Three times in Scripture, Jehovah affirms that the nation of Israel is "the apple of His eye" (Deut. 32:10; Lam. 2:18; Zech. 2:8). The last verse promises to punish those nations who mistreat His people: *"For thus says the Lord of hosts: 'He sent Me after glory, to the nations which plunder you; for he who touches you touches the apple of His eye'"* (Zech. 2:8). God's tender affection for the Jews and His care of them explains why Esther's request of Xerxes was granted and their incredible victory. In one day 75,000 enemies of the Jews were slaughtered in the provinces outside of Shushan (v. 16). It is noted that the Septuagint provides a number of 15,000; this may be the correct amount (as 15,000 fits better, proportionately speaking, with the 800 slain in the capital region).

The text states a second time that the Jews did not plunder any of their fallen foes; this would prove that they were only interested in protecting themselves, not profiting from their fallen enemies. The Jews rested the day after the fighting ceased to celebrate their victory with joyous feasting (vv. 17-19). This meant that those Jews in Shushan met on the fifteenth day of the twelfth month, while the Jews in remote regions gathered on the fourteenth day.

As previously mentioned, the Feast of Purim draws its name from the *pur* (the lot) that was cast in chapter 3 to determine the day Haman's evil plot would be executed – the thirteenth day of the twelfth month. The irony of the situation is that Haman actually chose the time that the Jewish nation would annually celebrate his defeat, the fourteenth and fifteenth days of the twelfth month. Mordecai sent letters to the Jews in all the provinces to ensure these two days would be set aside annually to commemorate their deliverance (vv. 20-22).

The annual Feast of Purim was to be a festive event including the exchange of presents and gifts for the poor. To ensure that the reason for the holiday would not be forgotten, Mordecai rehearses all that Haman did against the Jewish people and how his conspiracy against them was thwarted (vv. 23-28). Their victory resulted not only in Haman's death, but also in the demise of his ten sons and thousands of their enemies.

It is noteworthy that there are three separate prayers offered by Jews during the Feast of Purim: In the first, they thank Jehovah that they are counted worthy. In the second prayer, they thank Him for preserving their ancestors. In the third prayer, they thank Him that they are able to enjoy another festival. Though specific prayers of thanksgiving to Jehovah are not expressly stated in the book of Esther, Jews since that time have continued to praise God for His providential protection.

Esther, along with Mordecai, wrote a second letter which was circulating throughout the empire to again confirm that the Jews should keep the Feast of Purim (vv. 29-30). Though God was hidden from His covenant people in Babylon at this juncture in time, they did acknowledge His faithful watchfulness and care for them.

Meditation

A state of mind that sees God in everything is evidence of growth in grace and a thankful heart.

— Charles Finney

Mordecai's Greatness
Esther 10

The book closes by summarizing the far-reaching power of Ahasuerus' (Xerxes') kingdom, but more importantly to Jewish readers the extoling of Mordecai, Xerxes' minister (vv. 1-3). While it was true that Xerxes had promoted Mordecai to be second in command of the empire, that was not what made him great in the minds of his countrymen; rather, it was the good that he did in that high office. He was known for *"seeking the good of his people and speaking peace to all his countrymen"* (v. 3).

Not only had the Jews been delivered from all their distresses, but one particular Jew, Mordecai, had achieved nearness and the favor of the great Gentile king. As a result, the one who had been hated by Gentiles was now in a powerful position to protect the seed of Abraham and execute vengeance on any who would seek to harm them. In this sense, Mordecai reminds us of the Lord Jesus, who as Head of the Jews is connected with the heavenly throne that rules over all things. This association ensures that God's covenant people will be preserved as promised in Scripture.

Perhaps this is why Mordecai's death is not recorded and no obituary is found in the book. We are left with the impression that this highly-favored, powerful Jew lives on to champion the cause of his people. Although there were times during this story that all seemed lost, God was working His plans within the evil plotting of Haman to ensure the preservation of His people and to achieve the utmost blessing for them.

Why has God been so patient with the Jewish people through the centuries despite their frequent idolatry, lapses of faith, and disobedience? Because Jehovah is a covenant-keeping God and He has established irrevocable promises to Abraham and his descendants that He must fulfill. Accordingly, the vast wonders of divine mercy and His providential care of them will be witnessed again and again, until the nation of Israel is finally restored to Him through Jesus Christ. God's ongoing devotion to Israel is clearly demonstrated in the fascinating story of Esther.

Meditation

We may not see the way, but we know the God, we see the God, we can draw near to the God that controls all things in our favor. In short, therefore, the providence of God is a universal truth, till the day come when the dealings of God will be public and manifest, and His name will be named upon His people. Meanwhile, we can count upon this for Israel. We know that now they are dispersed – that now they are in a wholly anomalous condition, but the day will come when God will set aside the Gentile, and bring in Israel once more, and our hearts can rejoice. It will be no loss to us even if that were the motive. But, in point of fact, it will be no loss to us. We shall be with the Lord Jesus on high, and it will be only after that that God will judge the Gentile and call back the Jew.[1]

— William Kelly

Endnotes

Ezra
Preface
1. H. A. Ironside, *Notes on the Book of Ezra* (Shiloh Christian Library, no date); pp. 5-6

The Decree of Cyrus
1. Ibid., pp. 13-14
2. Edward Dennett, *The Christian's Friend Magazine* (1885) http://stempublishing.com/magazines/cf/1885/Ezra.html
3. P. L. Tan, *Encyclopedia of 7700 Illustrations* (Bible Communications, Garland TX; 1996, c1979)

Homeward Bound
1. Edward Dennett; op. cit.
2. H. A. Ironside, op. cit., p. 24
3. P. L. Tan, op. cit.

The Foundation Laid
1. Edward Dennett; op. cit.
2. John A. Martin, *The Bible Knowledge Commentary : An Exposition of the Scriptures* (Victor Books, Wheaton, IL; 1983-1985), p. 659
3. H. A. Ironside, op. cit., pp. 8-9
4. P. L. Tan, op. cit.
5. Ibid.

Progress Invites Attack
1. C. H. Mackintosh, *Genesis to Deuteronomy – Notes on the Pentateuch* (Loizeaux Brothers, Neptune, NJ; 1972), p. 47
2. Ibid.

Stop Rebuilding Jerusalem
1. William MacDonald, *True Discipleship* (Gospel Folio Press, Port Colborne, ON; 2003), p. 155
2. P. L. Tan, op. cit.

The Work Resumes

Threating Accusations
1. Ibid.
2. Ibid.

The Temple Completed
1. Edward Dennett; op. cit.

Prepared Hearts
1. Ibid.

Seeking the Right Way
1. H. A. Ironside, op. cit., pp. 72-73
2. William E. Allen, op. cit.
3. L. B. Cowman, *Streams in the Desert* (Zondervan, Grand Rapids, MI), April 1
4. Edward Dennett; op. cit.

"Give Us a Reviving"
1. H. A. Ironside, op. cit., p. 82
2. William Kelly, http://stempublishing.com/authors/kelly/1Oldtest/ezra.html
3. J. C. Ryle, *Christian Leaders of the 18th Century* (Banner of Truth, Carlisle, PA; 1978)
4. William MacDonald, op. cit., p. 159
5. William E. Allen, op. cit., chp. 1
6. Martin Moor, *Boston Revival 1842* (John Putnam, Boston, MA, 1842), p. 6

Confession and Separation
1. Edward Dennett; op. cit.
2. Duncan Campbell, *The Lewis Awakening* (Faith Mission; April 1954), pp. 9-10
3. Ibid., p. 12

Nehemiah
Introduction
1. H. A. Ironside, *Notes on the Book of Nehemiah* (Shiloh Christian Library, no date); p. 11
2. John C. Whitcomb, *Nehemiah*, in *The Wycliffe Bible Commentary* (Moody Publishers Chicago, IL; 1962) p. 435
3. Iain Murray, *The Puritan Hope* (Banner of Truth; Carlisle, PA; 1971) p. 92

The Cupbearer
1. Xenophon, Walter Miller (Harvard University Press, Cambridge, MA; 1914), 1:3:9
2. Frank Charles Fensham, *The Books of Ezra and Nehemiah* (Eerdmans Publishing Co., Grand Rapids, MI; 1982), p. 157

264

The Cupbearer (cont.)

3. A. T. Olmstead, *History of the Persian Empire* (University of Chicago Press, Chicago, IL; 1959), p. 217
4. Dr. Howard Taylor, *Spiritual Secret of Hudson Taylor* (Whitaker House, New Kensington, PA: 1996), p. 368
5. Warren Wiersbe, *The Bible Exposition Commentary, Vol. 2* (Victor Books, Wheaton, IL: 1989), p. 416
6. H. A. Ironside, *Notes on the Book of Nehemiah*, op. cit., p. 12
7. http://www.revival-library.org/catalogues/genhistory/allen.html

The Petition

1. Gene A. Getz, *The Bible Knowledge Commentary: An Exposition of the Scriptures* (Victor Books, Wheaton, IL; 1983-1985), p. 659
2. H. A. Ironside, *Notes on the Book of Nehemiah*, op. cit., p. 12
3. Anna Abrams, "The Conversion of Hudson Taylor" from *Touching Incidents and Remarkable Answers to Prayer* (TGS International, Berlin, Ohio; reprint 2007), p. 80

The Wall-Builders (Part 1)

The Wall-Builders (Part 2)

1. Hamilton Smith, *Nehemiah* (http://stempublishing.com/authors/smith/NEHEMIAH.html)
2. C. H. Spurgeon, *Spurgeon's Morning and Evening Devotional*, July 11th Evening (Parsons Technology, Inc. - electronic copy. 1995-1999)
3. http://ldolphin.org/daniel/neh01.html

Opposition

1. Josephus, *Wars* (Book 5, Chapter 4, section 4)
2. BargilPixner, "Jerusalem's Essene Gateway" (*Biblical Archeology in Review*; May/June 1997).
3. Philip J. King, "Jerusalem" in *Anchor Bible Dictionary* (Doubleday, NY; 1992), pp. 751-753
4. Gene A. Getz, op. cit., p. 682

Internal Problems

1. Matthew Henry, *Matthew Henry's Commentary on the Whole Bible* (Electronic Edition STEP Files Copyright © 1998, Parsons Technology, Inc), Jas. 4:7
2. Ibid., Acts 5:3
3. Stanley D. Toussaint, *The Bible Knowledge Commentary – New Testament* (Victor Books, Wheaton, IL), p. 365
4. Warren Wiersbe, *The Bible Exposition Commentary, Vol. 2* (Victor Books, Wheaton, IL: 1989), p. 421
5. H. A. Ironside, *Notes on the Book of Nehemiah*, op. cit., p. 67

Attack on Leadership
1. H. A. Ironside, *Notes on the Book of Nehemiah*, op. cit., p. 71
2. Charles Stanley, *Nehemiah*
   (http://stempublishing.com/authors/stanley/Nehemiah.html)

Delegation and a Census
1. H. G. Mackay, *Biblical Financial Principles* (Christian Missions in Many Lands, Inc., Spring Lake, NJ; 1970)

The Water Gate Revival (Part 1)
1. H. A. Ironside, *Notes on the Book of Nehemiah*, op. cit., p. 87-88

The Water Gate Revival (Part 2)
1. A. B. Earl, *Bringing in the Sheaves* (J. H. Earl, MA; 1868)
2. J. G. Bellett, *Nehemiah 8*
   (http://stempublishing.com/authors/bellett/MED29.html)
3. http://gloryofhiscross.org/revive28.htm
4. William E. Allen, op. cit., chp. 1

A Long Prayer
1. H. A. Ironside, *Notes on the Book of Nehemiah* (Shiloh Christian Library, no date); p. 96
2. Roy Hession,*The Calvary Road* (Christian Literature Crusade, Fort Washington, PA; 1950), pp. 21-22

Consecration and Service
1. Albert Barnes, *The Bible Commentary Vol. 5* (Baker Book House, Grand Rapids, MI; reprinted 1879), p. 194
2. Irving L. Jensen, *Jeremiah, Prophet of Judgment* (Moody Press, Chicago, IL; 1966), p. 59

Decision Time
1. William E. Allen, op. cit., chp. 1

The Dedication of the Wall
1. Matthew Henry's Commentary on the Whole Bible: New Modern Edition, Electronic Database. Copyright (c) 1991 by Hendrickson Publishers, Inc.
2. Frank M. Cross, "A Reconstruction of the Judean Restoration," *Journal of Biblical Literature* 94:1 (March 1975), p18
3. H. A. Ironside, *Notes on the Book of Nehemiah* (Shiloh Christian Library, no date); p. 117
4. William E. Allen, op. cit., chp. 1

Spiritual Declension
1. Charles Stanley, *Nehemiah*
   (http://stempublishing.com/authors/stanley/Nehemiah.html)
2. Hamilton Smith, *Nehemiah,* op. cit.
3. P. L. Tan, op. cit.

Esther
Overview of Esther
1. J. Sidlow Baxter, *Explore the Book* (Zondervan Pub., Grand Rapids, MI; 1960), Esther Introduction
2. John N. Darby, Synopsis of the Books of the Bible, Vol. II (Stow Hill Bible and Tract Depot, Kingston, England; 1949), p. 18

Too Much Feasting
1. F. C. Cook, *Barnes Notes: The Bible Commentary – Exodus to Ruth* (Baker Book House, Grand Rapids, MI; reprinted from 1879 edition), p. 490
2. Herodotus, Histories 7.114

Esther Becomes Queen
1. James Vernon McGee, *Thru the Bible* Vol. 2 (Thomas Nelson Publishers, Nashville, TN; 1981), p. 546
2. Josephus, *The Jewish Antiquities*, 11.6.1-13 184-296
3. F. C. Cook, op. cit., p. 492
4. Matthew Henry, *Commentary on the Whole Bible, Vol. 2* (MacDonald Publishing Co., McLean, VA; 1985), p. 1126
5. F. C. Cook, op. cit., p. 494

Haman's Conspiracy
1. F. C. Cook, op. cit., p. 495
2. William Kelly, *Esther*, STEM Publishing:
   http://stempublishing.com/authors/kelly/1Oldtest/esther.html [accessed July 2016]

Fasting and Courage
1. Matthew Henry, op. cit., p. 1132

Esther's Banquet
1. Matthew Henry, op. cit., p. 1136
2. William MacDonald, *Believer's Bible Commentary* (Thomas Nelson Publishers, Nashville, TN; 1989), pp. 501-502
3. *The Christian Friend's* Magazine (1875); Esther
   [On-line] http://stempublishing.com/magazines/cf/1875/Esther.html [accessed July 2016]

The King's Insomnia
1. Matthew Henry, op. cit., p. 1140
2. R. C. Chapman, *Robert Cleaver Chapman of Barnstaple*, by W. H. Bennet (Pickering & Inglis, Glasgow, Scotland; no date – 1st ed.), pp. 125-126
3. H. A. Ironside, *Proverbs* (Loizeaux Brothers, Neptune, NJ; 1995), p. 67

Esther's Urgent Plea
1. William Kelly, op. cit.
2. Matthew Henry, from *Matthew Henry's Concise Commentary on the Whole Bible [assessed via E-sword)*, Est. 7:1-6

The Royal Decree
1. John A. Martin, *The Bible Knowledge Old Testament Commentary*, edited by J. F. Walvoord and Roy Zuck (Victor Books, Wheaton, IL; 1986), p. 711

Vengeance and Purim
1. F. C. Cook, op. cit., p. 502
2. William Kelly, op. cit.

Mordecai's Greatness
1. William Kelly, op. cit.

www.ingramcontent.com/pod-product-compliance
Lightning Source LLC
Chambersburg PA
CBHW051945090426
42741CB00008B/1283